David,
A combo of things
I know you love...
baseball
a good story & Italy,
memories of Italy!
Enjoy!
Suzy/Xmas '08

BASEBALLISSIMO

ALSO BY DAVE BIDINI

On a Cold Road, 1998
Tropic of Hockey, 2000

BASEBALLISSIMO

My Summer in the Italian Minor Leagues

DAVE BIDINI

M&S

National Library of Canada Cataloguing in Publication

Bidini, Dave
    Baseballissimo : my summer in the Italian minor leagues / Dave Bidini.

ISBN 0-7710-1461-9

1. Bidini, Dave – Journeys.   2. Baseball – Italy – Nettuno.   3. Nettuno (Italy)
I. Title.

GV863.51.N472B43 2003   796.357'094562   C2003-902055-X

We acknowledge the financial support of the Government of Canada through the Book Publishing Industry Development Program and that of the Government of Ontario through the Ontario Media Development Corporation's Ontario Book Initiative. We further acknowledge the support of the Canada Council for the Arts and the Ontario Arts Council for our publishing program.

Typeset in Janson by M&S, Toronto
Printed and bound in Canada

This book is printed on acid-free paper that is 100% ancient forest friendly (100% post-consumer recycled).

McClelland & Stewart Ltd.
The Canadian Publishers
481 University Avenue
Toronto, Ontario
M5G 2E9
www.mcclelland.com

1 2 3 4 5   08 07 06 05 04

For C. Abel

"Listen up, because I've got nothing to say
and I'm only going to say it once."

– Yogi Berra

CONTENTS

NETTUNO PEONES, 2002

First base: The Emperor
Second base: Mario Mazza
Shortstop: Skunk Bravo
Third base: Chicca
Catchers: The Big Emilio, Paolo Danna
Right field: The Red Tiger
Centre field: Mario Simone, Solid Gold
Left field: Fab Julie, the Natural
Infield: Christian, Mirko, Fabio from Milan
Pitchers: Cobra, Chencho, Pompozzi, Pitò the Stricken

Manager: Pietro Monaco

I

STRONZO WITH A SMITING POLE

During a pre-game workout in Nettuno, Italy, Mirko Rocchetti, an infielder with the Peones, arrived at the park carrying a tray of cornetti, brioche, and biscotti. Simone Cancelli (the Natural) followed twenty minutes later with a large box, which he placed on the ledge of the dugout. He lifted the lid, pulled back a layer of crepe paper, and revealed a small mountain of fresh croissants, their light, flaky shells embossed with vanilla crema. A few minutes later Francesco "Pompo" Pompozzi, the Peones' twenty-one-year-old fireballer, produced two green bottles filled with sugar-soaked espresso, and passed out little white plastic cups. Ricky Viccaro (Solid Gold) – who looked, as always, as if he were standing in front of a wind machine – showed up a half-hour into the game, swinging a red Thermos of espresso, which he cracked in the fifth inning and refilled for the beginning of the second game. Someone else placed boxes of sweets on racks above the bench, and they were polished off in no time.

This sugar fiesta was typical for the Peones, Nettuno's Serie B baseball team. They believed – as did many Italians – that sugar and coffee were all you needed to get you through any game. Andrea Cancelli (the Emperor) munched on energy pills that tasted like tiny soap cakes. At a game in Sardinia, I saw Fabio Giolitti (Fab Julie) pat his rumbling stomach before fetching a box of wafer cookies from his kit bag, which he passed out, two at a time, to his teammates. Then Mirko asked me, "Davide? Are you hungry?" and promptly handed me two panini spread with grape jelly – the Italian athlete's equivalent of an energy bar. At the same game, Mario Mazza, the Peones' second baseman, gathered the team excitedly, as if he'd just cracked the opposing team's sequence of signs, only to pass out packets of sugar he'd swiped from a café. The players poured them down the hatch. I joined in, even though I wasn't playing, just watching the Peones, the team I'd come to Italy to write about.

I found language as much a cultural divide as the approach to food, though I was able to find my place among the Peones by spouting a combination Italo-Canadian-Baseballese, at the risk of becoming Team Stooge. At times, I wondered whether the boys were asking me questions just to see how I would mangle their mother tongue.

One day, Chencho Navacci, the team's left-handed reliever, heard me comment that a hit had been "il pollo morto."

"Tuo pollo?" he asked.

"No, la palla. La palla è il pollo. Il pollo è morto."

"Okay, okay," he said, smiling.

"You know, dying quail," I said, reverting to English.

"?"

"The chicken is dead," I said, making a high, curving motion with my hand. "The ball – la palla. La palla è il pollo."

"Il pollo?"

I couldn't understand why Chencho was so confused. I'd always assumed that *dying quail* – baseball's term for a hit that bloops between the infield and the outfield – was one of those universal baseball terms.

"Si! Il pollo è morto!" I repeated.

"Il pollo è morto? Okay, is good!" he said, turning away.

Later, I told Janet, my wife, what had happened at the ballpark.

"La qualia," she corrected. "You should have said 'la qualia.'"

"How was I supposed to know they had quail in Italy?"

"What did you think? They have chicken, don't they?"

"Ya, but quail."

"Yes, quail. And I don't think *pollo* is the right word for chicken. *La gallina* is how you say chicken. *Pollo* is what you order in a restaurant.'

"*Pollo* is restaurant chicken?" I said, mortified.

"I think so."

"So, you mean I was telling Chencho that the ball was like a piece of cooked chicken?"

"Yes, I'm afraid you were."

"Flying cooked chicken?"

For my first few weeks with the team, I probably sounded like a moron. I regularly confused the word for *last* with *first*, and used *always* instead of *never*, as in "Speaking good Italian is always the first thing I learn." I'd also fallen into the embarrassing habit of pronouncing the word *penne* (the pasta) as if it were *pene*, the Italian word for penis. But I was excused for saying things like "I'd like my penis with tomatoes and mushroom," and, to their credit, the team and townsfolk hung with me. After a while, the players must have noticed a pattern in the things I said at practice: *dying quail, rabbit ball, hot potato, ducks on the pond, bring the gas, in his kitchen*. They probably figured I was just really hungry.

Before leaving Canada for Italy in the spring of 2002, I bound my five bats together with black packing tape. They looked like a wooden bouquet and their heads clacked as I laid them on the airport's baggage belt: the brown, thirty-four-ounce Harold Baines

Adirondack, two new fungo bats, a red Louisville smiting pole, and a vintage Pudge Fisk hurt stick, with Pudge's signature burnt into the fat of the wood.

My bats and I weren't alone. There was also my wife, Janet; our two children, Cecilia, a curly-haired two-year-old blabberpuss, and Lorenzo, not ten weeks old; and for the first part of the trip Janet's mother, Norma.

Other than a curiosity to experience sport unblemished by money, I had a few more reasons for shipping the family off to Italy. First, I love the game of baseball, having committed the last half-decade of summer Sunday evenings to something named the Queen Street Softball League. I am the starting shortstop for a team called the Rebels, originally affiliated with a local brewery, which was both our strength and poison. I spend most games standing on the gravel in my white Converse low-cuts, waiting for some silk-screen print shop worker or bartender or anthropology student or record-store clerk to wail the ball to my feet, providing that no off-leash hound makes for the pitcher's mound, lovestruck couple promenades through centre field, or rapscallions riding their BMXs rip up the sod in the power alleys, which lie just to the right of the oak tree and slightly to the left of the guy selling weed out of his Dickie Dee ice-cream cart. Still, we compete like heck. As a weekend scrub, I give everything at the plate. I also try my best to keep my feet spread, arse down, and eyes on the ball when fielding ground hops, the way Pee Wee Reese might have. Stats-wise, I've hovered around .400 – a modest softball average – year in and out, having effectively learned how to slice a 25-mph spinball just beyond the reach of the guy in the knee brace, who's swatting a mosquito while trying not to spill his lager.

It's because of my shortcomings as a ballplayer that I couldn't possibly have tagged along with an elite, or even semi-elite, pro-level team in Italy. I had briefly flirted with the notion of following around a major league club, but ditched the idea after hearing about Nettuno, which had just the right combination of respectable talent level, rabid fan base, and casual sporting culture to allow a dreamy scrub like me to toss in my glove and wander among them.

Which is to say: they let me.

When I first arrived in Nettuno, a seaside town of thirty thousand on the Tyrrhenian Sea, just an hour south of Rome, the Peones' reaction to the idea of having a Canadian writer follow them around was mixed. The players occasionally quizzed me about the nature of my book, not asking, "Do you plan to deploy a post-modernist narrative or will the book be in epistolary form?" but rather, as relief pitcher Pitò the Stricken put it, "Your book? Peones? Vero?"

"Yes," I told him. "Most of it."

"Peones? You write, really?" he said, lighting a smoke and eyeing me with doubt.

"Yes, really."

Chencho, overhearing our conversation, said, "Chencho è in tuo libro?"

"Yes, Chencho, of course," I told him. "Chencho, e tutto la squadra."

"Photo?" he asked.

"Si."

"Photo nudo?"

"Maybe."

"Angalaaaaato," he said, using a Nettunese expression for love-making.

Another time, Paolo, the veteran catcher, asked me, "Dave, why you write about Peones?"

I gave him the same answer.

"No, you should write about a real team. This team is bush league. You should write about the other Nettuno teams. Real baseball."

"I'm not interested in real baseball."

"But, Dave, we just fool around. We play for fun, no?"

"That's why I like it."

"Noooo!" he said. "Really. Peones, this is not a normal team."

I had perfectly good reason to write about Nettuno and its beloved third-tier Peones. Nettuno is a charmed spot on the international baseball map. The game took root here in 1944, just after the Allied Forces hit the beach at Nettuno as part of Operation Shingle. Nettuno and its sister city, Anzio, sat square on the pathway to Rome, which the soldiers hoped to wrest from the Germans. After setting up camp on the beach and in the surrounding countryside, the American soldiers found the time to play a little ball, at least when they weren't being assaulted by V1 bombers and Messerschmitts. There's nothing better to take your mind off the inevitable blitzkrieg than a game of pepper, so Kip and Mouse and Sarge would break out the bats and scrub 'er up a little, sometimes right there in the trenches. This happened wherever American GIs went during the Second World War, but it took particular hold in Nettuno, where the locals were taught how to play by a pair of career military men – Colonel Charles Butte and Sergeant Horace McGarrity. No one I talked to could explain why the game captured the hearts of the Nettunese, other than to suggest that baseball represented hope and rebirth amid so much rubble and death. After the war, hundreds of Americans remained in Nettuno to build one of the largest and most beautiful war cemeteries in Italy. In the evenings there were endless games of cobblestone streetball, a sport that allowed the Nettunese to forget, if only for a moment, the ravages inflicted on their medieval town. As early as the mid-1950s, youngsters were given baseball gloves and bats upon taking their first communion, a tradition that continues today.

Nettuno eventually formed two local teams, and Prince Steno Borghese offered his grounds to be used to build a baseball field. Joe DiMaggio hit here, in 1957, driving in by jeep from Rome after hearing that baseball was close at hand. He showed up during a

The Yankee Clipper (in shirt and tie) comes to Nettuno. (Courtesy of Silvano Casaldi)

game between two Nettunese teams to face Carlos Tagliaboschi, the moustachioed local ace famous for taking his boat out at dawn on the days of important games, until fans burnt it to a crisp so that he might rest properly before a match against their provincial rivals.

DiMaggio, playing to a thrilled crowd teeming over the chicken-wire fencing of the old park, stepped to the plate in the same suit of clothes that he'd worn to the luncheon where someone had whispered in his ear about Nettuno. The small, rakish Nettunese pitcher settled into his caricamento (windup), his heart beating like a tympany, and offered DiMaggio his most biting fastball. With his long, majestic swing, DiMaggio reached for the ball and missed. The crowd paused for a moment's respect, then exploded wildly, incredulous that their five-foot son of a sailor had slipped a pitch past the world's greatest hitter. DiMaggio took off his jacket, folded it into a square, laid it next to the plate, rolled up his sleeves, and told Tagliaboschi, "More. Gimme some more." The tiny pitcher threw and DiMaggio made contact, sending the ball over the outfield wall, the neighbouring farmer's field, the seacliffs, and the

The great Tagliaboschi, in mid-windup. Note that there is no pitcher's mound, which is typical of many early Italian ballparks. (Courtesy of Silvano Casaldi)

beach until it splashed into the surf. Seconds later the sea was filled with thrashing scamps trying to find this cherished piece of history.

Which, of course, they did not.

DiMaggio hit home run after home run, astonishing the crowd and exhausting Tagliaboschi, who bequeathed the rubber to a few of his teammates, eager for the privilege of pitching to the sartorial giant of the grass game. Finally, someone shouted, "If you keep hitting, we'll have no more balls!" DiMaggio graciously stepped out and minutes later was back on the road to Rome.

By 2003, there were six ballparks in or near town – one more than the number of churches – and countless adult and kids' teams, the best of which, the Serie A Nettuno Indians, had won seventeen Italian baseball titles and supplied the Italian Squadra Nazionale with many of its best players. The Peones were more like the players DiMaggio encountered than any other modern Nettuno team. While the Indians of Serie A and the Lions of Serie A2 were stocked with a sizable American and Latin contingent – locals groused that these foreigners had blocked the advancement of young local up-and-comers – the Peones of Serie B were wholly Italian, with the exception of the visiting Canadian writer, whose name at least ended in a vowel.

Before committing to a six-month stay in Nettuno, Janet and I visited the town to make certain it was where we wanted to be. As we made our way from the small train station into the centre of town – Piazza Mazzini, with its modest fountain of Neptune astride an enormous fish, being pulled by two swimming horses – we ran into a deranged fellow in a ROMA bandana named Andrea who, within minutes, was making me squeeze his calf and forearm. "Strong!" he kept saying, raising his arms above his head like King Kong. He asked me what my business was in Nettuno, and when I told him, he said that, like everyone else in Nettuno, he too was once a baseball player, until a series of beanballs ended his career. He showed me three scars: two over the eye and one above his lip. "But still, I am strong!" he said, grabbing my hand and pressing two packets of sugar into my palm. While I stood there wondering whether this was a traditional Nettunese greeting (it wasn't), he patted me on the chest and said, "Eat. Very good. Be strong!" I thanked him and we walked on. He shouted once more and again raised his hands above his head like you-know-who, at which point I realized that if there were a handful of others like him in the town – not to mention a little bit of baseball – well, really, there could be a lot worse places to spend your summer.

My baseball adventure took shape after meeting Pietro Monaco, the Peones' coach/manager and one of the city's legendary old-timers.

*Pietro at
seventeen as a
rookie with the
Nettuno Indians.*
(Courtesy of
Pietro Monaco)

Pietro was fifty-eight years old, retired after twenty-seven years
starring at second base for the Nettuno Indians, and twenty-five
years as head teller at the city bank. This daily double had made
him one of Nettuno's most recognizable citizens. For nearly three
decades, when people weren't howling his name at the ballpark,
they were facing him across his marble countertop. I was told that,
during Nettuno's dominant baseball years in the 1960s and 1970s,
fans would open bank accounts so they could meet the prodigy,
whose baseball career had caught on fire when he was seventeen,
during his first year at second base for the big club.

Pietro had been a clever hitter with good bat control and
unmatched cunning on the basepaths. He still held the Italian league
record for steals, as well as for the number of times stealing home in
one season (four). He started playing the game at a time when it was

a given that every young Nettunese boy would join a baseball team, forgoing soccer and volleyball for year-round hardball.

Most days, Pietro dressed in a loud shirt (a requirement among Nettunese men) buttoned to his clavicle, shorts, and sandals, his car keys hanging on a shoelace around his neck. He moved in a slow, loose jangle, a pace that frequently slowed to a standstill while he exchanged words with another Nettunese. More often than not, the men and women he paused to chat with had a close connection to baseball, either as amateurs or professionals, coaches or players. During our first meeting, Pietro warned me, "Once you are in baseball here, everyone will want to talk to you about it. This is a town madly in love with game." The following summer, it didn't take me long to discover that the fellow from whom we bought our fruit had won two cadetti championships, the butcher's sister was married to a player who currently starred with Serie A Anzio, the chef at La Sirene trattoria could name the starting nine of the last twenty Nettuno Indian teams, the fountain codger with the smoker's hack – Sergio Serpe – had helped build Nettuno's first ballfield, and our cab driver's son played all-star ball at Santa Barbara. On any given night while strolling along Nettuno's seawall, I'd stumble upon someone who'd hit a famous home run at least once in their lives. On a typical Nettunese Friday night, the locals donned baseball jackets, Property of New York Mets T-shirts (as opposed to the Property of New York Dolphins shirt that a friend spotted in Germany), and hundreds of Indian pins and caps. Just in case you didn't get the hint, there was the Planet Baseball restaurant, and on the northern approach to the town stood two ten-foot murals, one depicting the 5th Army arriving on the beach on January 22, 1944, the other showing Giampiero Faorone, the old national team slugger, lashing at a high fastball.

Pietro was the face of Nettunese baseball. Though he'd lost the exquisite form of a young baseball star, he still cut a handsome figure, weathered not by wind or work or peril, but by time. His hair – no longer thick and brown, but frosted grey – was clipped short, giving his head the resolute squareness of a cinder block, a physical characteristic that best illustrated the stubbornness of his character.

Whatever competitive drive lingered in him, Pietro's blue eyes made gentler. They weren't the kind of piercing blue that tacked you to your chair, but a soft azure that tempered his expressions and softened his fiercest words. His eyes were never quite capable of delivering the kind of cruel stare that, as a manager, he desired, and whenever he'd force his brow forward and jut his jaw in anger, they would make the target of his anger feel that, even though it had been bad, it was not as bad as it could have been.

Baseball was forever on Pietro's mind. Even on those afternoons when we took lunch at his third-storey city home – where his wife, Maria Pia, prepared feasts of rigatoni with lupini, grilled calamari with cabbage, and fried eggplant – he'd push away his plate in an instant to clasp his hands in a batting grip and explain how to hit a sinking curve.

After his retirement from pro ball, Pietro took to managing. He worked his way up and down the coast before stopping at nearby Aprilia, where he took the job of manager/pitcher, leading his team through three ranks of Italian ball – C to A2 – before leaving them to embark on another project. He worked as coach with the Serie A Indians under national team manager Giampiero Faorone, but found the job of running mundane drills for players thirty years his junior on the same field upon which he'd once played too awkward. In 2001, he'd signed on as manager of the Serie B Nettuno Peones.

In better times, the Peones would have been a feeder team for the Indians. The Indians' top brass would have scouted the games at San Giacomo – the Peones' home field, due north of the beach – and kept their roster fluid to include the occasional rising star. But since the Indians' lineup was dominated by imports, there was little room for local players. Modern Italian clubs have become afflicted with a serious case of the wins, designing their teams to succeed at all costs, even if it means alienating local supporters. The Indians' management defended themselves by pointing to their half-dozen local players, but the position players the fans came out to watch – catcher, centre fielder, shortstop, and two-thirds of their pitchers –

The Emperor (left) and Fabio from Milan. (Cathy Bidini)

were almost all born elsewhere. The only notable Nettuno player on the 2002 Indians roster was first baseman Roberto de Franceschi, whose family owned Silvana Sports on the main drag. This store, with its great wall of leather mitts, faced the very spot where the first Allied landing craft had stormed the beach.

The Peones had been the Serie C champions in 2001, and the summer of 2002 would be their first season in accelerated ball, Serie B. In Serie C, they didn't even keep player stats. Serie B, by contrast, provided formidable teams from around Italy stocked with athletes who'd competed for the nation's elite pro teams. The Peones were formed by Andrea Cancelli, whom I nicknamed the Emperor because of his imperial air. He had a classic Italian face, every hair angled perfectly in place, and he walked at a regal pace, slow and careful, with his chin tipped to the sky, turning his head from side to side as if to take in the full breadth of what lay around him. The Emperor's family had been part of Nettunese society since the quattrocento, and his father, Gianni, had played alongside Pietro in Serie A.

Along with his friend and teammate Fabio Sena, the Emperor had built the Peones more or less as a lark. They'd invited players who'd become frustrated – as they had – with the political nature of Nettunese baseball, men who had suffered at the hands of tyrannical managers and a tribal baseball society. They offered the weary a club formed in the spirit of those teams who'd first taken to the Villa Borghese – the teams of their forebears – and a chance of succeeding simply by playing the game for the joy of play.

Pietro was the ideal figurehead for this family of hardball misfits. Even though he was one of the town's greatest stars, he was not offered a job at the town council like so many others (including Giampiero Faorone). Pietro's family had owned an alimentari (grocery store) in town, but had never made it into the elite of Nettunese society the way others had, whose names hung on a myriad of shops and businesses around Nettuno.

With the Peones, Pietro could be around baseball without having to deal with the trials that came with top-level local ball. Like his players, he wanted to pitch batting practice, hit fungos, field groundballs, ride the buses, go to team dinners, tell stupid stories. One afternoon, he told me, after agreeing to let me travel and practise with the team, "Dave, maybe we win, maybe not. But still, I tell my players the same thing: The games mean nothing if you don't learn from them."

The Emperor told me one day, "We are the Peones. Our name is like a funny joke, you see?" (I hadn't, at first, but once I'd seen it in the context of Italy's soccer teams, who were nicknamed the Wolf and the Eagle, I understood.) By naming themselves after impoverished Mexicans, the Peones were sending up the machismo of sport, no small feat for young men raised in a proud, patriarchal society. "The Peones," mused the Emperor, "we just like to be together, and that, for us, is beautiful." In a town where ballplayers are lionized, and where baseball is vital to its regional identity, the Peones' flip attitude about competing is controversial, and, at times, a joke. When word spread that the writer from Canada had chosen to document them over other teams, the locals scratched their heads and asked what this stronzo's problem was: Didn't he know baseball at all?

2

THE PASTA GHETTO

It wasn't easy growing up Italian in Canada. Like any teenager, I'd simply wanted to vanish into the crowd, but the culture into which I was born prevented easy assimilation. My surname was the first obstacle. My teachers enunciated it like they were reading a street sign from a distance, surprised to have made it across all six letters: "Bi . . . dee . . . nee?" I imagined each syllable as a small, winged insect flying into the towering constructs of "Smith! Jones! Bolton!" while Scottish names, such as MacDonald, were angry jaws snapping over my three little i's. I suppose I didn't have it as bad as Phillip Zinko, Karen Pocock, or Winsome Losesome – a South Asian girl in my driver's education class – but in Anglo Toronto in the 1970s, it was enough to make me realize that I would never join the Hudson Brothers nor start at left wing for the Toronto Maple Leafs, whose Armstrongs and Harrises and Stanleys carried the day.

My father used to tell me, "If people can't spell your name, tell them, 'It's just like *bikini*, only with a *d* instead of a *k*!'" That, of course, was beyond reason. I might as well have announced at assembly: "Hello, my name is Dave Bidini. That's just like *bikini*, only different. Hey, would anyone like to punch me in the face?" After I learned that Hollywood had immortalized our name in film, I calmed down. For a while, I thought Bidini might be a fearsome street fighter or black-hearted villain or courageous champion of small causes. But Señor Bidini, a minor character in Fred Astaire's *Top Hat*, turned out to be a flamboyant tailor with a high-pitched trill who flitted gaily at the other end of the manly chart.

The other issue that caused me great consternation was my nose, which looks like it's peering around the side of my face to see what's behind me. As a teenager, my proboscis always felt more like a foot than a nose. The Joneses, Jaspers, and Smiths may have felt burdened by their pink skin and button noses, but theirs were features in retreat. My nose was in danger of poking the person in front of me in the back of the neck. While I could always anglicize my name (Daniel Bennett!), dye my hair strawberry, and dress like a cricketer to mask my heritage (at this point, let me wish Lorenzo August Morassutti-Bidini the best of luck), my nose was a resolute Rushmore.

I knew very little about the history of my name. All I knew was that my grandparents were among the huddled masses who'd come over between the wars. The first story I ever heard of my maternal grandmother's life – my sister and I called one pair of our elders Gramma and Grampa (the Palermos), the other Nonno and Nonna (the Bidinis) – was that she'd flung her Italian passport into the Welland Canal days after arriving in Canada. She rarely said anything about life in her hometown (Foggia, in the south), vowing never to return to Italy, where, she said, it was dirty and people stole. Playing to shock us, she'd throw up her hands – one of which was usually holding a large knife for dramatic heft – and announce, "They can go to hell over there!"

Gramma was diminutive and loud, with the footfall of a Yeti. As a boy, I once watched her prepare a chicken for dinner. She dug her fingers into the bird's body and wrenched its heart out, devouring it in front of me with a sparkle in her eye. It was Gramma who, one summer's afternoon in her backyard, laid down her shovel and showed me how to make the sign of the horns with her hands, explaining, "In Italy, this is how you say 'Bullshit.'" Then she mimed a series of equally explicit gestures, right there among the tomatoes, cucumbers, and peppers, which she tilled in her drooping socks and old dress.

My Grampa, a quiet, sullen man named Leonardo, was a devout unionist who came to Canada via the U.S.A. in the back of a truck, buried under a mountain of potatoes. He rarely did anything more than growl at the dinner table. I suspect that he was a constant worrier – he chain-smoked and died of a heart attack at age eighty-two – though he was a sworn teetotaller, drinking nothing stronger than warm water with his meals. Grampa's idea of bliss, I think, was to sit in his favourite chair on a Saturday afternoon, sucking on a Du Maurier watching wrestling. The set was always on at the Palermos. I watched countless sporting events – the Red Sox–A's American League Championship Series in 1975; the Reds' World Series victory a year later; the Montreal Canadiens 3, the Central Red Army 3, on New Year's Eve 1975 – lying on my stomach on the cool hardwood floor, the shades dimming the light of the early evening as Grampa smoked behind me.

It couldn't have been easy for any of my grandparents to emigrate from Italy, where things had remained unchanged for centuries, to stiff, cold Orange Toronto – home to the Dullest Sunday in the World, according to Pierre Berton. Forget the fact that there was very little street life or indigenous culture, short of the Group of Seven and hockey, but back in the 1930s in Toronto, you could be arrested in a bar for carrying a drink from one table to another. Provided you could find a bar.

The Bidinis, by comparison, made Gramma and Grampa Palermo look like Mr. and Mrs. Diefenbaker. Even their names suggested a greater depth of Italianness. Nonno was Augustino or "Gus," and Nonna was Delfa, a word that sounded like an element on the periodic table, which was to me as mysterious and difficult as Italian culture. Both of my nonni came from Rassina, a small town in Tuscany. There were few Tuscans in Toronto when they arrived – there still aren't many compared to the number of Calabrians – since they rarely emigrate, finding no good reason to leave a place so beautiful, green, and warm. However, my nonno set out to see New York City when he was twenty-six. My aunts say that this wander-lust had less to do with wanting a new life than it did with playing cards, gambling, and hanging out with the compari who'd come before him. Like so many Italian immigrants, he ended up on Mulberry Street in the 1920s but left when it was pointed out to him by a friend that he stunk at cards, never getting so far ahead that the future looked better than it had the day before.

Gus didn't return to Italy for long. He and my nonna were married in Rassina – she was twenty-six, he was ten years older, which was old for betrothal in those times – and, instead of settling in New York, they came to Toronto. My nonna was a small woman, but her presence gathered around you and she used her voice like a chisel, intending every word to leave a mark. She was the God's-gonna-getcha type. The Bidinis observed all of the churches' sig-nificant occasions, particularly Palm Sunday, which brought with it a shocking no-television edict. Sacrificing a pig would have seemed more normal to me. Palm Sunday was a little like Christmas, only the toys, eggnog, evergreen, carols, and snowball fights were replaced by a single crappy palm stalk. At the end of mass, an atten-dant would hand it to me with a twinkle in his eye, as if it were some kind of glorious reward. I would have had more fun with an old cable clutch.

Visits to the Bidinis meant sour chocolate and scratchy church pants, plastic-encased furniture, and uncles with voices like creak-ing doors. Compared to the fab world of my teenagehood – "Rock and Roll Hootchie Koo," Don Kirshner's Rock Concert, *James at 16*, and "Life's Been Good" – Italian culture felt sepulchral and slow. My nonna – and later my aunts – drew great pleasure from watch-ing the Pope conduct mass on television, an event that makes a tel-evised political debate look like an episode of *American Gladiators*. I longed for comfort from AM radio, but my grandparents favoured stations featuring an eighteenth-century hit parade, which I toler-ated until I grew tired of waiting for the fuzztone lead guitar break that never came. In hindsight, of course, I wish I hadn't been such an arrogant doofus, and had tried to accept all of this for what it was. After all, my nonno, an aficionado of opera and an amateur singer, was clearly nuts about music, an obsession I've inherited, setting the table for Lorenzo to one day dream of wrapping my Pavement CDs in a cloth and hammering them to dust.

As a teenager, I renounced almost every facet of my Italian heritage (except pizza). I looked for Italo-Canadian role models who had escaped their past, men in whom I could see myself. If they existed at all, they were usually populist parodies of the type. There was wrestler/Grey Cup hero Angelo Mosca, a gorilla of a man whose face had the pallor of a potato, scrubbed with mud, grass, or blood, depending on the season's sport. His celebrity was based on talk-show appearances in which he threatened either to hoist the host over his head or to eat him. Another celebrity I thought was Italo-Canadian was prizefighter George Chuvalo, who fought Ali twice, taking the champ fifteen rounds before losing. Despite this acclaim, Chuvalo, who lived a stone's throw from me, and wasn't Italian, was cursed with a low, sonorous drone and the verbal agility of a vacuum bag.

On the entertainment side of things, there was even less to offer. In the 1970s, Montreal's Gino Vannelli was one of the country's pop Lotharios, and while his ability to create solid-gold hits suggested real talent, his image as a bedroom creeper in gold chains and groomed chest hair suggested otherwise. As a nervous kid too frightened by girls even to consider talking to them, I felt woefully inadequate compared to Gino; his songs implied that he had all it took, while I had none of it. Vannelli's cross-city equal, Michel Pagliaro, was less motivated by lust, but the assuredness of his hip-shaking stage moves still left me feeling acutely insecure. Altogether, my teenage search for an introspective Italian songwriter trying to come to terms with his Mediterranean roots was in vain, except for a brief moment of hope that I might find my worries addressed in the musings of Jim Croce, who died in a plane crash too soon for me to ever know.

It wasn't until the mid-1970s that I was able to see myself in other Italians – if not Italo-Canadians – despite, and sometimes because of, their cultural trappings. Hockey star Phil Esposito did wonders for my appreciation of the Italian character (not to mention the impact he had on Loyalist Canada as a whole), but there came a trinity of others: the Fonz, Rocky Balboa, and, for a fleeting moment, John Travolta.

The thing about the Fonz was that, even though his last name – Fonzarelli – ended in a vowel, he wasn't required, as I was, to pay heed to the culture into which he was born. It was as if he'd selected the charming aspects of being Italian – the hair, the complexion, the ability to fell girls with a single twitch of the lip – while discarding the Pope, opera, and all of that ass-biting furniture. Shockingly, he was even able to cast his Mediterraneanness against the pale Cunninghams and use it like a flare. The Fonz somehow managed to stand out in a good way, an achievement that was as mysterious to me as the rings of Saturn.

The Fonz was a powerful symbol: he scored with girls, was tough, people were awed by his cool, and he had an almost pathological love for cars and bikes, a characteristic shared by every other Italian kid who went to my high school, except, of course, me. But as the characters on *Happy Days* became more interesting and involved, the Fonz revealed himself as a loner whose cool was simply a way of covering up his massive insecurities. I lay on the carpet in my parents' bedroom one evening watching the New Year's Eve episode where Richie Cunningham tries to guess the kind of wild scene that is likely taking place in Fonzie's loft. Later in the show, he dares to climb the stairs to the Cool One's place for a quick eyeful, only to find our anti-hero sitting alone in the difficult silence of his apartment. To me, it was a profound and deeply sad portrait. I believe it was the first time that I understood how a story is supposed to work – that craft exists in peeling back layers to reveal the greater truth about a person. Fonzie's loneliness made him real to me.

At first, I felt a similar attachment to Vinnie Barbarino, *Welcome Back, Kotter*'s classroom cut-up, haltingly voiced by John Travolta. Like the Fonz, Vinnie's strut was all an act, and, at the end of the day, he was no better than the rest of the Sweathogs, teenage fuck-ups to the last. It's a shame that the noted Scientologist couldn't sustain his hold, for his next career move – *Saturday Night Fever* – provided endless hours of misery for any Italian kid who wanted to escape the disco-and-pasta ghetto. The film was released while I was in high school, at a time when you were more or less defined by your taste in music. My school was split into two camps – Rock and Disco – and while I abhorred the latter (even the word, ending in a vowel, sounded embarrassingly Italian), my name pegged me as someone for whom gold chains and a white suit was the sartorial apex. If anything, Travolta's fame and the film's popularity made me try even harder to separate myself from the platform-heeled pack.

I adopted a serious, unwavering two T-shirt rotation (T-shirts being the most obvious form of self-expression in the days before the lip stud and tattoo), wearing either RUSH I TORONTO, a tribute to Toronto's imperial prog-rock mavens, or ROCK AND ROLL WILL NEVER DIE, which showed a cartoon skeleton slashing a Les Paul over a tombstone bearing the words DISCO RIP. While most of Etobicoke's Italo-Canadian kids crowded the weekend dances at the Etobicoke Olympian, I stayed in the darkness of my bedroom, head-phones strapped on, listening to *Houses of the Holy* or *Boston* or *Heaven Tonight*, and hardening my resolve to distance myself from a heritage that was becoming ever more mainstream and unavoidable.

Rocky was released just in time. While *Saturday Night Fever* was set mostly in Manhattan dance clubs, *Rocky* took place in the dim living rooms of crummy shoebox apartments, its characters choking on an oppressively old and airless culture. For its stark drama, I put *Rocky* right up there with *The Battleship Potemkin*. There's a moment in the film where Rocky's future brother-in-law, Paulie, played by Burt Young, takes a baseball bat to the living-room bureau. It's one of the most poignant and disturbing scenes I've ever witnessed on film. Young's apartment, which he shares with his sister – the timid

shopkeeper who becomes Rocky's muse – could have been fur-
nished by my aunts and uncles: drab, stiff-backed furniture, reli-
gious shrines sharing the top of lemon-waxed wood cabinets with
faded photos of strange relatives. In the scene, Paulie arrives home
bitterly drunk and furious because Rocky, the perennial loser thug,
has been given a shot at cultural liberty while he's left in a shitty job
at the meat-packing plant. He destroys the photographs of his late
parents, spraying glass about the room, froth bubbling at the
corners of his mouth. Once he's done, Rocky wrestles him to the
chair and pins him down. Paulie throws his hands over his face and
loses himself in despair.

After this scene, the film's characters turn the corner. It's as if
the filmmaker – the movie was written by Sylvester Stallone – is
suggesting that it's not until you destroy the ghosts of your past
that you are able to be yourself. The scene frightened and moved
me, standing high in my thoughts whenever I felt tight and choked
by the closeness of that same culture. That an Italian had taught
me this truth was something too.

I saw *Rocky* for the first time in Dunedin, Florida, with my dad.
It was 1977 and I was fourteen. We went to the movies one afternoon, having spent most of week watching the Blue Jays at their
first spring training, our reason for the trip. When I was young, I
navigated the world of baseball alone, in another guise. Baseball
allowed me to liberate myself from, well, myself. It was as far from
the pasta ghetto as I could possibly imagine. The players were hip,
funny, wild-haired, rogue, stoned, troublesome, free, black, white,
Latin, and cracker, even the squareheads, like Jim Kaat, Kent
Tekulve, and Tom Seaver, and the fossils, like Casey Stengel, Bill
Veeck, and Yogi Berra. Renegade stars like Dock Ellis, Dick Allen,
Reggie Jackson, Al Hrabosky, Carlton Fisk, and Curt Flood were
perfect icons for a kid trying to rocket out of his form. Everything
about the baseball stars of the 1970s was wild and free: Willie
"Pops" Stargell and his great windmilling forearms; Mark "the Bird"
Fidrych, his Horshack afro pressed under the Tigers' gothic T,
holding the ball aloft and engaging it like Hamlet addressing Yorick's

skull; Pete Rose diving headfirst into third base like a cat at a windup toy; Bill Lee, Luis Tiant, and Charley Finley. Like Curt Flood and the reserve clause, baseball gave me a place to break free, to *be* free. The ballpark let me dream of becoming a six-foot slugger with billowing afro sideburns and opaque sunglasses, hammering the phantom ball as if born from the dust of the diamond's red clay.

But just as the game offered me a way out, it also helped me to find a way back in. On the ride from the movie theatre to the ballpark in Florida I experienced a kind of spiritual frisson – *Rocky*'s Italo art fusing with the free world of the ballpark – and began a baseball journey that years later delivered me, leather mitt in hand, to the place that I once wanted to destroy.

3

BOB DYLAN AND THE DRAG BUNT

Before seeing it, Janet and her mom were a little apprehensive about the apartment that Pietro had rented for us. "It's a few feet from the beach, with a view of Fort Sangallo," he'd told us over the phone, making it sound a bit too perfect. But when they discovered that his wife, Maria Pia, had checked it out, they felt more at ease. They were probably worried – as I wasn't – that Pietro would rent us a giocatore flophouse with rank jerseys flung over door handles and empty Powerade bottles piled everywhere.

It turned out that Pietro and Maria Pia's instincts were bang on: our second-floor apartment (which, technically, was located on the third floor) on Via della Resistenza Nettunese indeed faced the sea, sitting just below the main road (Viale Matteotti), not fifty feet from the beach. From the rear window in what became my writing room, we could see straight out to the sea and, to the side, Fort Sangallo's burnt-red walls and turret, which rose gracefully like a woman's neck. Our landlords – two brothers named Matteo and Simone, who usually wore matching Adidas track suits (Matteo's was red; Simone's blue) – told us that the building was made from a rare local rock, macco, which lent the neighbouring Fort Sangallo its distinct ruddy-brown hue. The turret had such a bold presence in Nettuno that every time you looked up, it found you. The fort's exterior walls were smooth and round at the edges, designed so that cannonfire would glance off the building and, in past times, whenever a visitor was received on shore, a staircase was lowered by pulley to fetch him. Once collected, he was deposited on a platform as the steps folded back into the castle, at which point the letter box in the great door slid open and the caller tried to remember the quattrocento equivalent of his PIN.

The building had been home to both Pope Alexander – who commissioned its construction in 1503 – and Benito Mussolini, who'd kept an apartment there in the 1930s, putting to use its crenellated rooftop terrace that loomed over the sea. The fort and the Borgo Medievale – Nettuno's walled old quarter, built sometime between the tenth and eleventh century – were the oldest surviving parts of the town. It felt strange to be surrounded by such deep history, coming from a city where last week's *TV Guide* was considered old. There were times when I'd be out on the town chatting with someone only to realize suddenly that I was leaning against a wall where Spartacus might have stood after busting out of his gladiatorial cell.

The history of the area was almost too rich to comprehend. Both Nero and Caligula had been born in neighbouring Anzio (back then, Anzio and Nettuno were one city, Antium), while, ten minutes up the road, Roman emperors once bred elephants for show and sport. In the nearby Alban Hills, Pius IX had kept a summer palace, where he roamed among the dryads and chestnut woods on a white mule. The presence of the past first struck Janet, who, on hearing the Nettunese greet each other with a two-thousand-year-old Roman salutation ("*Salve!*"), realized that she could use her Latin degree in everyday life.

With the exception of the Fort and the Borgo, the rest of city was modern, large sections of it rebuilt, out of necessity, after the war. The colours of the buildings – pink, Tuscan yellow, taupe, white, sandy brown, salmon, peach, and light red – changed tone with the rising and falling of the light. Viewed against the blue-black night sky, Nettuno – a city illuminated by yellow lights fixed high on its medieval walls – was a beautiful gold lizard stretched out along the coastline.

At the foot of our apartment was a bar, Señor Frog, that staged Friday-night karaoke contests, pretty much guaranteeing that anything you read in this book was written on any day except Friday. In front of the bar was a beach: Bagne Vittoria. When we first arrived, it was an empty swath of sand, but a few months later, it was dotted with hundreds of blue-and-white ombrellone. The proprietors of the beach constructed a fully enmeshed soccer field, a grass hut that housed a horseshoe of cackling arcade games, a card tent and coffee terrace, a kid's park with swings, an above-ground pool, a kiosk that sold everything from grappa shots to Nutty Buddys (Cornetto Classico), and a huge flower box with Bagne Vittoria spelled out in geraniums. In May, only a handful of swimmers tested the waters, but July and August brought a swarm of locals – guys named Ivano pulling foam surfboards and women parading in tiger-stripe bikinis – and an assortment of tourists from every part of the Boot.

There were few nights when I didn't stare out the window, chew my pen lid, following the sea to the horizon, my eyes falling on the small lights of a fishing boat netting chernia, swordfish, orata. For a city dweller for whom a brick wall choked with weeds is a natural vista, this view was a blessing. In the early months, during those low times when the words wouldn't come, I noticed that a few of the female sunbathers had unstrung their bikini tops and were reclining au naturel. From time to time, I found myself leaning through my open window, and, um, musing awhile about my work. After I discovered, with a start, that I'd written only fifteen pages in two weeks, I realized that Pietro had rented us the world's worst apartment, after all.

But, you know, I lived with it.

Cecilia and Norma shared a room (and, often, a bed; it was the little snipe's first time sleeping without fencing), while Janet,

Lorenzo, and I took the other camera. As you might have guessed, *camera* is the Italian word for bedroom. Perhaps this gives you an idea of how difficult it was for me to grasp the language. I'd taken lessons in Toronto with an instructor who was eager to teach me at first, but later confessed, "You know, I think Janet, she will be fluent in Italian by the time she comes home. And even Cecilia will be speaking a little!" And he stopped there.

With certain words, I detected clever etymological clues (*week* is *settimana* because there are seven days – *septo* – in a week), and others just reminded me of stupid things (*guidare* is to drive – I once had a friend named Guido, who was really into cars; and *mela* means apple – the boxer Eddie Melo had a head like a bruised apple). But with words like *camera*, I was lost. I mean, in no way does it make one think bedroom (unless you're in a relationship that encourages cameras in the bedroom. I'm not. Never mind). I had no better luck with *piano* and *stanza*. *Piano*, my friends, means floor, while *stanza*, yup, means room. Not bedroom, mind you, but room, as in, "I'm going into the camera to stanza on my piano," or something to that effect, which is actually a sentence I might use. In English. Only we were in Italy. I didn't own a camera, but I slept in one.

Go figure.

The day after we arrived, Pietro collected me in his Land Rover to take me out to practise with the Peones. Pietro and Maria Pia had arranged everything for us, from ironing our bedsheets and setting up a local bank account to letting me use Pietro's citizenship card to pass unmolested through customs. Since I had no idea how to repay him, I presented him with a box of balls from Canada (made in China, actually), which had been unkissed by either wood or aluminium, and my red Louisville bat, which, after a few practices, would be referred to by the team as *il legno rosso*, a much prettier way of saying "big hurt stick." One of the first Italian phrases I was able to master was: "Ti piace mio legno rosso?" ("Do you like my red, wooden bat?") This worked quite well on the diamond, but was confounding for whomever was making my espresso.

The Peones' home diamond was located in San Giacomo (the

Serie A Nettuno Indians played at a newer ballpark closer to the water), an older suburb north of Nettuno. We got to the ballpark by walking down a gravel lane below the road, passing a cement wall where two badly faded paintings promised what lay ahead. One was of Goofy hitting what appeared to be a billiard ball with a baseball bat, the other was a crudely rendered Major League Baseball insignia. The ballpark was surrounded by metal fencing held together by scavenged wire, as if the field were merely an extension of the grassy farmland that stretched out beyond left field. Behind home plate sat a playground with rusted swings and climbers that were as suitable for children as the musings of Foxy Brown, and a row of tall trees paralleled the first-base line. Beyond centre right, the ravine that divided San Giacomo from Nettuno East was home to sparrows, crows, and cornacchia, a constellation of fluttering bugs, and high tufts of sugar cane and bulrushes. At the base of the outfield fence, wildflowers and weeds rampaged up from the valley. Whenever there was a lull in the team's workout, I liked to walk to the lip of the ravine and peer down. Sometimes there'd be two dozen pecore (sheep) making their way down the shaggy banks, other times a cow, a bunch of kids playing soccer, a pack of dogs. Atop the other side of ravine sat a half-built church that had been half-built when we'd come for our look-see the previous October. I figured that having half of a church watch over the team was better than having no church at all.

One of the diamond's charms was that it was possible at times to stand in the parking lot at the end of the gravel path and inhale the scent of peppers and veal shank wafting from a nearby kitchen. Later in the year, while I was walking in from the outfield with Paolo, the veteran catcher, he stopped dead in his tracks, clasped his hands, and closed his eyes in rapture, sighing, "Ahhhhh . . . barbecue chicken!"

The Peones' diamond gear had been wearied and bitten by the weather. The bonnet of the hitting cage and mesh pitching fences used for batting practice creaked when you rolled them across the grass, slowed by rusted wheels and bent metal, while the shovels and hoes used for tilling the bullpen mound – which was mottled with weeds and clumps of dirt – looked like old gravedigger's tools, their handles bowed and rough. When I first arrived, the field was being mowed by a sleepy-eyed man wearing a dark rumpled suit, who pulled his John Deere across grass spotted with small white flowers, which the Peones were reluctant to weed themselves (they left the poppies, lilacs, daisies, and other flora surrounding the park to bloom). The players were similarly laissez-faire over a dead mole that had become entangled in the hitting cage's mesh, which none of them wanted to touch, leaving it to grow maggoty as summer ripened.

That said, the infield was a lovely, deep-red clay, and it was regulation size, not at all like the bandbox rinks I'd encountered on my exotic hockey tour a few years earlier. The concrete bleachers, which stood impossibly high – perhaps forty feet – above the field and behind home plate, were bleached grey-white, exactly the kind of quirk you'd find in a field built by a person unaware of the problem a light background might present to an infielder trying to track a speeding white pill. The dugouts were also made from concrete blocks, and while you could tell that every Nettunese ballplayer who'd ever scratched himself had once sat there, they weren't altogether horrible places to sit and spit. There was a small sink at one end with a piece of garden hose plugged over the tap, however the bottom and sides of the sink had turned black and green with algae, so I was careful not to put my face against the Mesozoic sludge when quenching my thirst. The floor of the dugout was well below field level, with three or four steps at one end that brought you out to the field. I was reminded, for an instant, of the old, sunken grottos of Tiger Stadium and Fenway Park, so, as if I were Don Zimmer or Johnny Pesky, I sat down on the bench in the Peones' dugout and pulled on my glove as Pietro introduced me to the players.

Here I'll start with the team's largest player, for he was the most noticeable. This should not be considered a slight, for I've always held that one of the things that separates baseball from other sports is that the male fan can look down and see himself more or less represented on the field, which is to say they still let fat people in. Baseball is not just the domain of the pumped and ripped, but also the heavy and the hipped. Anyone who's ever pulled on a glove – with the possible exception of Michael Jackson – knows that baseball is not a sport that requires players to be body-toned, or even fit, to compete. For much of their careers, relief pitchers only have to stride a few hundred feet from their bullpen chair to the mound (sometimes they're even driven across the field in a golf cart). Ex-Phillie John Kruk, whose lifetime batting average of .300 suggests equine strength and grace at the plate and on the basepaths, possessed a body like a teapot. When derided by a woman in a restaurant for not looking enough like a bona fide ballplayer, he told her, "Lady, you don't have to be an athlete to play baseball." It's players like Kruk who give the game its everyman pull. At heart, we're all a bunch of Shanty Hogans, the formidably waisted old Giant who used to avert the suspicions of his manager, John McGraw (who regularly reviewed Hogan's dinner bills), by striking a deal with hotel waiters so that pie à la mode appeared on paper as asparagus. Babe Ruth, like Hogan, was also a famous destroyer of foodstuffs: it's said that a typical breakfast comprised an eighteen-egg omelette with three slices of ham, six slices of toast, and two bottles of beer. It's no wonder that Yankee owner Jacob Ruppert suggested the team wear pinstripes to make Ruth appear thinner.

The roly-poly representative on the Peones was the man I called Pitò the Stricken, who, typically, also bore the brunt of much of the team's humour. Pitò had been a star pitcher in his youth, but an arm injury had robbed him of his potential, waistline, and mop of blond hair. His family had originally hailed from France (Pitò only ever whispered this), so he possessed little of the swarthiness of his teammates. Instead, he had the pallor and shape of a salt-and-vinegar potato chip. This is not to say that Pitò was defensive or at all sensitive when the team poked fun at his weight, skin tone, or lack of pitching tools (although, later, I think it got to him) because, during that first practice, he was repeatedly lifting his shirt and

Chencho.
(Cathy Bidini)

rubbing his belly, drawing cries of amusement from the rest of the
team. When I tried to ask Chencho Navacci, the club's dyed-blond,
spike-haired left-hander, what was Pitò's best pitch, he mimed a
hurried eating motion with his hand.

"Forkball," he said, grinning.

Chencho was the flakiest pastry in the tin. I expected nothing
less from a left-handed reliever. Whenever I dropped Chencho's
name in the company of other local ballplayers, it was met with
hiked eyebrows and a demented rolling of eyes. It seemed that as

many players in Nettuno knew Chencho as knew Pietro, but for different reasons. While the veteran coach's reputation had been staked by years of championship baseball, Chencho was famous for holding the ballpark earthworm-eating record, and other diversions of bullpen life.

Perhaps it was his fondness for cacchione – Nettuno's strong vino bianco, which Chenco said enhanced one's sexual abilities – but wild expressions were always bouncing across his face. They only ever settled down when he was pitching, at which point his body took over, using a swooping three-quarter delivery that lifted both of his feet off the mound when he threw. When Chencho wasn't pitching – which was often, since he worked in relief – he killed time by heaving his skull into a locker from a running start, or singing into one of his shower sandals. He led the team in pretending to have intercourse with inanimate objects, favouring batting gloves, helmets, cement poles, and empty ball boxes.

The Peones had two players named Mario (they also had two Fabios and three Alessandros). To confuse matters further, the Marios were, for a time, the only two players who ever brought their girlfriends around. If that wasn't enough, both of these women bore a resemblance, as did many young Nettunese, to Cher, or at least the young Cher. Each had long black hair, full lips, and wore tight pants pulled just a little below their hips. I could barely tell them apart. What distinguished their boyfriends from each other was Mario Simone's nose. His was like a lavish hood ornament pointing out from between his wraparound shades. Once, when we saw him in tight bathing trunks at the beach, Janet remarked that Mario looked like one of Madonna's dancers, but his stars-and-stripes bandana gave off a lost 1960s *Easy Rider* sort of vibe. Surprisingly, his knowledge of 1960s American iconography was quite limited. He told me that, a year before, Anzio had hosted an outdoor concert by a very popular American musician whose name he simply couldn't recall.

"Rock? Folk? What was it?" I asked.

"It was . . . rock. I think. Was very good."

"And you can't remember who it was?"

"No. Ummm . . . He is very famous. Very well known."

"And American? You're sure?"

"Yes. I even worked as part of the security."

"Rock, you say? Rock and roll?"

"Kind of, yes . . ."

"Bob Dylan?" I asked, taking a stab in the dark.

"*Yes! Yes!* Bob Dylan!"

Mario Simone constantly sung fragments of English and Italian songs, as if his brain was a radio dial hopping from one frequency to the next. Sometimes when he showed up early for practice, I'd watch him throw in the distance with another player along the left-field line – the birds chirping, butterflies tumbling through the air, a goat braying from beyond the ravine – to have this baseballian reverie broken by "*I am simpalee da besssssst!*" A construction worker by trade and a centre fielder with the Peones, Mario was an Italian hoser. Pietro once described Mario as not as smart as the other players, but perhaps he was biased because Mario was among the handful of Peones who confronted him on the field, finding it impossible to internalize a single emotion. Mario wasn't one to let an umpire's questionable call go, either. Sometimes his at-bats were a slapstick opera, an opera buffo. If he didn't like the call, he'd bend over as if being pulled backwards by his hair, thrust his hands in the air, and belt "Puttana!" at the sky. If the umpire took exception and shouted back, Mario would wave him off before settling back in the box, where, once his feet were righted, he stood as stiff as a Stop sign. Because he wore his socks hiked halfway up his knees, Mario looked like a prewar ballplayer who'd configured his stance before anyone knew anything about weight distribution or the hind flank being the power zone (or even used terms like *power zone*). His bat loomed way too high above his helmet. Any experienced batting coach would have been all over it, but any experienced coach wouldn't have been coaching him in the first place.

Whenever I made Mario Simone search for a word in English, he would tighten as if he were about to get poked with a needle.

Mario Mazza, on the other hand, spoke quickly and recklessly. Mario was the team's knothole kid (and second baseman). He had a small, boyish face, a quick smile, and his voice was forever on the verge of cracking into laughter.

Despite his sunny disposition, Mario was prone to episodes of deep funk, which usually came after fielding errors or troubling days at the plate. Post-strikeout, he'd often sit by himself on the bench, staring into the dugout's cement ledge and rubbing his gammy leg, which had slowed him considerably, and had prevented him from blossoming into one of Italy's best young talents. Mario was a spinning weathervane of emotions, a raw, bipolar nerve. If he committed an error, his bright, round face would sharpen into an insolent triangle. He had little or no emotional rebound after booting a play in the field or flailing at a third strike, responding like a child who'd just had his tricycle taken away. But when fortune smiled on the Peones, he was overwhelmed with happiness, often to the point of breaking into tears. He participated hard in practice, chasing down every ball that was hit to him. The first thing Mario Mazza ever said to me was, "Do you like the drug?"

I wasn't sure that I'd heard him right – or that he'd actually said what he'd said – so I got him to repeat it.

"Do you like drug?" he repeated.

"Drugs? Ya, I like drugs."

"No, no, the band. Do you like the drug band?"

"Bands? Yes, I like bands. Which ones?"

"No, no, not band: bunt."

"Ancora, lentamente," I asked him. Again, slowly.

"Do . . . you . . . like . . . the . . . drug . . ."

"Drug?"

". . . bunt?"

"The drug bunt?"

"Si! The drug bunt!"

This was the second time the drag bunt had been mentioned to me. Fabio Sena – the Emperor's best friend, who played a myriad of positions – had spoken to me before about baseball's element of surprise. He asked me flat out, "Do you know one way there is to win a game?"

I ventured a guess: "Drag bunt?"

"Si!" he said, thrusting his finger at me.

To keep the two Fabios distinct, I called Fabio Sena "Fabio from Milan" and Fabio Giolitti, "Fab Julie." This came to pass when Mario Mazza shouted, "Il morta che tua!" after robbing someone of a hit in practice. I asked Mario to illuminate the nature of this phrase, and he said that it meant to kill one's family. I must have expressed a certain dismay, because Fabio from Milan rushed up to me and said, at what sounded like 78 rpm, "No, not like that! Not so serious, but, in a funny way." I still wasn't buying it, so he said, "They say it up north, in Milan! I know this because I am from Milan. We kill your family all the time in Milan!"

Chicca was the Peones' third baseman, and no one knew where Chicca was from. At thirty, he was the oldest of the Peones. He looked perpetually weary – which was ironic, considering that he ran a cappuccino stand on the other side of town – and was the only member of the team to show up scruffy and stubble-chinned, dressed casually in a T-shirt and jeans. He fielded groundballs like a toy skeleton, the kind with a string you pull to make its arms and elbows shoot out. This odd style tended to work, and the players respected him for his formidable play and mysterious nature. Chicca was the one player who didn't say a word to me for the first month of my visit. He showed up alone at practice, walked over to his position, sucked up every ball that Pietro hit to him, then disappeared, like one of W.P. Kinsella's spectres in *Shoeless Joe*. To this day, I cannot tell you whether he drove because I never noticed him leaving.

Paolo Danna, whose stomach was only slightly flatter than Pitò's, was the one Peone who spoke good, if not polished, English, so I was constantly asking Paolo to translate what was being said. He did this with great patience – not once did he shift to the end of the bench to avoid answering questions about Chicca's socks or Chencho's motorino.

Paolo's soprannome was Sheriff, a name he'd inherited from an old Nettuno Indians' catcher, Jeff Ransom, who'd also given him his first glove. He had strong legs and a broad chest – good catcher's stock – and his forearms were fat little hens. He had a wide face with sympathetic eyebrows – the kind of face that kids are drawn to, for it hides nothing – and a welcoming gap between his teeth. Paolo was the type of player who could mentally adjust either to smiting the ball with a vengeance or pausing to take in the wild-flowers blooming in the outfield. Chencho – a staunch Communist who took to singing party hymns when he could no longer think of ways to rhyme *Bidini* with a farm animal's reproductive organs – used to ride Paolo about his political convictions. Paolo had cam-paigned and given speeches as a member of the Green Party and was studying to get his degree in oceanography and meteorology. While his concern for the Earth didn't stop him from eating the dust of home plate when required, I valued Paolo because I could drop Hemingway's name while talking to him without being looked at sideways.

Paolo was the team's aging catcher, even though he was only twenty-seven. He'd quit baseball for six years after playing for the national team as a prized eighteen-year-old prospect, and his brother, Gonfreddo, had caught at Serie A Nettuno for a number of years. Paolo had been absent from last year's division winners and was aware that he had only a year or two left in him to win a league title. Because of his layoff, the early practices were hard on him and his body. It's one thing to try to regain your form at the plate, but it's another to step into a position that requires constant physical intensity and intellectual command.

At the beginning of the season, Pietro wanted Paolo to backup Emiliano Conti, a tall, handsome player with a devastating power stroke, who rivalled Chicca as the quietest Peone. To quote Sparky Anderson on Jose Canseco, the Big Emilio, as I called him, had the body of "a Greek Goddess." Each day he arrived for practice on his motorino, the essence of cool in a glittering blue helmet as he bar-relled down the gravel path, spraying dust and stones and smoke in his wake. The Big Emilio was a pure hitter, with a batting stance – legs spread, bat waving, weight adjusted to his back foot, elbow pointing like the crook of a bow at the pitcher – that said power. Like Fred White once said of slugger Don Baylor, "He looked like an RBI standing up there."

The middle infield was tiny, lithe, and quick. Mario Mazza and Giampiero "Skunk" Bravo traded off between second and shortstop (or interbase, as the Italians called). Skunk Bravo was the smallest Peone. He was a whispering presence, only ever speaking – at least to me – after being asked a question. Skunk was blessed with what scouts like to call "a tender glove." He also was the possessor of a thick mop of black hair that never moved – not when he dashed to his left to scoop the ball with his mitt, nor pivoted atop second to launch the ball for the back end of the double play. Because of his hair, at first I wanted to call him Porcupine, but it didn't sit right because there was no roundness to his shape whatsoever. I'd fancied Chicken – like Fred "Chicken" Stanley, he was also fast-moving and small – but it was kind of disparaging, so I settled on Skunk. I decided that his hedge of dark-black hair was like a skunk's haunch, and whenever he got to a ball, he "skunked" a hit away from the batter. It was imperfect, but it would have to do.

Left fielder and designated hitter Simone Cancelli (the Natural) – and the Emperor's cousin – had a barrel chest for a kid of twenty-three, and could slug the ball with power. He had a soft face with long lashes and wore his sideburns trimmed to a fine point below his jawline. Though he wasn't tall, he moved with confidence, making him appear bigger than he was, possibly the result of his day job as a traffic cop. The previous year, he'd polished the bench for a Serie A team in Anzio, but was back this year taking his cuts in Serie B. He was the one Peone who seemed driven to achieve something in baseball, to make his mark.

The Natural was also an aficionado of the game, and more than any of his teammates, he seemed aware that, by playing ball in Nettuno, he was part of the city's grand sporting continuum. Each time we spoke, he explained how he and his girlfriend were connected

The Natural.
(Cathy Bidini)

to Nettuno's baseball past. His girlfriend's uncle, for example, was Fausto Comusi, the fellow who brought the game to Grossetto, in Tuscany, founding a club that would challenge Nettuno's baseball supremacy. The Natural's own grandfather played for Nettuno in the 1940s and 1950s, and had been in action on the day Joe DiMaggio showed up at the prince's field in the summer of 1957 to take his cuts.

The Natural knew enough about baseball that we were able to talk a little about the inside game. One day, he asked me, "Superstitione?"

I told him yes. I had a series of rituals not uncommon to players of all stripes, both scrub and trillionaire. Whenever I showed up at my home park, the first thing I did was to empty my pockets of all money (a gesture that, I'd guess, is much easier for the scrub than the star), which I hid under the end of the players' bench nearest to the dugout entrance. Once I'd done that, I felt ready to hold a bat, which, game in, game out, had to be wood, never metal. (Once, I cracked my blond Cooper stalwart, but rather than forfeit my folly at the plate, I chanced to use a teammate's metal lance. Yup. Game-winning double.) On my way to the game, I bought the same energy bar (blueberry granola, until it was, horror of horrors, discontinued) from the same store (7-Eleven), and took the same route every time.

I told the Natural this, and I told him how Wade Boggs ate chicken and cheesecake before every game (and two hot dogs, a bag of barbecue chips, and an iced tea afterwards. Unless you have a swing as even as a Saskatchewan sunset, as Wade did, you probably don't want to try this at home). One day, his cheesecake came topped with strawberries, and he hung an o'fer. Never again.

"Boggs, è campione?" asked Simone.

"Campione," I said. "Of baseball, e pollo."

"World Series?"

"Uno, I think. But lots and lots of batting titles, for sure."

The Natural nodded his head and showed me the inside of his glove, where he'd written a tiny number, twenty-one, in black ink.

"Perché twenty-one?"

"It was the day that my girlfriend and I met," he said. "September, twenty-one."

"That's swell," I said.

"And my calze," he said, pointing to his socks. "Never change. Never."

"I'll remember that the next time I'm sitting beside you in the dugout," I said. He cocked his head quizzically. It was a joke that would have to wait till later.

4

MIA PALANCA, MIA AMORE

I challenge anyone who's ever played a sport to convince me that they like to practise. No one likes to practise. I know what they say – the great ones are great because they work harder in practise than anyone else – but even Maurice Richard said, "I get paid to practise. I would play the games for free." Much of my discontent comes from having been forced to practise as a kid, all of those repetitive drills, which soaked up so much precious time when I might have been doing something more valuable instead, like locking David Moore's head to a sewer grate. When I think of practising, the image of a pylon comes flying at me, bringing back the pain of sore legs and arms and the sound of a middle-aged man in sweatpants blowing into a whistle.

But practising with the Peones was fun. I didn't play with them, but I was allowed to practise, and enjoyed it even though the routine was commanded by a middle-aged man. Pietro wore not exactly sweatpants but what you might call sweat underpants. Well, sweatshorts. And he didn't brandish a whistle (an absurd tool in a nation so in love with the sound of its own voice), but he carried his fungo like he meant it, working the players through a series of drills designed to make them il campioni of Serie B ball.

Sadly, these drills included running. I have not run voluntarily since 1974. When Pietro asked, "Dave, you run with us?" my first notion was to chuckle loudly, but then I thought that the team might better accept me if I participated in all of the drills (turned out, it mattered not a whit). And as we charged over first base and turned towards the clubhouse, I decided that running wasn't bad at all. Turned out, I was only half-right, because Pietro looped us back, and we ran from first to second, second to third, and third to home, four or five times.

I survived, and happily this modest sprint was as gruelling as the practice would get. Otherwise, my two hours were spent behaving like a dog off its chain, flying around the field picking off (or not picking off, as was often the case) fly balls, retrieving errant throws to home plate, and playing catch. The outfield was so much wider than at home (you could have fit our entire softball diamond in the San Giacomo infield) that when I ran under a looping line shot, I found myself travelling a surprising distance, which may or may not explain why I was panting like Cicciolina with every plucked fly (or unplucked fly). More often than not, I'd track the ball feeling like Devo White or Andy Van Slyke, only to arrive far too late. It served me well to watch a few of the Peones – Solid Gold and Mario Simone, to name two – who swallowed pretty much everything that was hit to them, rarely breaking into anything faster than a lope to get to where they had to be to make the outs look automatic. Near the end of the drill, I finally managed to track one ball down, and was met with cheers. The play was half forty-yard dash – my heart jumping through my skin, shoes skipping across the grass like locusts – and half balletic catch, the ball falling into my glove. I tucked my leather under my arm and slowly galloped to a stop at the edge of the ravine. I sighed a long sigh, then turned to Pietro and proudly showed him the ball before slinging it into the clouds above his head.

Pietro usually stood about five feet behind second base, fungo in hand, the one I'd brought him from Canada: black, with white hockey tape wrapped around the handle. Baseball has given us many delightful words and phrases – *chin music, the frozen rope, waggling the bat, the suicide squeeze, banjo hit, the sweet spot, bitten to death by ducks*, et cetera – but *fungo* is among its finest. Hardball scholars the world over are stumped over the etymology of *fungo*, which only adds to the charm of this lightweight hitting stick. Tapered at the handle and with a nubby barrel, the fungo ostensibly allows the batsmen greater control and prolonged use, due to the weight of its body. Working a good fungo is like being able to hit a housefly with a wad of gum. You've got to be able to strike the ball precisely so that your player gets the proper workout. Need three hops to short? No problem. Texas Leaguers behind first? Okay. Doubles off the wall? Can do 'er.

Modern major leaguers have testified that no one handles a fungo like Jimy Williams, the former Red Sox and Blue Jays boss, and long-time third-base coach for Bobby Cox's Atlanta Braves. Jimy also had the disconcerting habit, when managing, of stuffing all ten fingers deep down the front band of his pants. Although he kept his hands out of his pants, Pietro was a pretty good *fungattore* in his own right, running the Peones hard while hitting the ball to all fields.

At work, Pietro tried to be a disciplinarian, which was no small feat while wielding an instrument with a name like Snow White's eighth dwarf. Every now and then his "Vai!" or "Veloce!" sounded serious. When shouting at the top of his lungs, he had a commanding voice, even though it climbed the musical scale. He also had a powerful swing, having long ago smoothed away the choppiness that burdened a few of the Peones, notably Mario Simone and the Emperor, who moved their bats through the strike zone with all the stiffness of an old cellar door. Pietro hit the ball tirelessly – fifty consecutive swings, perhaps more – and as the sun dimmed over the third-base line, he cut an impressive figure in the burning orange light, an ageless Olympian slugging against the march of time.

Pietro lined up half the team in right field, the other half in left, and had them move like a duck gallery across the outfield, where he whopped fungos just far enough in front of them to make the catch difficult. Every now and then, a flychaser would get a late start and Pietro would yell, "Mascalzone!" (rascal). Whenever they missed a ball, he made them repeat the drill, and since the guys grew tired after only an hour of work (it was still early in the year), this happened a lot. Pietro started to get annoyed, and when Fabio from Milan missed his catch – a rare occurrence – the coach laid into him, with singsong rhythm and melody. As Fabio from Milan was standing about two hundred feet away in centre field, I wondered how much of an impact the coach's words would have. Turned out, not very. After Pietro finished his rant, Fabio shouted back – "That ball was too far! Why don't you give me a chance!" – which made Pietro yell some more. This went on for quite a while – one voice rising above the next like duelling violins – until Fabio from Milan shouted more words in succession faster than I've ever heard spoken by a single person. It was like a performance piece by the Four Horsemen. I had no idea what he'd said, but was impressed by his verbal speed. So, obviously, was Pietro, who pointed his fungo upfield and commanded firmly, "Vai."

Fabio from Milan jogged into left, his point won. Pietro sliced the ball into the air. This time, Fabio from Milan ran velocemente, all kicking legs and long arms, and trapped the ball in the heart of his glove. His run collapsed into a jog, slowed to a trot, and ended in a few long steps before he rested his hands on his hips and leaned over the grass, the sun sinking behind him.

Pietro gave him very little. But he gave him something: "Okay. Was that so hard? Questo allenamento è finito."

In the car after the practice, Pietro admitted, "This is a good team. These are good guys."

"There's a good balance," I said. "You know, Fabio from Milan, Chencho on one side; the Big Emilio and Chicca on the other. Some guys up the middle."

"Is what makes a team," he said, navigating us through the narrow streets. Despite the late hour, the shops were busy. We passed baskets of plums, cantaloupes, red and green tomatoes, figs, cherries, grapes, apples, and nectarines (pesca nuda, the naked peach) laid out in crates across the cobblestone walk, a crowded gelateria, bar after bar after bar, including both the Blues Club and the Jazz Club, neither of which had any live music, LA DOLCE NOTTE sweet shop, whose speciality was something called la bomba calde – a hot bomb – which I thought might have gone nicely with a pesca nuda; and a handful of busy cafés, each of them rattling with colour and life.

"A team is many parts. Cinque dito è una mano," I said, spreading my fingers, then folding them into a fist to illustrate my point.

"Ah," he said. "Si. Cinque diti è una mano."

"Cinque diti, yes," I said, correcting myself.

He opened and closed his hands a few times, perhaps imagining a team coming together, stretching apart.

It was during an early practice that Paolo helped me to compile a list of Italian baseball expressions. I'd started to lean on the backup catcher for translation, and he was more than happy to help, as was his way. Paolo possessed a great deal of selflessness – a quality that I've found to be common among talented veteran athletes. One of the reasons clubs like the Peones draft such players is because they are a steadying force. I appreciated Paolo's help even more after learning that he sometimes suffered long, sleepless nights studying for exams (Italian students write their finals in late July and early August), often showing up at the park looking as if he'd spent the night sparring with the ghost of Primo Carnera. Combined with the fact that his power stroke seemed none too eager to return – there were days when he'd lift the ball with authority, only to see it fly straight over second base – I would have understood had he waved me off whenever I approached him. But he never did. He put up with my constant natterings about whether *faccia di cazzo* was a term of derision or endearment, or where in Nettuno I might buy the local version of Toilet Duck. I was grateful.

Together, we drew up a list. Italian and English, it turned out, share a lot of baseball words: foul was *foul*, pick off was *pick off*, grand slam was *grand slam* (not *grande salami*, as I'd hoped), and bunt was *bunt*, at least when it wasn't *stoppa*, which is what the fans, not the players, called it. Hit was *base valide* (if you were under thirty) or *singolo* (if you were older). Double was, of course, *doppio*, and triple was, you guessed it, *trippolo*. Home run was the first term I learned: *fuoricampo* (literally, "out of the field"). Stolen base was *ruba*, as in "Ruuuubbaaa!", which the players shouted whenever a baserunner was set in motion. Catcher was *ricevitore*, while pitcher was *lancetore*, meaning, literally, "he who throws a spear" ("Like a fisherman who uses a stick," said Paolo. "Like a knight who throws a lance," corrected Mario Mazza).

Fastball was *fastball* (it was also, sometimes, *diritto*, meaning straight), curve was *curva*, and slider was *slider*, except when it was *cuciture*, a word that referred to the point in the ball's rotating stitches. They had no colloquialism for screwgee (i.e., screwball) or spitter, mostly because they didn't throw one. However, *cambio* was the word that pitchers gave to their changeup, at least to Chencho's changeup, which, when it was working right, would come at you like a grapefruit, only to fall through a trap door in the air. At one practice, with Paolo catching, I stood over the bullpen dish and faced him, providing a dummy batter to help il matto sinistro find his location. It was then that I learned two other phrases, or rather, taunts – *pia la palanca* and *pia la guitara* – both deriding hitters lugging slow bats. Being a musician, I found the taunt double-edged. Not only did I have a slow bat, but it only stood to reason that I might occasionally hold it as if it were my long-time instrument of choice. Maybe it was the rock 'n' roll in me talking, but I mused aloud to a few of the boys that, given the right circumstances, this guitar-playing non-slugger might relish the opportunity to defend the honour of baseball-playing musicians everywhere, from Garth Brooks to Geddy Lee. Later that week, I got the chance.

I'd like to report that my days with the Peones got off to a flying start, however the first game I was scheduled to write about – at San Giacomo, against a team from Sardinia – was rained out. The day was swamped by a great storm. It was so thrilling that I almost didn't begrudge the huge tower of grey that gathered over the town, nor the jellybean-sized rain pellets it unleashed on us. But, like any scrub on his first day of ball, I still hoped that the darkness would soon crack and the spirit of Rube Marquand would appear to blow-dry the field. But it never did. Pietro and I drove to the park anyway, and spent the better part of the morning standing in the doorway of the clubhouse watching a river pour along the sunken pathway between first and second base.

Every Peone was deflated, but the team from Sardinia felt considerably worse. They'd travelled an hour by air, only to have to turn around and go back. Their day consisted of bus-plane-bus-clubhouse-bus-plane-bus, and I don't think their spikes ever touched the field.

The first practice after the rainout, Pietro called for a game of scrub, and yours truly was grateful to be included. I thought it was a smart move on Pietro's part to run a loose, carefree practice. There was no sense in demanding a physical workout when the guys had been well prepared for game action, only to be left hanging. Scrub – or workups, as others call it – gave the boys a chance to take their licks at the plate, and to observe and measure the skills of the Canadian import.

I started the mini-game in left field, *esterno sinistre*. Naturally, the afternoon's first hit came my way, a high, screaming liner that deflected off the webbing of my glove. I make no excuses for the error – the general rule in baseball is that if you can touch it, you should catch it – but I was playing with a new, blue-and-red Heart of the Hide mitt (Raul Mondesi model) whose webbing was considerably less malleable than my old Joe Torre first baseman's glove, which had been my regular leather for the last twenty-seven years.

I'd brought the vintage Torre glove to Italy but after so many years sweeping across diamonds and fields – to say nothing of the hours I'd spent grinding it into the pavement as a street-hockey goaltender – it was actually less like a glove than two pulpy mango skins stitched together. There were times, while playing with the Rebels, that opposing players found it lying against the fence and nudged it with their foot as if it were a dead squirrel. I figured that a final, symbolic trip to Torre's homeland was the least I could do for its years of service. I was determined to give it a little bit of work too, and after flubbing my first chance with my new mitt, I thought that maybe my hand, suddenly encased in hard blue-and-red leather, was telling me something.

No thanks to me, my team got out of the inning down by only one run. As I jogged in – without even being ordered to – I looked to see who I would be facing in my first Italian at-bat. Pietro had deployed the four pitchers to rotate between the two teams: Pitò the Stricken, Pompozzi, Cobra, and Chencho. I would have forfeited my at-bat against Pompozzi. There would have been no point. The young hurler was only twenty-one years old, and had a hot, lively arm. While he seemed like too nice a kid to bury one under the chin of a stranger, I didn't want to find out the hard way. Pitò the Stricken concerned me less. He'd started the game pitching for our side, and had had a rough go of it. His change didn't change and his fastball wasn't. Coming off his hand, the ball had no zing, and from my perspective, it looked like it hurt him when he threw. Pietro ordered him to sit. Pitò never threw another pitch that day.

We sent four batters to the plate before I hit, but I have no idea what they did because I was too busy listening to a cautious inner voice, warning me not to strike out. It probably wouldn't have meant a thing to the fellows if I had, but there was my pride to consider and, really, I was determined not to suck. I'd already E-7'ed, and adding a strikeout to my Mediterranean debut was the last thing

I wanted to do in front of the players I'd be travelling around Italy with over the next five months. Feeling tight as a zither string, I stuffed my head into a batting helmet and grabbed my redwood Slugger, waggling it in mock confidence as I strode to the dish. I looked out.

Chencho.

As a rule, I've been told always to take the first pitch: *lascia la palla.* So I did: strike one. The ball slapped into Paolo's glove, who was crouching behind the plate, murmuring the odd word of encouragement: "Waiting on the ball . . . good, Dave." Still, it felt pretty good to be playing even though I was in the hole.

For the next pitch, Chencho came inside, and, this time, I swung: strike two. "See the ball!" yelled Pietro from first. "Concentrate," said Paolo, almost whispering. They were both right. After I'd swung, I knew that I hadn't seen the pitch. I was trying too hard to hit the damned thing to really hit it at all. At that point, two suggestions ran through my head: stay back – *aspetta* – and see the ball into the catcher's glove. I wasn't really sure how to do either in the heat of a swing, but I'd heard it said so many times on television, it was like a double mantra. I stepped back and, for a second, gazed out at the field. *Don't strike out. 0-2. That's one pitch away from striking out.* From the hill, I heard Chencho huffing. His face was still and his eyebrows – which were usually so buoyant and expressive – had fallen into a bold line, an underscore across his forehead. I watched him as he peered in for the sign. Chencho drew the ball into his glove while I considered, at the last moment, that the two Peones with whom I'd made a personal connection were trying to strike me out.

The pitch sailed outside. I heard Paolo grunt as he stretched and caught it. I felt a little indignant that they'd taken me for someone who would've fished for such an obviously wasted pitch, but was grateful for staying alive.

"Chencho is sexy!" I shouted.

He gave a slight laugh, then collected himself.

"Chencho is beautiful!"

He watched for the next sign.

"Mascalzone."

I didn't know how far I was supposed to take my at-bat – or, rather, how far Pietro wanted me to – but I was willing to test the limits. So when Chencho gathered himself into his delivery, I put up my arm and stepped out. I saw Chencho blow out a breath. I stepped back in. So did he.

The next pitch was a weird one, che strano. Afterwards, Chencho told me that it was high, that he hadn't meant to throw a hittable pitch. When he saw me swing, he thought he had me, the fisherman, biting at the high, hard one. Coming in, the ball looked fat and lazy, growing bigger as it approached the plate. Major leaguers talk about "seeing" the ball, and that's what it was like for me. For a moment I could see the rotation, the stitching, even the cartography of dirt and scruff on the pale rawhide. I realized that Chencho had not prepared his pitch's trap door, so I reacted. I slapped at the ball and it shot up, blooped over Mario Mazza's head, and dived for the shaggy field. I ran down the chalk line, watching the ball until it rolled to a standstill, at which point the outfielders converged upon it.

Someone yelled, "Salvo!"

It was a good word to hear.

5

NETTUNO AT MONTEFIASCONE

The evening before Nettuno at Montefiascone, Pietro gathered the team on the steps of the San Giacomo dugout and said, "We are now one team, una squadra. Everyone plays for each other, okay? This year is different. Because why? Because many things, many reasons. One of those reasons is here," he said, gesturing with his neck to the far end of the dugout, where I loitered with my notepad and tapedeck. The team turned and looked at me. "This year, someone has come to write about you. Think about that when you're in the field or at the plate. Give him a good story to tell."

The suspicious look on a few of the players' faces suggested that they didn't quite understand why, precisely, this writer had chosen to document their season of third-division ball in the first place. In fact, I'm not sure that my intentions were ever clearly explained, although I did catch Pietro mumbling something to them about il libro sportivo, and, I hoped, its validity as a serious literary form.

Before we broke practice, Pietro announced, "We leave at 6 a.m. tomorrow. Okay? No being late. The bus leaves at 6:15, not a minute later." So it was that, at 7 a.m. the next morning, the coach threw his first little shitfit, right there at the side of the road outside the ballpark, as the fifty-seater pulled up an hour late. The driver, inching his six-wheeled behemoth forward, held out his hands, then brought them together in an arrow and drew them towards his chest, where he tipped them back and forth in a plea for mercy. Pietro called him a cazzone (big dick) and spent his anger dragging the team's luggage – bats, helmets, spikes – towards the bus. If the late start hadn't been enough to sandpaper the manager's ass, three players had failed to show: Sandro Valentini, a heavy-hitting out-fielder who was one of those rare Italians – red-haired and freckle-faced – whom I nicknamed the Red Tiger; Davide Calabro, another outfielder, who would later be cut for missing the game; and Solid Gold, the team's regular centro campo. When I asked the Natural why Solid Gold was missing (he was, by far, the most talented of the absentees), he told me, "Last night, he was at the disco, proba-bly, till five o'clock in the morning. He is always there, even on the nights before important games." I asked what he made of this.

"Some players," he said, "don't try hard enough because they don't love the game."

I'd only ever been on one team road trip before, with my hockey club, the Morningstars, and I was voted Most Totally Wasted Dude for my post-game achievements. During the trip to Montefiascone, I became aware that everything about the process – the vehicle you take, the route, the field itself, the clubhouse, the lighting, the sound, smell, and feel of the playing surface – makes playing on the road different. Playing at home, you can usually predict what your day is going to feel like – one of the advantages of knowing a field, rink, or court is that you're familiar with the patterns of the sport in that location so that you can perform your best within them – but playing away is always unpredictable. Add to that the horror of waking at an ungodly hour to get there and the whole activity takes on a strange spin. As the bus rolled through the village of Campo di Carne, I knew I'd reached a new personal benchmark in world sporting travel when Paolo told me, tapping the window with his knuckle, "This village, it was given its name after the Second World

War. It means 'Field of . . . ,' how do you say?" he asked, tugging the skin on his arm.

"Skin?" I said.

"No. Not quite."

"Flesh?"

"Yes, flesh. Field of Flesh. Eight thousand soldiers were slaughtered here by the Germans."

North of Campo di Carne, farms spread out for as far as the eye could see. Then after about an hour the landscape suddenly changed, and thick forests swallowed the sky. We rumbled down narrow roads under a ceiling of interlaced branches. I was thrilled by the bounty and darkness of the country, a scene that in Canada would have been commonplace. Every now and then, we cruised through a medieval village buried in the lap of the forest, passing rows of ancient houses splashed with sunlight. For most of the trip, my hands and face were pressed against the window while the team slumbered quietly at the rear of the bus, their legs stretched out, newspapers flipped over on their laps, ball caps shading their tired eyes.

Many of the villages in greater Lazio were rich with lore (much of it about food and drink), and Montefiascone was no exception. The best and most famous story was about the town's local wine, Est! Est!! Est!!! The story is from the year 1110, when German Cardinal Johann Fugger sent his steward, Martin, to scout the inns that lay in Johann's path as he made his way to Rome for the coronation of Emperor Henry v. Martin's instructions were to write the word *Est* ("it is," in Latin) in chalk on the door of whatever osteria served wine suitable for the cardinal's rather prodigious consumption. In the olden days, this kind of assignment was considered to be a pretty good gig – even nowadays, you wouldn't complain – so Marty, obedient servant that he was, embraced his mission with great zeal. He didn't make it past a certain joint in Montefiascone, where he was found sprawled on the ground outside, drunker than Yeltsin. Above him, on the door, he'd written, *Est! Est!! Est!!!* The cardinal, rather than punish his bilious servant, bettered him, sampling the wine to its fullest breadth, not resting until he'd been poisoned by the very drink that had taken down his scout. The manner of his passing became such an oft-told tale that word of Est! Est!! Est!!! spread, making it one of southern Italy's most popular wines. In fact, everyone I spoke to before heading to Montefiascone told me I was obliged to kill a bottle or two in the old Fugger's honour. I told them I would try. Maybe the Most Totally Wasted Dude would go two for two on road trips.

The team from Montefiascone had no name, though I was hoping against hope for the Est! Est!! Est!!!s (the Peones seemed to be the only Serie B team to be called anything other than where they were from). The M-Birds (they had no nickname? I gave 'em one) held down first place in Serie B. Last year, they'd competed one level higher – Serie A2 – but had been relegated after a poor run against the bigger, better clubs. I asked Pompozzi at the start of the season what team was the one to beat in Serie B, and his face tightened when he said, "Montefiascone." Paolo had also told me, "Montefiascone have two very nice pitchers. And they have a very nice catcher. He is very nice, very good." *Nice* didn't sound too daunting, but I got the picture. I had joined the Peones three games into the season, and already Montefiascone was running away with the division, having lost only once, to Sardinia. In a previous engagement with the Peones, the M-Birds had swept both ends of the doubleheader – reports had them crushing the ball to all fields – and as we left the main road and swung into the town of the division leader, I felt a little guilty that I'd treated the trip like a Sunday outing, when it might have been a ride to a place where RBIs went to die.

The Montefiascone ballpark was a beautiful spot. The town was perched above the field on the rim of a volcanic crater, its buildings rearing over the park. It seemed as if only the glue of history was holding the town in place. In the centre stood the duomo of Santa Margherita's Cathedral, the third largest dome in all of Italy. The cathedral had been built to accommodate the remains of Santa Margherita (a lesser saint, Lucia Fillippini, was buried there too), and had given Montefiascone its name, "great flask mountain."

From centro campo, the dome dominated the park's backdrop like an enormous marble skull, a daunting sight for any ballplayer to blot out. Throwing the ball into such a view would be like flicking a pea into time's chasm. It was all I could look at as I walked around the outfield.

A few days before the game, I asked Pietro if he'd chosen his arms for the games against Montefiascone. Pietro shook his head for a second – Pietro shook his head a lot when discussing his team – then moaned about his pitchers and the skeletal nature of his staff, which comprised Pompozzi, Pitò the Stricken, Chencho, Fabio from Milan, Solid Gold (who was good for only a handful of innings a year), and the veteran pitcher, Cobra Spera.

Alessandro Spera – Cobra – was the crafty elder of the Peones' pitching staff. Chencho possessed a certain craftiness in his pitching too, but Cobra seemed craftier by nature. Chencho had given Cobra his nickname, an allusion to the fact that Cobra had, apparently quite heroically, got his wife pregnant. Chencho was forever explaining the name to me, as if I didn't get it. "Angallaaato . . . ," he'd say, dragging out the penultimate vowel and winking.

Cobra was a small man, all shoulder and breastbone. Before each pitch, he'd take a breath and his entire chest would heave, lifting the balls of his feet off the ground. He was so small, I wondered how he'd ever deliver the ball over the plate. But he was a wry veteran of local ball, authoritative, cunning, and cool. The Italians had a term for how he pitched – *spregiudicato* – which means using whatever means are at your disposal. The Peones leaned on him for quiet leadership because, unlike the rest of the flakes and misfits and reclamation jobs, Cobra was steadfast, not to mention good. And clever. He gave the batter very little with which to judge him and rarely got upset with his fielders (unlike Chencho). In the dugout, he wore a perpetual look of concern. But then he'd walk out to the mound, his head lowered, trying to draw the other team into believing that they could end his career with one swing. This gave him all the advantage he needed.

Cobra.
(Cathy Bidini)

As soon as we got to the park, the players hit the dressing room, and, once tucked into their spit-clean divisi, the Peones metamorphosed into ballplayers. I was thrilled to find that they wore blue and white, the colours of my home team, the Blue Jays, and their winter sisters, the Maple Leafs, to say nothing of the Brooklyn Dodgers, baseball's most fabled club, renown for losing pennants rather than winning them. The Peones' Dodgerdom was further invoked by their choice of chewing gum, Brooklyn, the most popular brand in Italy, which featured the Brooklyn bridge on its wrapper.

For the first time since I'd met them, the Peones were all wearing their cappelli, which they hadn't during practice. At first, the Peones refused to offer a good reason why they wore their caps only during games, but eventually I got them to admit what I'd suspected all along: they didn't want to mess their hair. Even on hot days with the sun beating down like Keith Moon's floor tom, the Peones refused to subject themselves to a condition that has long afflicted the North America male – hat head.

Being a traditionalist, this disregard for classic baseball style bothered me at first, but after a while it was actually refreshing to be among young men for whom wearing a baseball hat wasn't the pinnacle of fashion. (Their desire to look like Fred Durst or Eminem was quite low too). Black, shoulder-tight T-shirts with zippers up the front were another matter, but not to come across a constant horizon of bad band tattoos, face piercings, and a sea of bobbing ball caps made me feel pleasantly far from home.

I know that, at some level, wearing a baseball cap makes one feel like Honus Wagner, but a hat is a hat when it's sweetened with ball-park sweat and doused with beer, not spit-clean with something like CONDEX '97 inscribed across it. Ever since ball caps became popularized by balding Hollywood actors, they ceased to be the domain of fans supporting their favourite teams, and instead were worn by Gerald in softwood lumber, who was told by his boss to put the damned thing on, or else. Ball caps used to define the look of ball-players and truckers, who were in the habit of salting in a little sweat to make 'em look and feel just right. Imagine their disgust at those pale pink-and-green numbers that are sold for, like, fifty bucks at the Gap. Used to be, in trucking country anyway, that what you found at Bumpy's Eggs 'N' More was good enough to wear with pride on your noggin. But no longer. Cap wearers today have to sport the right logo to give them a certain identity, even though, right now, there are thousands of Florida Panthers caps being worn by people who have no idea just how badly that team sucks.

There was another, more obvious, reason why the Peones weren't attached to their caps. The logo, which a friend of the Emperor's had originally drawn on a napkin (while under the influence of a carafe of cacchione, I assumed), was supposed to be a smiling, leather-skinned Mexican peering out from under his sombrero. But it looked like a turd being squashed by a giant foot.

Really, it wasn't nice at all.

Even the way the ballplayers moved seemed to have changed. On the field, they carried themselves like athletes, which, by association, made me feel a little more like the real deal too. With a serious team in competition to write about, I felt like my job was finally in play, inspiring me to do what any serious sportswriter would do, which was to find a seat in the shade, pull my hat down, and grab twenty quick ones while the fellows ran their windsprints.

I was woken by Pietro, his cleats scraping the dugout's concrete floor, walking over to Cobra and telling him that he would start the first game (Pompo would go second), whereupon the veteran moved to the end of the bench and sat by himself, applying liniment to his right arm and shoulder and trying to steady his nerves. Pietro sat on the ledge and dictated the starting lineup to the Emperor: "Cancelli, Simone, Mazza . . ." The Emperor, as part of his executive capacity, ran a copy of the lineup to the official FIBS (Federazione d'Italiano Baseball e Softball) scorer sitting under an umbrella behind home plate, as modest a task as had ever been undertaken by any Italian emperor.

Once Pietro had set the roster, he cupped his hands to his mouth and bellowed to the players warming up on the field. They hustled back into the dressing room, and once everyone was seated, Pietro moved into the middle of the room. "Alora," he said, swinging into a pantomime. "Touch chest is bunt. Touch arm is batticorre [hit and run]. And touch belt is steal." Then he pinched two fingers to his cap. "Eh, and this, this is take a pitch." And that was all he said. We sat in silence for a spell until Pietro finally sat down, at which point the Peones, realizing that there would be no pre-game speech, sprung from their seats and hurried back to the dugout. As Pietro walked past me, I grabbed his arm and asked, "Hey, coach. What's the sign for three-run homer?" He sighed. "Dave, this is all they can remember," he said.

Just after ten o'clock, Montefiascone's starting pitcher climbed the mound. The local players were all about a foot taller and twenty pounds heavier than the boys from Nettuno. They wore green-and-white uniforms of different shades, as if they'd simply fallen out of bed, pulled on whatever doubleknits were at hand, and walked through a field of nettles to get to the park. The first player I noticed was a tiny goat of a man – Cuccari – who wore a long beard and a ratty afro, and who threw with a kind of jerking motion that lifted his whole body off the ground. I can't put my finger on it, but he looked very pagan. The team seemed to follow an entirely different tradition – perhaps one of old-time country ball played at the Festival of Lammas, with the odd human sacrifice thrown in – and their postures had none of the Peones' élan. They walked to the plate hunched over, their feet shuffling through the dust. The differences between the two teams couldn't have been more marked. The Peones represented the ancestral home of Italian baseball – and, if that wasn't enough of a burden, the birthplace of Western civilization – but the M-Birds' legacy lorded over the game, high on the hill. While the visitors were required to play well to flaunt their historical pedigree, all that Montefiascone had to do was stand at home plate and point back at their dome, like Babe Ruth in reverse. Even before the first pitch, the visitors were visibly nervous, and for good reason: the M-birds had already beaten them twice this season. There was none of the lightheartedness of the Peones' practices in the dugout at the beginning of the game. The bench was almost sullen.

Despite the fact that Pietro had been required to field a Scotch-taped lineup, with Mario Simone and Mario Mazza playing the outfield and Fabio from Milan at first – Solid Gold would've been in centro campo, and the Red Tiger probably would've designated hit, if they hadn't been AWOL – the boys in blue kept pace early and actually took command of the game in the middle innings with a

surprising 8 run 4th. The M-Birds' pitchers ran into a case of the
wilds, walking four Peones before Skunk and the Natural hit
screaming back-to-back triples. This action seemed to ignite the
day, and, with it, the Nettunese players forgot what it was they were
supposed to be uptight about.

From near silence, the Peones' bench bubbled into a fountain
of voices led, unsurprisingly, by Chencho, who shouted "Buon'
occhio!" ("Good eye!") and "Bella palla!" ("Good ball!") with the
force of a man hollering down a well. Pietro, urging Cobra with
"Buono Sa!" and "Sa. Tranquillo!", had a naturally deep tenor that
boomed out to the field. Skunk and Mario Mazza and Fabio from
Milan and the other smaller players added a hurried tom roll of
"Guarda la palla's!" and "Buono tiro's!"

I thought it was only polite to join in – it sounded like so much
fun, and it was a way of both ingratiating myself with the boys and
learning the Italian language via the dugout. My favourite word to
yell was *ruba!* (steal). Together, the Peones and I rolled the first *r*
like a humming outboard motor, then skated long and smooth
across the *ahhhh!* We must have looked great singing this word as a
group, rising off the bench and leaning forward like a team of ski
jumpers, hollering our sudden, terrifying howl.

Even when we weren't shouting, but merely talking, we were a
cacophony of voices, Italian bouncing off fractured English,
English pausing for the occasional moment of butchered Italian.
After a while, I tried my hand at "Forza Peones!" while the players
attempted "Atta boy, Fabs!", my best contribution to the Nettunese
lexicon thus far. Every now and then, whenever an error was committed or an M-Bird reached base, the dugout grew heavy with
groans and huffs of incredulity, but it was only a matter of seconds
before the bench found its voice again. As the Peones marched
their way to what appeared to be certain victory in the first game,
I noticed only one player not cheering: Chicca, the Peones' third
baseman, who said nothing all afternoon, choosing to sit alone at
the far end of the bench, his dark eyes trained suspiciously on
the field.

Somewhere around the seventh inning, the M-Birds, frustrated by Cobra's changes of speed, tried to get the better of the Peones by insidious means: they started cooking lunch. The kitchen was to the right of the dugout, and so was the dining room, where photos and trophies from the M-Birds' conquests filled the walls and a huge trophy case. When I went to investigate, I found a man with a shaggy Vandyke beard moving an enormous wooden spoon around a frying pan the size of a radial tire. I made some comment about the food – not "I've seen better pasta fagioli chucked into a dumpster," as the Peones would have hoped – and was promptly invited into the kitchen. So, with the bianco e azzuro safely in the lead, I chanced a trip into the enemy's den, where the cook proudly lifted the lid off the pan to show me his bubbling creation: spezzatino alla cacciatore. When I asked him what he'd used to make his sugo, three women who were helping prepare the meal explained excitedly, "Rosmarino, salvia, sedano, carrota, alio." The room was hot with the scent of the veal sweetening in its stew, and I was nearly taken by its intoxicating perfume. I managed to pull myself back and announced that I should rejoin my team on the bench lest they think I'd crossed over to the other side. But before I could get through the door, a fellow with a scrabbled beard, Freddie Mercury teeth, and a midriff the shape and size of the Santa Margherita duomo, gripped my arm, pulled me towards a small table set up in the corner of the kitchen, plugged a glass into my hand, and slapped the tablecloth with his fist, bellowing "Est! Est!! Est!!!"

Karma policeman that I am, I wondered what it would mean in the eyes of the baseball gods to sit down and indulge in the opposing team's drink of choice while the club to whom I'd committed my summer was less than twenty feet away staring into Montefiascone's offensive cannon. I decided it wasn't proper, but, as the glass was already poured, I drained it and sucked in some air. The fellow refilled it. I glanced through the window at the field, and there was Chencho, staring back at me.

"Davide!! Est! Est!! Est!!!" he said, giving me the thumbs-up before, no doubt, running back and telling Pietro that, right there in the enemy's den, the Canadian writer was turning into the Most Totally Wasted Dude.

It never got that far. I left the kitchen to the cheers of the chef and his crew and strode gaily back into the Peones' dugout to discover that the blue and white were barely hanging on to a three-run lead. Chencho was sitting near the end of the bench biting a nail, and Mario Mazza was staring at the floor, rubbing his gammy leg. It was the bottom of the ninth inning and Nettuno were leading 12-9, having hacked up a five-run furball in my absence.

The scoreboard in the outfield was painted in Roman numerals. Underneath them, a little light flashed whenever a run was scored, and once I'd settled back in the dugout the light began winking like a lascivious barfly. No sooner had I shouted, "C'mon! Forza, Peones!" than the M-Birds lead-off hitter singled, was pushed to second, and, moments later, came wheeling home on a stand-up double by the host side, whose sudden change in play was equivalent to a giant yawning and stretching.

Cobra was weakening. His disciplined pitching style – a clever mix of curve, fastball, sinker, and slider married to an acute sense of what to throw when, where – was melting as quickly as candle wax. His command had kept the M-Birds off balance for most of the day, but now he was slinging each pitch with self-doubt and fatigue. The Montefiascone batters had spent the morning studying Cobra's sequences and were well prepared for their final at-bats.

With each run, the entire Peones' team – me included – waited for Pietro's decision to make a pitching change. But since he only had five pitchers at his service, he was loath to burn Chencho – his fireman – whom he needed for game two, scheduled half an hour after the end of the first. So, instead of acting, he sat on his hands and watched as one of the M-Birds' barrel-assed sluggers, Zerbini, cut the Peones' lead by homering off Cobra to dead centre field.

The Peones moaned. At the beginning of the at-bat, it looked like Pietro's non-move might play itself out as genius undermanagement, for Cobra had slipped ahead of the slugger 0-2. But instead of busting the batter inside, he hung a ripe curve, which the green giant destroyed, one of five fuoricampi the M-Birds would clobber that day. The ball was hit so far and high that it seemed to hang in the air forever. It gave Cobra a long time to think about what he hadn't done, and when Mario Simone, playing centre field, hid his face in his glove and knelt on the ground, you could feel the promise of the day leave the dugout like so much stale air.

Pietro huffed through his nose and stared at the floor. Chencho's command split the silence: "*Paolo!*" The backup catcher grabbed his glove and ran with the reliever down the left-field line, where they warmed up in haste behind third base. Cobra was trying to make eye contact with his manager. Pietro finally raised his eyes and looked back. Realizing that the M-Birds were all over Cobra like rhinestones on Elvis, he harumphed in the disgusted way that only a beleaguered hardball manager can and rose to take his long walk to the mound.

Soon, the entire infield was crowded on the hill. Those of us in the dugout – the Natural, the Emperor, Fab Julie, Christian (the rookie), Pitò the Stricken, and me – assumed that by leaving Cobra out there for a few extra seconds, Pietro had been stalling for time until Chencho got loose. But they assumed wrong. Pietro, looking over the next batter, decided against making a move. Cobra, his weary body goosed with renewed hope, straightened his shoulders and nodded. Pietro turned and headed off the field as the next hitter, the tiny Cuccari, walked to the plate.

Cuccari leaned back on his heels and pointed his front elbow at the pitcher. I walked over to Pietro and, casting off all journalist-player protocol, warned him, "Watch out for this little dickhead. He might bunt." Pietro just waved his hand in front of his face and said, "He is no problem. This batter, he is nothing."

Cuccari barely touched Cobra's first two offerings, but on his third look the small infielder doinked the ball between first and second. His swing had all the force of a spatula hitting a raisin, but contact is contact; you put the ball in play and anything can happen. Fabio from Milan just missed getting a glove on the ball. Mario Simone kicked it around a little, and by the time the boys in the dugout had raised their faces from their hands, Cuccari was jumping up and down on third base. He'd put the M-Birds' winning run in scoring position.

At this point, it didn't matter how loose Chencho was or whether he would pitch in the afternoon, because with the score tied Pietro had no choice but to use his reliever. Cobra walked sullenly off the mound, and once in the dugout, he sat silently and stared at his shoes. No one said a word. Instead, we turned our attention to the field, where Chencho made an easy groundball out but lost the next hitter.

Game tied 12-12.

It looked like extra innings, but the M-Birds weren't done yet. The baserunner advanced on a loud out – a fly ball that nearly handcuffed Mario Mazza in centre field – and was in scoring position for another one of the Montefiascone bangers, Danielle Cappanella, a behemoth who, to steal a phrase from Lefty Gomez, looked like he had muscles in his hair. He glowered at the mound from under the plastic brim of his batting cap. Chencho glowered back like a feral cat. With his first few pitches, Chencho made the M-Bird appear awkward, his swing wrapping around him as he sliced the air.

Chencho did what he had to do: he made the batter put the ball on the ground. Bouncing across the diamond, it headed towards second base. Skunk reached down to grab it and stood to throw the ball to first, only to discover that he didn't have the ball. It was still on the ground. The time it took for him to retrieve it was enough to give the runner a chance to beat the throw. Rushing the play, Skunk missed Fabio's waving leather target. The runner on second turned towards home and scored.

13-12, M-Birds.

Coming off the field, the Big Emilio whaled his catching armour against the dugout wall, and with that, all manner of gloves and hats flew through the air. Chencho swore repeatedly to himself, proving that losing sucks in any language.

The M-Birds had hotfooted out of the dugout and were slapping each other in delight. After we stumbled to the clubhouse, we could still hear them. Pietro stood in the middle of the clubhouse floor and, instead of painting the air blue, told his team, "Forget about this morning. It is over. Finito. Put the game away, don't think about it. We still have another game to play. Okay? Okay?" He looked around the room for confirmation, but there was none. The damage had been done. Forty minutes later, the Peones took to the field for the second game, which they lost 16-9. Pompozzi, the young fireballer, lasted all of three innings. As I sat in the dugout watching the team flail away in their last at-bat, I noticed one of their sponsors' logos printed in black on the back of their shirts. It was the silhouette of a crane hoisting a slab of concrete over a construction sight. To me, the message was clear:

There was still a lot of work to do.

6

THERE CAME A ONE-ARMED MAN

War.

As a child in Canada in the 1970s, much of my life was spent under a sugary mountain of happypop and Lik-N-Stik, *Baseball Digest*s, and orange Hot Wheels track. War for me was only something I saw on Saturday-afternoon TV movies, or played out with plastic soldiers whose ears and hands I'd chewed off moments after getting them. In my teenage years, war was a song by Edwin Starr, a funk band, a movie about Vietnam starring Bruce Dern, the khaki pants that the Clash wore, the combat boots favoured by two punks who went to my high school, a long Dylan song that I didn't understand, War Amps commercials, Uncle Sam's pointed finger (and Alfred E. Neuman's), and Hitler, or rather a guy playing Hitler. My understanding of the Second World War – to say nothing of the First, Crimean, 1812, or Seven Years – was cribbed from a textbook read with one eye on the clock, or seen through Hollywood's rosy filter. I saw it, but I never tasted it.

Twenty years later, I was finally hit by comprehension. I was walking with Silvano Casaldi, the erudite historian who curated the small war museum inside Fort Sangallo. As we passed the seawall, he pointed out pockmarks in the yellow brick.

"You see this," he said. "This is one of the things that reminds us of the war.

"When the Germans first arrived, they moved everyone out to the country, forcing them to live in shacks and hovels. Some stayed in barns and lived like animals, with very little food, comfort, or proper sanitation, while others went up into the hills and lived in caves. Not everyone complied with these orders, however, and some were caught in town, living among the rubble, when they were supposed to be out in the fields. Once, a boy from Armellino was found with a pair of pliers, which he'd planned on using to repair his cattle enclosure. But the Germans suspected him of spying, of working for the underground, so they brought him out to this spot against the wall.

"Here," he said, pointing at the dented brick, "is where the bullets hit. The Germans lined up these so-called informants so that they faced the sea – looking out at the water where they used to swim and fish as children, where their grandfathers had swum and fished. It was here that they killed them."

"They shot them right here, in the open?" I asked.

"Yes. Against this wall," he said, drawing a phantom rifle to his eye. "The boy was taken past a lineup of people – women mostly – trying to get their travel permits from the barracks office."

"They killed lots of people?"

"Well, not lots. But, Dave," he said, "even one is too many."

We moved farther down the wall, where it curved towards our apartment. We stopped in front of a grille set into the wall, behind which was a generator that supplied power to the surrounding buildings. The grille vibrated, as if something alive were shaking in the small space behind it. Silvano talked about how a Nettunese man, accused by the Nazis of providing information to the Allies, had once hidden here, cowering in the room until he guessed that it was safe to move on. But the Germans had been waiting for him. They arrested him, wrestled him into handcuffs, and threw him back inside. The Nazis returned later and tossed in a live grenade.

It was hard to imagine this kind of horror. Very little about the golden town suggested the terror that had once ruled here. The reality of war was as distant and unreal as a Tolkienian fable to me until then. Had Silvano not pointed out the places where the deepest evil had left its mark, I might well have spent my entire time in Italy oblivious to the region's pain, never once pausing to acknowledge the irony of cavorting on a beach where, fifty years earlier, thousands of lives had been lost.

That evening, I looked through my window onto the still waters of the Tyrrhenian Sea, trying to imagine what Prince Steno Borghese – Nettuno's former land baron – saw when he walked out onto his balcony in his dressing gown one winter's night in January 1944 as a slow fleet of steel drove through the tide. The Allies' plan – dreamed up by Winston Churchill – was to attack the Italian coast on three fronts, using the British to the north, the Americans to the south. None of the soldiers, sailing from Naples, were aware of their destination, and as they headed out to sea, many of them must have figured it was the last they'd see of Italy. Then the twenty-eight destroyers, cruisers, minesweepers, and submarines bearing them turned back towards the Boot.

The Italians called the invasion lo sbarco, or beach-head landing, and it was among Europe's bloodiest and most costly offensives. It could have resulted in liberty – and the end of the war – had Allied commanders decided to march on Rome as originally planned, rather than wait and move their troops forward across the Alban Hills. On the morning of January 22, Operation Shingle, lo sbarco's code name, landed some thirty-six thousand men on the beach in an attempt to divert the Germans from the Gustav line, drawing vital troops to the coast. Author Raleigh Trevelyan remembers it as "a miraculous, clear, still night."

Once the landing craft ("enormous, open-mouthed whales," writes Trevelyan) had ferried their jeeps, trucks, and men to the shallows, and a cluster of eight hundred British rockets had bombarded the mine-infested beaches with a "howling, shrieking madness," the

Allies mobilized by direction of pin lights and loud speakers only to find that there was no resistance whatsoever. There were no Germans to be found, not even by the reconnaissance teams from the 5th Army who were sent in the direction of Rome – fifty-two kilometres away – to chart the German's advance. Only thirteen men of the 36,034 who landed died, killed by floating mines or when their vehicle was toppled by the waves. When the soldiers reported that the inland roads were empty (except for three drunken German officers out for a joyride in their jeep, and a few other soldiers who'd crept into Anzio to shoot cattle for food), General John Lucas, commander of the 5th Army, could have sent his men marching on Rome.

He didn't.

Four months later, thousands of men were dead.

General Lucas, an American southerner who favoured a corncob pipe, was a man of caution whom, Trevelyan remembers, "acted as if he were ten years older than Father Christmas." During the invasion, he'd ridden in an armour-plated cabin on the deck of an aircraft tender, writing that "I think we have a good chance of making a killing." This just days after General Patton had warned him: "John, there is no one in the army I'd hate to see killed as much as you, but you can't get out of this alive." As the Allies' assault crafts moved through the surf unmolested, Lucas suggested confidently to a fellow officer, "We have achieved what is certainly one of the most complete surprises in history."

The Allies encamped on the coast, waiting for orders to advance on the Alban Hills and then Rome. It seemed a no-brainer, but Lucas's sleepy trigger finger and General Mark Clark's advice not to "stick your neck out, Johnny. I did at Salerno and got into trouble," prevented the obvious from happening. Ignoring reports of a free pass along the Appian Way, Clark told Lucas, "You can forget this goddam Rome business." By dawn the next day, the Germans had amassed ten thousand men on the perimeter of the town, making Clark's suggestion moot. Four months later, the Allies remained pinned on the coast.

Perhaps it's too simple to say that the Germans mobilized in the time that Lucas – and his superiors – fretted over their decision, but it certainly appears that way. Even Eugen Dollmann, of Rome's ss, said that, after landing, "The Americans put up their tents, said their prayers, had a good meal, and then lost a unique occasion for finishing the war within the year." The loss of life was a devastating price to pay for the supposition that the enemy was lying in wait, when in fact most of the Germans captured around Nettuno were found asleep in their beds.

The battle turned Nettuno into an eyeless, toothless town of shattered buildings. Silvano remembers the town as having "un viso spento, senza occhi," a face without life. In almost every photo from that time, a shock of black smoke is curling around the walls of a demolished building as soldiers tramp through the wreckage, putting out fires. In their heavy greatcoats, their tired, sunken eyes staring out from under muddied helmets, their shoulders pinched from lugging guns and ammunition, the men on both sides of the conflict look like living shadows.

Despite the fighting, the number of casualties suffered by the Nettunese was remarkably low. Silvano was reluctant to put a number on it, but thought it was probably no higher than one hundred because most of the people had been forced out to the country. Required to remain a minimum of five kilometres from the town, the Nettunese were exposed to a different kind of war. The Nazis often enlisted local men to help plant mines, while, as Silvano writes in his bilingual book *Those Days at Nettuno*, women and children led "a life of stray dogs," forced to live in cellars and caves and deprived of food. Some women, Silvano wrote, "made the hazardous journey to Rome in search of oil for the pan or a few kilos of pasta, in exchange for sheets and gold earrings."

Still, compared to most of Italy – and Europe – and considering the horror of the battles that were fought around it, Nettuno was not as badly damaged by the war as Anzio, which was largely obliterated by the bombing and had to be rebuilt after the war. The closest Nettuno came to suffering destruction – except for a

A soldier at Fort Sangallo. Our apartment is just beyond the far turret.
(Courtesy of Silvano Casaldi)

September 1944 Stuka attack, which ripped off most of the city's rooftops – was when a German bomb hit Fort Sangallo. But luckily, its chassis had been filled with sand by Italian saboteurs. When the Nettunese returned after the war, they were encouraged to see that their town was relatively unscathed. Because life here returned to normal sooner than in neighbouring towns, the Americans decided to stay in Nettuno, building the largest military cemetery in Italy, and teaching the people to play baseball.

Baseball was introduced to Nettuno on the beach and in the country, at the front line and in the trenches. Most Nettunese from that time have a memory of how and when they first encountered the game. One afternoon, Silvano and I met the Cittadino (the Citizen Man), a septuagenarian firebrand with four teeth and quick, suspicious eyes. Shaking hands with him was like slipping my fingers into a vise. Before sitting down for a late-afternoon drink, he gripped my hand, pulling me close to his face as I grimaced in pain.

"See? Cittadino is still very strong," said Silvano, who knew better than to offer the elderly man his mitt.

"Ha, ha!" said Cittadino, finally releasing me. "Forte!"

"Si, si," I said, counting my fingers to make sure none had remained in his fist.

Cittadino has a reputation in Nettuno for being among the city's most intense and notorious baseball fans. In the 1950s, he'd been involved in an infamous basebrawl, in Rome, during which he'd leapt onto the field and assaulted members of the opposing team with a bat. The attack made all of the Roman papers. It resulted in suspensions for players from each side, and a bounty on Cittadino and a few other fans, who were hooligans before hooligans existed, if there are such people as baseball hooligans, fans of the New York Yankees notwithstanding. After the game, Cittadino and his two fellow combatants were pursued by the carabinieri, but they fled on foot, hiding out in a ditch until nightfall before walking back to Nettuno, where they were welcomed as heroes.

As a boy during the war, Cittadino ran weapons and other supplies from the beach to the front line. One day, he noticed a group of American soldiers dragging a long green box out of a tent to an abandoned field just beyond the battleground. He followed them in case they needed his help assembling a gun. When they wrenched off the top of the crate, Cittadino says, "I looked at what was inside and thought, How are they going to use these? How powerful are they? The equipment didn't look like guns, but you'd never take a grenade for a weapon, so I assumed that the gloves, balls, and bats were clever, new fighting devices. I was anxious to see how they would work.

"When they picked up the balls and started to throw them

around, my first reaction was to jump back in fear. What if they were explosives? What if the soldiers mishandled them? I thought they were mad, being so reckless with these new weapons. Then, when they put their gloves on, and used the bats to hit the balls, I was even more confused. I had no idea what was going on, but I was sure of one thing: there was simply no way they were playing a game, not with the front line just metres away. When I finally realized that it was indeed a sport they were playing, I yelled at them furiously, 'The Germans are bombing us and here you are, playing a game!' Before I knew it, they were showing me how to hold the bat, what to do with the ball. Then I understood. Afterwards, whenever a game broke out, I was there, learning this strange new thing called baseball."

This scene was played out across Europe, North Africa, and Asia: games of baseball being waged in the face of war. Participation was encouraged among troops abroad and at home by the United States army, which distributed thousands of bats and balls to their servicemen. As word of the games reached home, it wasn't uncommon for soldiers leaving for battle to tuck their gloves, perhaps a ball, inside their kit bags. Baseball would relieve stress, help the soldiers stay sane, and with major league stars like Joe DiMaggio, Hank Greenberg, Bob Feller, and Stan Musial joining the forces, a handful of star ballplayers saw action. Ted Williams was a naval recruit and Yogi Berra survived the Battle of the Bulge. Baseball and the war were entwined in Franklin D. Roosevelt's "Green Light" speech, in which he stressed the importance of keeping major league baseball alive so that the war workers of America would have a place to turn for a respite from the world's madness.

Because so many players had been drafted, the calibre of play in the majors dropped dramatically, allowing the previously woeful St. Louis Browns to capture their only title. It was during the war that athletes like one-armed Pete Gray starred for the St. Louis Browns, getting fifty-one hits and striking out only eleven times despite swinging the bat with one arm. Joe Nuxhall was fifteen years old – the youngest pitcher ever – when he started for the Reds in 1944, dressing alongside forty-three-year-old Guy Bush and forty-six-year-old Hod Lisenbee, retreads made necessary by the great player shortage. Tommy Brown was another kid who, at sixteen, replaced Pee Wee Reese as shortstop for the Dodgers, chipping in with a pair of home runs. At the time, every dinger-hitting Dodger received a carton of Old Gold cigarettes for his achievement. After Brown's clouts, however, Dodgers' skipper Leo Durocher intercepted the deck sliding down the screen to the Brooklyn dugout. "Give 'em to me," he told the attendant who'd fetched the smokes. "He's too young to smoke 'em, anyway."

As Richard Goldstein notes in *Spartan Seasons*, his wonderful book about wartime baseball, a Chicago traffic policeman, John Miklos, took leave from his job to try out for the Cubs. He got the gig, pitched in two games, and, within a year, was back managing his street corner. Denny Galehouse, who worked at a Goodyear aircraft plant in Akron, would take the train to St. Louis every Sunday and pitch for the Browns, returning to his factory shift the next morning. In another instance, Eddie Basinski, a bespectacled violinist with the Buffalo Philharmonic, played with the 1945 Dodgers. Fielding or hitting never gave him as much trouble as his Dodger teammates, who refused to believe that he was actually a musician. Answering a wager of a suit of clothes and ten dollars, he sent for his violin and played in the Dodgers clubhouse before a game. The war also opened the door for U.S. baseball's first Cuban players, who were scouted by an Italian-born minor leaguer, Joe Cambria, the man responsible for testing the colour line before Jackie Robinson broke it.

Not only did the shortage of quality ballplayers prove problematic for owners, but broadcasters were faced with their own set of obstacles. Announcers had to be careful, for instance, to avoid talking about the weather for fear that the enemy would intercept them and design a North American attack based on the meteorological conditions. Once, during a rain delay, Dizzy Dean and his partner were required to fill hours while waiting for the skies to clear with talk, none of which mentioned the rain. Fearing that the confusion

George Maurer from the Bronx spanks one at Nettuno-Anzio in 1944.
(Courtesy of Silvano Casaldi)

among listeners tuning into the game would prove too great, Dean, no longer able to contain himself, said, "If you want to know why we're not calling a baseball game, look out the damned window!"

On the front line, baseball provided a means of escape. The lone photo of Nettunese war ball that hung in Silvano Casaldi's museum is of a soldier from the Bronx, George Maurer. In the picture, he's taking his cuts in the Anzio trenches, under the cover, no less, of an anti-aircraft gun pointing at the sky over his shoulder. His face is darkened by the shade of his helmet, and the bulk of his bomber jacket ripples as he swings at the pitch. He's surrounded by dark mounds of dirt, with the odd bush reaching its bony fingers through the earth. It's the middle of the day and, from the lip of the trench, ten soldiers poke their heads out, laughing at Maurer's laboured swing. "Gimme that bat!" he might have said when the reporter from *Stars and Stripes* asked for a picture. "I'm a regular Pete Reiser, I am."

Perhaps, as the ball sailed towards him, the war faded in Maurer's vision, just as the roaring Ebbets Field crowd must have become a backdrop for Reiser, Duke Snider, Dixie Walker, and the others. Maybe, for Maurer, the war thinned into sixty feet, six inches of pure solitude, if only for an instant. It's impossible to know. George Maurer was killed in action and his body was never recovered.

According to Paolo Dinese, the late Nettunese war historian, one of the first things the Allies did was to construct a POW pen for the German prisoners, then they built a ballfield of sorts right next to it. Whenever the soldiers weren't required at the front line, they took to the makeshift diamond in the sand and played ball at all hours of the day and night, sometimes by the light of the enormous Roman moon. It's ironic that, while the game was brought to the liberated nations of Italy, Spain, and the Netherlands by American GIs, it was also shown to the enemy behind the metal fencing of the POW compound. It couldn't have seemed any less strange to them than it did to Cittadino. Perhaps, like the ballplaying soldiers, the POWs' thoughts also became lost in the movement of the ball and the swoosh of the bat; perhaps those seaside games provided a momentary respite not only for those who played them, but for those who stood and watched. While the games were, in one way, an Allied taunt to their prisoners, perhaps it fed their yearning to return to the homeland to watch Fritz Szepan, Ludwig Durek, Josef Gauchel, or other Rhineland soccer stars, or it filled them with the possibility of a new sporting life beyond the war.

It was largely in makeshift settlements near the Padiglione Woods outside Nettuno where the GIs played ball. While the beach provided a serviceable terrain for the game, the grass and dirt inland was much better. It was near one of the fields that Silvano's cousin, Mariano Casaldi, first encountered baseball. Casaldi, who would go on to pitch for the early Nettuno teams, talked to Silvano and me one morning in the courtyard of Fort Sangallo. We sat in a cool sliver of shade against the fort's eastern wall, where, below us, Silvano had wrenched open a great door to provide a view to the sea. Bespectacled, with a thick upper body and a slow, dramatic tenor, Signor Casaldi told us that the first time he saw a baseball, it was being thrown by an American soldier against the side of an old wooden building that had been used as provisions barracks for Italians living in the country.

"When I first saw the soldier, two things struck me," he remembered. "First, he was playing with this small, round ball, which he threw with great strength, and second, he had only one arm. He'd fall into his delivery, throw the ball against the wall, pick it up, and do it again. Like a normal pitcher, really. He must have noticed me, because he immediately invited me over. He gave me the ball, and I squeezed it in my hands. That was the first time I'd ever touched a baseball.

"Pretty soon, that's how I spent my days, just watching him pitch, the sleeve of his missing arm batting in the wind. He'd lost it in combat, but because he'd always been a baseball player, he didn't want to stop playing. He showed me his curve, changeup, how to throw a fastball. He wasn't among us for a long time, but it was enough to have a very big impact on my life."

Silvano asked him, "Did you ever find out his name? Where he was from?"

"No. I did not speak English. He did not speak Italian. Really, I didn't say much. I just watched and learned. Still, I would have liked to have told him that, because of what he'd shown me, I'd become a baseball player myself. I wonder what he would have thought. I wonder what his reaction would be if he knew that, ten years after I first saw him, I was out there, standing on the mound at Villa Borghese, pitching to one of his great countrymen. To Joe DiMaggio."

It became a custom for departing American soldiers to leave their equipment behind for the Nettunese. And since there were thou-

sands of Americans stationed along the Tyrrhenian coast, the game
grew at a quicker rate here than anywhere else in Italy. After the
liberation of Rome, baseball also blossomed in the Eternal City,
providing Nettuno with a natural rival. Giulio Glorioso, the great
Roman pitcher and former Nettuno manager whose colourful name
deserves a place alongside Birdie Tebbits, Oyster Burns, Ivy Wingo,
Lu Blue, Orator Shaffer, and many others, told me over a plate of
risotto con spec, "The first time I saw baseball, soldiers were
playing it on a soccer field that the naval reserve had converted into
a diamond. They used a portable mound, which they rolled on and
off the field on wheels. There was no outfield fence, just a backstop. Once we started to learn the game ourselves, the Red Cross
and the YMCA donated equipment. Later they brought over players
like Frank Crosetti, Whitey Ford, Early Wynn, Jim Bunning, Jim
Egan, and others to hold indoor clinics. Back in the 1940s, there
was a forgotten man named Guido Grazione, who'd played baseball for years in the States. He was a catcher for the YMCA Rome
team in 1920 who organized getting equipment to us, and who
wrote booklets in Italian about how to play the game. Because of
his efforts, there was lots of enthusiasm for baseball and softball
after the war. In 1946, in Rome, there were more than sixty softball
teams; it was very popular among young men. We used to pick up
bats, gloves, and occasionally balls at Porta Portese [Rome's largest
outdoor market], which soldiers had traded for other things or had
left behind. I used to find old balls there, which I'd sew back
together myself so that they'd last longer. At that time, I had a
Nacona fielder's glove [from Texas], that cost me six hundred lire –
six dollars – which I managed after selling two yards of books that
I'd stolen from my father's library. I watched him for weeks, months,
and only took books that I thought he wouldn't miss – theatrical
books and magazines mostly. Lucky for me, my father never found
out. My father didn't even know I played baseball until much later."

A tall, elegant gentleman with a great wisp of white hair whose
grasp of English was such that he used the words *rhubarb* and
pigeonhole freely, Glorioso said, "Back then, we had no uniforms

and, sometimes, no shoes. They were very hard to find after the war; any kind of shoe, really, even for wearing in normal life. They were a luxury. Some players even wore wooden shoes to play, it was all they had."

Glorioso told me that he'd played in Italy's first-ever international game against Spain. The night before the match, at a dinner to honour the players, one of the officials of Italian sport leaned over to him and asked, "Tell me. In baseball, what kind of horses do you use?"

When I told Mariano Casaldi about Glorioso's pursuit of second-hand equipment, he told me, "In Nettuno, we used old pizza boxes for gloves. We'd cut them to fit our hands and build a strap around the wrist. They worked fine. Sometimes, we'd take a soccer ball and tear it open, and then use the rubber to make gloves. (We had no need for a football in those days. The kids in Nettuno only wanted to play baseball.) If you were lucky, you'd get rubber from an old bicycle tire – but that was rare – and tie bits of it together with string to make a baseball. For bats, we used old broomsticks, pieces of furniture, whatever. We dreamed of real baseball bats in those days."

Silvano added, "At one time in Piazza San Giovanni, there were one hundred kids living in the apartments around the square. You can't imagine the games we had. There were games every day, at practically every hour. The piazza was laid out like a natural diamond, with home plate in one corner and the bases fanning out the way they would on a real diamond. The only problem was the outfield ran into the steps of the church. Most of the priests didn't mind. Father Don Vincenzo was the first person in town to get a television and he let us watch soccer on it. He enjoyed our games, I think. The police were the ones who gave us the most trouble. They'd try to stop our games when they became a little too hectic – sometimes you couldn't walk through the piazza without finding yourself on one basepath or another – but we always kept playing. We knew the little alleyways surrounding the piazza and down along the beach where we could hide and wait them out. Almost every player from the famous Nettuno teams of the 1960s played there. They learned it on the street, right in front of the church, playing with their pizza-box gloves and balls made of rubber."

Before coming to Nettuno, I'd telephoned Colonel Charles Butte, decorated veteran of the Normandy Invasion and architect of the Villa Borghese ballfield, at his home in Riviera Beach, Florida. He told me, "When I arrived in Nettuno to help build the cemetery, the Italians remembered seeing some of the soldiers hitting a ball around, and they asked me about the game. I think they'd also seen newsreels about baseball, and they certainly knew about DiMaggio. Also, a lot of families had connections to America, and, one way or another, they'd been told about this sport and how terrific it was.

"First, we started with softball, and, of course, the men were very eager to learn. I think they saw it as a challenge too. This was right after the war, so baseball was a way of starting over, which made sense considering that so much of their past was just lying there in ruin at their feet."

I asked the colonel – it was the first time I'd ever addressed a man by his rank – about building Nettuno's first diamond. He cleared his throat. "Well, you see, we played in a soccer field at first. It was fine for a beginning, but pretty soon the players, as they improved, wanted something more like the real thing, real baseball. So we went to the prince, who was a very intelligent, soft-spoken man, not the slightest bit aggressive or argumentative. When he spoke, the Nettunese listened because he commanded their attention. So when he granted us the land upon which to build our park, those who didn't know about baseball were immediately interested in what was going on. If the prince could get behind it, then anyone could.

"The Nettunese did all the work. Those who were employed at the cemetery worked on the diamond in their off hours. Lots of them were kids or young men quite eager to get involved. We sweated pretty hard to build that field, we really did. The townsfolk used to show up with picks and shovels to help any way they could.

Hardball on the prince's grounds, around 1954.
(Courtesy of Maria Antonietta Marcucci)

We used leftover pierced steel planking for seats – the kind they'd used in airfields during the war – and stuffed bags of canvas to make bases. I believe that we cut off a tree trunk to make home plate, embedding it in the dirt. Because I had experience building and landscaping the cemetery, I more or less used the same techniques. I showed the Italians how to level off the field and plant the sod."

Butte's wife sewed team uniforms out of requisitioned khaki, while a few of the local scrubs found military fatigues at nearby markets, which they tailored to allow easy movement under the scorching Mediterranean sun. Once the stone bleachers had been set, the field was ready. The prince held a dedication ceremony in honour of Colonel Butte, and, in the summer of 1949, the first game of ItaloBall was played. When I asked the colonel whether he'd ever paused to consider the poetry of having traded a rifle for a baseball bat, he jumped in: "Not at all. We were asked to do a job, and we did it. I have no feelings at all about that. It was something that had to be done."

Trying for another angle, I asked, "What do you think of the irony that, out of something as savage and desperate as war, came this beautiful, peaceful game?'

"What do I think?" he said. "Son, you put that nonsense right out of your head."

Giulio Glorioso said that, because of Nettuno's relationship with the American army, it was only natural that the game first take hold there. "Because of the cemetery – not forgetting the local munitions range, which they'd had well before the war – and Nettuno's relationship with the U.S. army, there was always employment and security for the people there. This allowed them to embrace the American game perhaps a little more easily than in other places. This relationship helped in other ways too. The film *Cleopatra*, with Elizabeth Taylor and Richard Burton, was shot there too, at Torre Astura [Nettuno's medieval fortress at the far end of the beach]. A lot of the Nettuno players – Bennedetto was one – posed as Egyptian soldiers in the film. The shoot was supposed to take six months, but it lasted two years. The Nettuno people wanted to make the event last as long as they could. But that's the Italian way too.

"Nettuno likes to think that it was the first place where the game was played, but it's not true. Officially, the army first started playing baseball in Milan, though softball had been around for many years, as well. Remember that, at the 1936 Olympics in Munich, the Americans played baseball in front of 110,000 people. The game was allowed by Hitler to appease the American Olympic Federation, who were at first reluctant to compete at the games because of what was happening to the Jews in Germany. Really, with baseball, there are many things to consider when trying to identify the origin of this sport.

"Baseball was a by-product of the war in Europe and elsewhere, but it wasn't necessarily brought there because of the war. I believe that it had already started to spread before 1944. Gold miners took baseball to South Africa and Australia; sailors took it to Holland, to Antwerp in Belgium; missionaries introduced it to Japan and China. In Japan, baseball started after 1853, with Admiral Perry. There's one theory, you know, that cricket really started in Naples, and when you consider that the two games are very similar, it only stands to reason that Italians might have played catch there too. It's an instinct, I feel, baseball. The chimps at the zoo could play it. There is something in the animal – we are all animals, believe it or not – where, I think, you can find baseball.

"In Russia, they call it lapta. When they first saw the game played by Americans in the 1950s – perhaps even the soldiers saw it before – they said, 'That's our game. That's lapta!' The Poles, too, they play a game called pilkaw, and in Germany, they call it stool-ball [in the Netherlands, it's honkball]. It depends. In Iran, in old Persia, they were playing polo: a stick and a ball. In Afghanistan they played too, and also in Mongolia, where Ghengis Khan was a champion, only instead of a ball, they used a human head. Take lacrosse. It's the same principle: a stick and a ball. There is something that occurs in man – out of the caves, down from the trees – when you give him a stone or a ball. There is something appealing, for some reason, which is outside, immaterial. All popular games involve balls. I have no reason to argue with the best researchers who think they know when or where, but . . . baseball is like language. It just happened.

"It's impossible to know the father of Italian baseball. Forget it. Forget trying to find him. Max Ott – Massimo Ottino – was the first person to register an Italian baseball club, in Milano. I would say the first Italians to play the game were in Sicily because they were the ones who were in contact first with the U.S. army. I know for sure that softball and baseball bats were used during the war not only to make fires in the winter, but also to build boats. Bernardini, the famous soccer manager of the 1950s, even played some baseball at the Fascist academy in the 1930s – la mazza fascista – as an athletic experiment by Mussolini. What do you think – 'Mussolini: the Father of Italian Baseball!' I know some people – one of whom was my old coach – who, as a prisoner of war in North Africa, became familiar with the game. You ask Rollie Marchie, the writer from Trento. He was a POW in the United States, and that's how he learned about baseball. All of those people wrote home about what they'd seen, so who knows where or how it might have taken hold. But, as the Romans say, 'Mother sempre certa.' [You can always be sure of the mother, if not the father.] It is for sure that the mother of Italian baseball was the 5th Army. You cannot go wrong. As they say, you can look it up.

"In the First World War, in 1917, the Americans came to the rescue of France against Germany. That's how they brought the game to France, for sure. History shows that that same army was rushed to fight in Italy. You'll remember that Hemingway was among them, he was the driver of a Red Cross ambulance. When I think about Hemingway I get pimples. No, not pimples. What do you say? Goosebumps! Goosebumps, yes? I have goosebumps when I recall *The Old Man and the Sea*, Joe DiMaggio, and Hemingway. All of those things are important to me.

"I was at spring training with the Cleveland Indians in 1953. I was taught how to throw by Rocky Colavito. That man was so strong. He was a giant. When I was at camp, I received a package through the mail to Daytona Beach, Florida, where the Indians worked out. In this package were three books: a Bible, *How to Pitch* by Bob Feller, and *For Whom the Bell Tolls* by Hemingway, in English. I read all three books, and the book by Hemingway became very important to me."

"I've been thinking about him a lot too," I told the old pitcher. "Every time I look out through my window at the water, I think of Hemingway and *The Old Man and the Sea*. I think of what he said about DiMaggio, who played in Nettuno."

"This is it!" he said. "DiMaggio, Hemingway, the war, Italy. These are the things that have created the very subject we are discussing today. Hemingway came to Italy with the Red Cross and he wrote about being here in his books, and about baseball. Dimaggio too. The Red Cross was present to support the U.S. army, and, of course, they played some baseball."

"What do you think, my Canadian friend?" he said.
"What do I think about what?"
His eyes lit up.
"Perhaps it was Hemingway who brought baseball to our country."

7

1975

The tradition of catch has been around for as long as there's been dirt and coconuts. In fact, I have no trouble conjuring up the image of a pair of Cro-Mags pitching a dodo skull across the scorched earth (a mere glimpse of the lunkering Tampa Bay Devil Rays will evoke such an image), and while many a sporting pundit may suggest that calcio (soccer) was the original sport, I'd remind experts that, in the early days of mankind, those mastodons, wild boar, large snakes, and other predatory jungle beasts were more than likely repelled not by a citizen's assault of fluttering toes and flying feet, but by an early version of the high hard one, thrown by cavemen as unkempt and hirsute as John Kruk, which might very well have been one of their names.

The way I see it, the ball is pretty much there from birth. It is among the first playthings we're interested in because of the way it moves. Just after Lorenzo turned four months old, he lay on our bed trying to spin a blue soccer ball with his feet. Legend has it that a family friend once put a baseball in Dock Ellis's crib. Presto: major leaguer. The same kind of story is told about Doc Gooden, who, as a child, used to toss a baseball in the air from his bed until he fell asleep (from a firm konk on the noggin, I'd suspect). And it was David Cone who told Roger Angell that, when he was growing up, he was told never to throw something at nothing. A cherry stone, peach pit, apple core, nub of chewing gum – he was instructed to choose a target and try to hit it.

While the finer points of soccer, rugby, tennis, and cycling escaped me until I was an adult, the opposite was true with baseball, which I was into, as Early Wynn used to say, from the git-go. As a boy, I'd spend endless, knee-aching hours throwing a yellow tennis ball against the side wall of our house until the street lights came on. Baseball was my summer activity – no camp, no cottage, no warm-weather hockey school – just baseballs pitched into a phantom strike zone, the voices of Curt Gowdy and Tony Kubek chattering in my head. Joseph Epstein once wrote that, after he did the math, he realized that he'd heard Gowdy's voice more often than his father's. Whenever I imagined I was Ellis Valentine, Catfish Hunter, Woody Fryman, or the improbably moustachioed Rollie Fingers, who looked like a loony barbershop crooner, it was Gowdy's flat drawl that described the *poinging* of my ball against the house.

That strip of grass where I pitched against imaginary batters was Crusoe's island in the sun for me. My time there was a splendid, busy-minded solitude away from adult coaches, tough kids, cruel teachers, parents, girls. It's not that I was a young misfit who'd turned away from the world – in fact, I liked the teams with whom I played, had lots of friends, and probably spent as many hours playing catch with my father as I did my teammates – but the headspace of baseball was my own. I decided what and what not to allow inside.

Practising with the Peones three or four times a week, then participating, if from the dugout, in Sunday doubleheaders, was the first time since I was twelve that I'd been so deeply involved with baseball. And while you had to squint to pretend that I was anything

My first baseball team, Martingrove Park, Etobicoke, around 1972.

more than a team mascot who, at times, was embraced simply for my ability to mock opposing teams in blue English, there were many occasions when I felt I'd stumbled into the baseball life I'd always dreamed of.

In a way, baseball is the ultimate kids game (I take that back: tag is the ultimate kids game. Keep an eye on those 2070 Olympics). Because the ball fields of my youth were part of the playgrounds and parks I occupied all summer, it made the game easy. You learned the game simply by running across the grass in your Cougars or Keds, a much easier routine than squeezing into hard-shelled ice skates. And because everybody was hanging around in parks anyway, it was never an effort to find or get into a game, even if you had only a gardening glove or vague sense of the rules or skill level lower than Johnny Ramone's guitar strap.

Unlike the crowded, claustrophobic hockey rinks of my suburb, baseball fields were often the sole domain of kids, at least on weekday afternoons, when grown-ups were away at work. While the small scale of the rink often forced you under the heavy gaze of parents, coaches, and peers, baseball fields were so vast it was easy to get lost.

Baseball generously harbours all kinds of kid athletes. In my day, there were more knobby-kneed nerds and fat kids on the diamond than in any other sport, a phenomenon that continued until the Internet and video games stole the youth of our nation. Since failure is an inherent part of baseball, it shortens the distance between the great and the not-so-great, allowing room for everyone. Take the at-bat. Not only does it offer the possibility of atonement – giving a hapless player a second, third, and fourth chance – but its one-to-nine hitting carousel ensures that every player takes a turn. Hockey offers scant scoring chances per game, but baseball guarantees several trips to the plate, fostering confidence. I was always much better at baseball than hockey for this reason.

Unlike cricket – where everybody scores, but nobody wins, at least not until a game has spanned the passing of two civic holidays – baseball is as much about failure as success, whether it's Ralph Kiner or Yogi Berra's failure at words, a hitter's failure to hit, a pitcher's failure to throw strikes, a runner's failure to steal a base, or a fielder's failure to field, which, in yet another of the game's quirks, are inventoried and entered as errors on a player's permanent record. Baseball is baseball because, to be good, you must also be bad. Success in the game – as in life itself – is fleeting and rare, something to be savoured when, and if, it occurs. For a kid finding his way in the world, I was never too young to learn such a lesson.

Growing up, I was devoted to one team: the Cincinnati Reds. They were the dominant National League team of the 1970s and, as far as I could tell, fielded a lineup of decent, heads-down guys, unlike such modern-day athletes as that firecracker-flinger Vince Coleman, or Giants pitcher Livan Hernandez who, as I write this, has just been arrested for allegedly beating an elderly man on the street with a golf club.

In 1975, my Reds, coached by Sparky Anderson, made it to the World Series after beating the defending champion Pirates (my second favourite club) in the National League Championship Series in three games. The Reds' opponents in the World Series were the Red Sox of Boston. Cursed in post-season play since 1918, the year

of their last World Series title, the Red Sox went into the Fall
Classic with a lineup nearly as formidable as the Reds, featuring a
pitching staff of Bill "Spaceman" Lee and Luis "Señor Smoke"
Tiant, and an outfield of Jim Rice in left, Fred Lynn in centre, and
Dwight Evans in right. The teams matched catching Hall of Famers
– slugger Johnny Bench with the Reds, and Carlton Fisk with the
Sox – an equality of talent that suggested both clubs were at the top
of their powers.

October 21, 1975, was the first time I can remember a baseball
game being about more than just who won or lost. In all of its gripping drama, game six hinted, instead, at greater lessons: the uncertainty of life, the magic of dreams, the fraud of the impossible. It
was this game in particular – the occasion of the Red Sox's improb-
able eighth-inning comeback and Carlton Fisk's famous twelfth-
inning, foul-pole homer – that taught me the importance of valuing
what is yours, lest it slip away as quickly as a sure-fire Reds victory
to a Bernie Carbo freak homer.

Most of what I remember of the game occurred in the late
innings, though the Reds must have played some fairly daunting
ball to have taken a 6-3 lead into the eighth. The clock had already
crept past 8 p.m., my bedtime, then 10, then 11. It was the latest I'd
ever stayed up to watch a sporting event, and while I tried hard to
concentrate, I edged towards dreamstate while the hot light of the
television flashed on my bedroom walls.

The drama began with pinch-hitter Bernie Carbo shuffling to
the plate with two-on in the bottom of the eighth, head down, his
blond afro stuffed under his batting cap. A smallish man, Carbo was
also a part-time hairdresser and noted eccentric who would buy an
extra plane ticket so that he could take his stuffed gorilla with him
on road trips. Like Joe Carter during his Series-winning at-bat for
the Blue Jays eighteen years later, Carbo appeared overmatched for
most of his turn at the plate, swinging wildly, which prompted Tony
Kubek to announce that Carbo was "a bit late on his swing," to
which Joe Garagiola added, "It was like he hit that [foul] out of the
catcher's glove!" (Gowdy simply watched and called the balls and

strikes, sensing perhaps that something heavy was upon us.) As a last-ditch hope for the home side – whose thirty thousand faithful fans stood in front of their seats in the raw Fenway night – Carbo promised little, perhaps a lucky double, a banjo hit, a freak single. Yet, after fouling off two pitches, getting immediately behind in the count, on his next swing, Carbo whacked the ball between the eyes. The ball sailed high over centre field and out of the park. I leapt forward in my bed, astonished that anyone – let alone Boston, let alone Bernie Carbo – had drawn equal to the vaunted Reds in the most important game, and inning, of the year. That they'd come back against the Big Red Machine seemed utterly impossible. But the impossible was only beginning.

Both teams took turns poking the unreal. First, Reds' left fielder George Foster gathered in a fly ball flush to the wall behind third base and threw out the Sox' speeding baserunner, Denny Doyle, at home. Minutes later, Boston answered with an even more audacious play of their own, a Dwight Evans catch that suffocated a late Reds' rally. The ball was hit by Joe Morgan, a compact man whose power, like Roy Campanella's, came from the bottom of his spine, through his neck and jaw. Evans turned to face the outfield fence, his heart carrying his feet across the grass until, at the last second, he leaped and caught Morgan's rocket in the deepest corner of the park, then pivoted like a dancer and hucked the pill to first. Baserunner Ken Griffey, convinced that Morgan's blast was gone, was easily doubled off base. The tie was preserved. The baseball world paced. Both teams had one hand on the prize.

Just after 12:30 a.m., Carlton Fisk walked to the plate to begin the bottom of the twelfth. It didn't take long. Pat Darcy threw once, then again. Fisk hit the second pitch, and it shot towards the left-field foul pole. Fisk moved up the line to watch the flight of the ball, waving his hands as if guiding a great ship into port, willing the white leather dot to hook towards the good side of a yellow metal toothpick. It did. The foul pole poinged and the ball sprung back towards the field. The Sox had won. The organist, as Roger Angell has remembered, leaned into the "Hallelujah Chorus." There was dancing and hugging. Fisk stormed around the basepaths, laying his shoulder into a few manic fans who raced to join him down the chalk line.

If the shock of the Red Sox comeback wasn't enough to rattle my senses, I felt like my allegiance to Cincinnati had been ripped away. Not that I became a Red Sox devotee after the Series, but I was frightened by their power, and when, one evening later, they took to the field at Fenway only to lose the World Series to Cincinnati, they became to me an even more madly complicated creature. That a team could create something as incredible as their performance in game six and simply bow out in game seven – in front of 75 million people, no less – was as awful as the miracle itself. Raised on paperback tales of heroic punt returns, overtime-winning goals, and championship home runs, I found the Red Sox narrative to be more dark and complicated than any storyline I'd known. It was as if their tale had been cribbed from a dusty book at the back of a magic store, one swept with spider tracks and bits of dried blood, and I was left with a notion it took me years to understand: In sport, as in life, we are chained to our gods.

8

ROMA AT NETTUNO

"Do you know where I can buy some baseball diapers?" I asked the Red Tiger.

"?"

"Diapers. Baseball diapers. I can't play without diapers."

I found out the hard way that, in the early stages of learning a foreign language, all it takes is one word to wipe out weeks of progress. I thought I was making great strides in Italian until I asked the Red Tiger about the you-know-what (having a son himself, he figured out that I'd meant pants, pantaloni, not pannolini). Janet had twice committed equally absurd malapropisms. During our first visit here, she'd tried to buy latte interno (breast milk), rather than latte intero (whole milk) and perplexed waiters throughout southern Italy by demanding that a mewling puppy – rather than a straw – be served with her Coca-Cola.

Still, I considered myself lucky to be spending so much of my time talking bad Italian, especially in the context of baseball. By butchering the language across the playing fields of the Boot, I was simply keeping one of baseball's grand traditions. The game is copiously decorated with wrong-brained word twisters, and to document all of them would soak up the whole of this book. However, I've got my favourites.

Ex-Phillies coach Frank Lucchesi, who, when confronting his team about certain scornful comments they'd made to the press, told them, "No one makes a scrapgoat out of Frank Lucchesi!" Dizzy Dean once commended a player (Eddie Lopat) for having "testicle fortitude," while ex-big leaguer Johnny Logan, upon accepting an award, told his teary-eyed crowd, "I will perish this trophy forever." Former Expo Andre Dawson once told the press, "I wan' all the kids out there to copulate me." Slugger-turned-broadcaster Ralph Kiner is on record telling millions of listeners, "Today is Father's Day. So, to all you fathers out there, happy birthday!" and, "If Casey Stengel were alive today, he'd be spinning in his grave."

Looking for words in a foreign language is like trying to trap a housefly with your hand: by the time you catch it, it's slow and half-dead, and of no worry to you any more. All you can do is file your phrase away until another similar moment arises, which it never does. It's an intellectual loneliness, really. To make things worse, the locals are always trying to get the foreigner to say something profane. With the Peones, it became a dugout tradition among Chencho and the boys to have me shout "cazzolino" and "angalato" and, wanting to be part of the intimate discourse of sports, I was more than happy to oblige. There was a lot I didn't understand, and I was starting to wonder how much I was getting wrong, when, one day at practice, I asked Fabio from Milan how long his family had been in Milan.

"Milan? No, Nettuno." he said.

"But you told me you were from Milan."

"No . . . I didn't say . . ."

"Yes, you did. It's how I distinguish between you and the other Fabio."

"?"

"I call you 'Fabio from Milan.'"

"But, I am not from Milan!"

So Fabio from Milan wasn't really from Milan. It presented a terrible problem. The only possible way of solving it was to rename him Fabio, No Longer from Milan. But that was absurdly long, so I decided to forget that we'd ever had our conversation. Still, between you and me, Fabio from Milan was not.

At the time, I was beginning to sense that Fabio from Milan was the glue that kept the Peones together. He was always first at practice and never had to be told to do anything. He was keen, but not a keener, and gave as good as he got. He was the most argumentative of all the players, but was the first to defend Pietro. On the field, he played four positions (1B, P, LF, RF) and even though he was the least natural hitter among the Peones, he managed to hit the ball at least once or twice per game.

On the morning of Roma at Nettuno – who hung two games above the Peones in the standings – Fabio from Milan ran interference for his coach after being confronted by the father of Davide Calabro, who'd been cut from the team for poor attendance. Peter Calabro had been the team's scorekeeper and had taken Pietro to task. "This isn't Serie A. You shouldn't take this game so seriously," he said, which only served to offend Pietro, for whom baseball was his life. Peter kept going back to this point in his argument with Fabio, which grew more heated. Their words cleared the rest of the team from the dugout, though a few players occasionally tiptoed over to catch a snatch of the argument, reporting back to small groups that had collected in the outfields. Pietro stood in deep left field, as far from the scene as possible.

I felt sorry for Peter and his son. The father was a slump-shouldered man in Coke-bottle glasses who wore a New York Yankees cap and matching windbreaker, both of which had seen better days. Davide was an ungainly kid with a jumbled face and few social graces. Whereas most of the Peones carried themselves with a certain finish or élan, Davide was a bag of wrong angles. Whenever he showed up for practice, he rarely joined one of the groups gathered in the outfield, and more often than not, he and I paired up to shag flies, two namesakes chasing loopers under the falling sun. I'd noticed that whenever the team ran laps around the field, he always did so in his socks. When I asked him why, he told me that his shoes were vecchio, old and rotten inside. I decided to give Davide the spikes I'd brought with me from home – I only ever wore my Converse to practice – but never got the chance. That was the last I saw of Davide all summer.

Peter, the father, left the park after losing the argument to Fabio. Before being dismissed, I heard him mutter, for the last time, "This is not Serie A, you know," to which Fabio responded, "We all work and have jobs, but when we come to the ballpark, it's serious. Davide isn't serious. He doesn't care enough." Later, I asked Fabio to elaborate, and he explained, "Davide, and his father, they are stupid. They've always been stupid. He knows when we have our games, but he doesn't tell his boss. We all work, but . . . ," and then he repeated what he'd told Peter. I asked Pietro why he'd cut Peter along with Davide. "Peter, sure, is a friend, yes," he said. "But a friend outside of baseball, not in baseball. Baseball is baseball. It's different."

"But wasn't Peter the team's scorekeeper for years?"

"Si, he was. But he always got it wrong."

Commitment is a tricky thing in middle-level sports, which offer neither financial remuneration nor guarantee of playing time. It's often hard to justify three nights of practice and two weekend games – often in other cities, miles away – when you've got family and work to consider. Then again, if the person has the right attitude to begin with – laying themselves on the line for the game and their team – it's easy to cut them slack when they have to turn their attention to home or work.

Maybe, by cutting Davide, Pietro was sending a message to his team – particularly in light of the two losses to Montefiascone – that no one would be spared. Perhaps Davide was sacrificed to show the team that their coach was single-minded enough to get them to win, even if it meant losing a good player who, last year, had helped them prevail in the Serie C championships. Perhaps Pietro was trying to tell them that this year was different.

This was real.
Italian League, Serie B.
Which says it all, both ways.

In a sporting sense, home is a friendly place. At least it's supposed to be. When you show up for a road game in a weird park in a strange city and find the visitors' dugout strewn with garbage, it's a threatening mess, as if wolves had been there the night before, and might return. But in the Peones' home dugout in San Giacomo – which the players knew as well as their bedside tables – all of those empty acqua frizzante bottles, discarded Kinder wrappings, claws of pizza crusts, and plastic gelato spoons looked like party junk, detritus from a week of circus catches, batting-practice dingers, and phantom triple plays.

The field was nostra casa, and the players and I were used to its discomforts: the splinters of the bench, holes and hidden drains, the sound the trees made when they rustled with the wind, the technique required to drink from the sink's tap without dragging your chin across its prehistoric algae. For us, there was nothing left to figure out. Instead, it would be Roma, not the Peones, who'd have to deal with the dugout drafts and sharp smells. Those were our wolves who'd left the bones.

On the day the Roman team came to play ball, at first it didn't appear as if the weather would co-operate. The rain had started before dawn, awakening me with its strange, foreign rhythm. Pietro collected me just after eight, and we drove to San Giacomo, where, at the stroke of ten, the rain finally stopped. The wet grass squished under the players' feet as they did what they had to do to get ready. Because they managed the park, this meant having to prep and groom the field themselves. Wheelbarrows of black dirt were brought in and strewn over the soft, muddy patches. Mario Mazza's father, 'Nando, took charge of measuring the field with a length of rope that he unspooled from what looked like a large yo-yo on

wheels and chalked the lines. Pompozzi and Pitò the Stricken tamped
the mound's dirt with their bare hands and punched drainage holes
with a grooved metal rod. The Emperor scrubbed home plate with
an old rag – a job better suited for a plebian, I thought – ridding it
of the red dirt blemishes that Pietro and the Red Tiger had left
after emptying two bags of pietrame rosso around it. Once all of
that was done, a fat kid on a motorino appeared in a corner of the
outfield dragging an old net, which he pulled across the infield clay
until it was smooth and pebble-free.

The way Pompo worked the mound reminded me of my grandmother tending her garden, working the dirt with the same arsenal
– an old hoe warped by the rain, a bent shovel, a toothless rake –
until it looked and felt right underfoot. Mark "the Bird" Fidrych
used to get singled out for grooving parts of the mound at Tiger
Stadium with his bare hands and the Peones' pitchers were just as
tender about theirs. They did everything short of taste it. Both
Pompo and Pitò pulled out a few thick clumps of weeds – spike grab-
bers, for sure – from the side of the mound, babying the path they'd
use to field bunts and groundball doinks. It revealed a greater attention to detail than I'd thought possible from the two young hurlers.

It was only right that I offered my help, and Mario Simone and
the Natural, who were loath to splatter their white uniforms with
gunk, were only too happy to have me mark the baselines. Being
young and fashion-conscious – and aware that their girlfriends, and
worse, their mothers, would be watching them that afternoon –
they'd arrived at the park with their pant stripes perfectly vertical,
their vests blooming evenly around their shoulders, their shirts and
stirrups and socks bleached and pressed. As I trudged into the brown
lake that had collected around home plate, the two players stepped
back, their arms folded, saying, "Grazie, Dave, bravo." If they'd
said, "The Canadese is already molto schifo . . . what's another
splotch of brown muck to him?" I wouldn't have blamed them.
Besides, as I pulled the serrated tire rim down the third-base line,
spitting muddy water over the grass, I realized it was the closest I'd
get to home plate all day.

After the clouds parted and the sun squeezed through, the day seemed ripe with possibility and, for the Peones, atonement. In an article in the weekly newspaper, *Il Granchio* (The Crab), the Emperor had said, in an eerie echo of the words of Augustus Caesar, "We are booked to redeem ourselves against Roma." The paper had used the quote as the headline for the game's preview. I thought it was great motivational fodder for the visiting Romans – ideal for taping at the front of the team bus – but Nettuno wasn't as concerned about the Emperor's prediction as they were with the accompanying story of their game against the M-Birds, where Chencho, not Cobra, had been credited with having allowed a team-record five home runs. Perhaps *concerned* isn't the right word. *Thrilled* is more like it.

Soon after the sun came out, fans, officials from the Federazione Italiana Baseball Softball (FIBS), friends, and families took their places along the fences and home-plate bleachers. They brought chairs, umbrellas, bags and coolers stuffed with food and drink. I busied myself filling in the scorebook that I'd inherited in the wake of Peter Calabro's dismissal (Cobra would start the first game, Pompozzi the second) as the dugout came to life: cleats crunching the floor's mulch, mitts pounded expectantly, blue batting helmets lined up on the dugout ledge like giant snails. An armful of aluminum bats were shoved into a vinyl rack roped to the fence, cigarettes were lit and nervously stubbed, and, finally, after a half-hour rain delay, the first ball hit leather.

I decided that the players who weren't playing should still contribute to the team's success. In the second inning, I asked Paolo if he knew how to steal signs, and he said he'd try. Within minutes, he'd cracked the Roman's code. "Go tell Pietro," I urged him. But Paolo didn't want to step on his coach's toes, to come across as too pushy. After a spell, I made him do it, but just as he did, Pietro figured out the signs himself. A few innings later, Paolo plucked a ball from the box of game balls and handed it to Pitò, telling him to hide the ball so that the umpire, should he request a fresh supply, wouldn't find it. When I asked him why, he grabbed the ball back and showed me its raised stitches. "This ball," he said, gripping two fingers across the seams, "is perfect for a curve. The Roma pitcher, he throws a curve."

I told Paolo that his perceptiveness and savvy gave the Peones a real advantage, but he just pursed his lips and shook his head. "Yes, but," he said, "I want to play."

For most of the first game, I hung out with the pitchers. I don't know what I was expecting, but I was surprised by how little of the game they actually watched. Pitò and Chencho were more interested in writing – unasked – a list of Italian words for *vagina* in my journal. Beside the list, Pitò drew a picture of a pig looking out a window, and scribbled *Chencho stay at window* beside it. It was quite nice. Every now and then, I'd wander away, only to return to find little penises drawn throughout the book. After tiring of drawing penises, Chencho tried out a new character on us, Super Chencho, which involved Travoltian gyrations of his arms and hips. Pietro eventually spotted his antics and yelled at him to stop, telling him that il strano sinistre's services might yet be required. It was a useless reminder. We all knew that it would take a stun gun to get Cobra out of the game.

Everything went right for the home blues. In the first inning, the Red Tiger made a wonderful diving catch, setting the tone for the day. He got a late jump on the fly ball, which fell heavily out of the sky. Everyone expected it to land for a single, but the Tiger chewed up the grass, getting to the ball in time. He pushed off with his feet, stretched out to glove the ball, slid across the grass, rolled into a crouch, sprung out of it, and showed the umpire the ball. This ended the inning, so he sprinted across the field and broke through a gauntlet of welcoming Peones who crowded around him and slapped him on the back, a buzz of blue and white in a corner of the dugout.

There were other heroes that day too. Mario Mazza homered, and so did Solid Gold. I'd first seen Solid Gold at Montefiascone – he'd made it in time for the second game, driving in from Nettuno, possibly setting a new land-speed record. Against the medieval

Solid Gold.
(Cathy Bidini)

backdrop of the city, he looked like he'd travelled back from the future, his jet black hair streaked with gold, a single diamond earring blinking in the sunlight. The Golden One moved with swagger and high confidence, and had the habit of winking at you to acknowledge your presence. Solid Gold never spoke much; over the course of the summer, he and I never had a meaningful conversation. Instead, he'd occasionally ask me, "Dave, facking yes?" or "Facking ya, Dave, facking ya?" For him, it was enough just to stand there, look good, and swear. We should all be so lucky.

Solid Gold was blessed with a tacklebox of baseball gifts. He had a mighty swing and a rocket of an arm, which afforded him an automatic place in the starting lineup, but I got the impression that sports, to him, was just a means of expressing his personality. Though he'd grown up playing little league ball with the rest of the Peones – yet another product of the San Giacomo kids' program – Solid Gold was a satellite, ignoring the team's many social gatherings in favour of a life of dancing and military service. Four nights a week, he guarded a Roman armoury, dressed in a royal blue uniform with gold epaulets and strapped with an air rifle like a cyborg warrior.

Because Solid Gold was a natural talent, few players ever questioned his chronic lateness. Even Pietro excused it on the grounds of his wearying military service, overlooking what the Natural had said about Solid Gold always being the last one to leave the disco. It's not uncommon for teams to have at least one player whose behaviour is tolerated because of his abilities, and Pietro was wise not to push the Golden One's buttons. When Pietro pencilled Solid Gold's name into the lineup – as a number-two hitter, no less – everyone else's name lit up around it. With Solid Gold – and to a lesser extent, the Red Tiger – in the order, the Peones' offence was far more aggressive.

With the help of Solid Gold's power surge, the Peones took command of the game. On the mound, Cobra was Cobra, pitching with the same authority as he had in Montefiascone. Hockey netminder Ed Belfour has stressed the importance of playing goal the same way no matter what the score. This was Cobra's method, and he kept to his change, curve, slider, fastball repertoire. This is not to suggest, however, that he was emotionless in his play.

Once, in the early innings, he walked ten feet in front of the mound to ask the umpire what kind of pitch he was expected to throw for a strike. The umpire told him, "Sopra il piatto" (over the plate). Cobra pressed two fingers into a point against his thumb and shook his hand violently, rather like a duck ridding its beak of water. "Then what do you think I've been doing out here?" he said.

The umpire dug into his hip pocket, pulled out a small black note-book, and wrote down the pitcher's name. Cobra asked him again, "Che lancia? What pitch?" The umpire sighed, "Managia," pulled off his mask, and stepped out from behind home plate. Their dis-cussion was voluble and protracted. It was like two people arguing across a kitchen table. They may as well have been wearing under-shirts and stabbing the air with forks wound with pasta. Chicca, looking into the dugout, announced, "This umpire's totally blind!" Finally, the umpire said something like, "All of you Nettunese are crazy!" and walked back behind the Big Emilio. From his half-crouch, he commanded "Play palla!", pointing at Cobra, who'd climbed back on the mound. After a derisive laugh, the pitcher unleashed a fastball that just dabbed the corner of the dish. The umpire called "Strike!" as if thanking Cobra for the argument. This prompted the batter to drop his bat, remove his helmet, and pick up the argument where Cobra had left off.

Almost all of the Peones' games were punctuated with rhubarbs of this nature. The Italian ballplayers just had to tease the game into a kind of Punch 'n' Judy show. For pure entertainment value, these verbal dust-ups between players on the same team, opposing players, fans, umpires, parents, and FIBS stats keepers were great to listen to and to watch. The combatants argued as much with their hands as with words. Cobra was one of the less demonstrative Peones, but he wasn't beyond waving his duck beaks or tapping the air to stress his words. Even while sitting on the bench, the team was constantly moving. Mario Mazza, for instance, could never tell me a story without first laying his hand on my shoulder, as if fearing that I would be sucked backwards in time during the long render-ing of his tale. He pushed the narrative along with a single raised finger, which he only ever lowered at the conclusion of the story, told excitedly with his face about five inches from mine.

The first thing the Red Tiger always did upon greeting me was slap my neck hard, as if a mosquito was about to draw blood. Then he'd grab my arm with his other hand and shake me violently. It was conversation by assault, in a not unpleasant way. The Emperor, by contrast, had the controlled gestures in keeping with his regal comportment, occasionally waving a hand, or pinching an imaginary coin, which he'd raise to his eye to underline his words. Paolo was prone to slower gestures, twisting his pointer finger in the air to make a point, or batting his hands at his chest as if fanning away smoke. The Big Emilio wagged duck beaks tight to his chin the way a nervous person nibbles on bread, while Mario Simone used a broad swooshing of his arms when he told a story, dramatic or otherwise.

Even though Pietro spent most of his time standing alone at third base or in a chair near the dugout, he was also constantly in motion. When he wasn't flashing signs like a robot checking for loose rivets, he was slapping his hands together in encouragement, whistling to his outfielders, waving Mario and Skunk across the infield, steadying Cobra by bouncing his hands at his waist, urging Pompo by clenching his fist, and so on. Sometimes, he went one on one with his players, other times he addressed them as a group. If he noticed an infelicity in their performance, he'd shout, "Why did you do that? Perche? What do you think you're doing up there? Why don't you ever listen to me?" The offender, of course, was obliged to defend himself at equal volume. Every few innings, he and one of his players sparred, and the scene was never dull. These were usually mild squabbles, unless they involved either Fabio from Milan or Mario Simone, in which case they'd extend over two or three innings, neither Pietro nor the player willing to back down. Only Paolo, Chicca, Cobra, Fab Julie, and Skunk Bravo – the veterans – were allowed to go about their business without Pietro undressing them in front of their teammates. Still, the others were forgiving. They'd shrug off the shit Pietro slung at them, saying, "Ah, that is Pietro. He is very serious about baseball."

The Peones' star catcher and cleanup hitter, the Big Emilio, usually rose above the coach's lecture, but in the fourth inning, the big backstop let his emotions get the best of him. After taking a ball to the wrist, he called for the team's canister of cold spray. At first, his request fell on deaf ears, so when it was finally delivered, he

The Big Emilio.
(Cathy Bidini)

thanked the player – Christian – for nothing. When he came off the field later that inning, still upset, he threw his equipment into the screen. Because Emilio was the lead-off hitter that inning, Pietro said nothing to him, but a few frames later, he called time and pulled the catcher out of his crouch, berating him in full view of both teams. You'd never see this in North American ball, but it is commonplace in the Italian leagues. Pietro coaxed Emilio up the third-base line and told him, "Think about what is happening in the game now! Forget three innings ago! Carry yourself like a real ballplayer, managia . . ." Being a man of few words, the catcher could only growl and return to his station.

Cobra threw nine innings, winning 10-5. The guys were loose and jubilant. In the second game, Pompo struck out ten Roma batters and won by the same score. The players didn't stop talking about their double win until the dugout had been cleared of all bats, balls, and gloves. With the falling June sun drenching the field with mellow gold, they filled their kit bags, greeted their families and friends, then made their way to the clubhouse, where Coach Monaco was waiting with a few parting words.

The Peones' clubhouse was a dank room painted utility grey, with a row of lockers and two pratfall benches. It was by far the mouldiest room I'd been in in Italy. It didn't even have a window. The room was only ever used by Pietro and the Emperor to shower after games – the rest of the players could not bear its filth – and, occasionally by Chencho, who'd reportedly launched his head into the lockers to pass the time during a recent rain delay.

Pietro stood in front of the team and spoke sternly in a low baritone. He said nothing about the games themselves. Instead, the issue was playing time. He told me later that he'd wanted to get things on the table before the problem got out of hand. It seemed like a strange time to scratch a sore, but it was probably better to do it with the team in a good mood.

The Natural had missed the first game – he'd also failed to show at any of the previous week's practices – and when he'd sat down beside me that afternoon in the dugout, the first thing he'd said was, "Dave, I not playing. Sorry, for your book," as if concerned about what his absence would mean to the narrative. He was visibly upset, and I could read everything that was going through his head – "I played fucking Serie A last year, who the fuck does Pietro think he is?" But the best I could offer was, "It's okay, maybe you'll get a chance to pinch-hit!" After the second game, I saw him leaning against his car in the parking lot, being consoled by his girlfriend. During Pietro's talk, he sat inside one of the lockers, unmoving, his eyes trained on the floor.

Everyone reacted a little differently. Chicca sat on one of the benches and watched Pietro with all the enthusiasm of a kid in detention eyeing the clock. Christian, at eighteen, the team's youngest player, looked scared, occasionally sneaking a glance at

Pietro to make sure the coach wasn't addressing him. Skunk Bravo sat in the middle of the floor staring at the ceiling, as if looking for a sign. (Turned out, he was simply trying not to vomit. He'd removed himself from the second game, holding his stomach as he'd walked off the field. When I asked Paolo what was wrong, he told me, "It is the influenza." I shuddered at first, until I realized that influenza is what Italians call the common cold.)

After such a banner day, it was strange to be huddled inside, being lectured by Pietro. The coach asked Mario Simone, "Aren't four practices enough for you? Do we have to schedule more for you to miss?" Then, to the Natural, "Why can't you get it straight at work? Do you work every morning and every night?" Then, backing off a little, to Solid Gold, "See what happens when you come to practice? See how well the team plays?" We sat there for five minutes, ten. Finally, Pietro set the week's practice times and then dismissed us. We filed out to the parking lot, and one by one, the Peones climbed into their cars and drove away. It was only then that I realized I hadn't had to sit there with the rest of them, getting yelled at as if I were a player myself. But, then, that was a small price to pay for a win.

9

A POCKET OF BRICK AND MORTAR

By now, I'd settled into a routine in Nettuno, more or less. Every morning, I pulled myself out of bed – when I wasn't pulled out by Cecilia – and strolled down to the newsstand, where I bought *La Gazzetta dello Sport*, or the *International Herald Tribune*, whenever it appeared. *La Gazzetta* – possibly the world's most famous daily sports newspaper – was a treat to if not read, then absorb. Which isn't to say that I understood nothing. The headlines were simple enough that "Totti: Trap, è buono per me" was decodable, even by me (thank God for dumb-guy sportspeak). For the record, Francesco Totti, the lynchpin of the Azzuri's (Italy's national soccer team) offence, was publicly announcing to Trap (Giovanni Trappatoni, the Azzuri's coach) that it was just fine with him if he coached the nation's side.

La Gazzetta was a self-contained paper – no annoying "Lifestyle" or "World News" or "Helpful Tips on Tax Returns" sections to shred through – with headlines in fat, black type. I couldn't get over my luck that I'd happened upon a daily paper devoted entirely to sports (albeit in another language, but still), and truth be told, it was a great way of sharpening my Italian, not to mention learning more than I ever needed to know about the beautiful game.

With the event not two weeks away, *La Gazzetta* was running ten pages of feverish pre–World Cup (La Mondiale) coverage, with forty pages in total. The text was printed on white rose newsprint – only in Italy, I believe, could such a pretty-looking sports paper have captured the nation's heart – and most sports, indigenous or otherwise, were given their due, from horse racing ("War Emblem sogno Triple dopo Baltimora") to tennis ("Serena regina a Roma") to, gratefully, hockey ghiaccio ("Detroit ha superato Colorado 5-3 con tripletta – tutta net 3 periodo – di Darren McCarty").

By subsisting on print reportage alone – there wasn't a single sportstalkwrapchat TV show, at least one that was about anything other than soccer – it was to relive an era when newspapers, and the odd, orphaned radio signal, were the only ways for fans to learn the fortunes of their teams. Suddenly, I found myself having to read between the lines, envisioning what "Kings Battono I Lakers Aiutati Da Un Cheeseburger" really meant, beyond the three-inch game report that followed the headline. Sorting through linescores and late summaries trying to imagine what might have happened, and how, was like collecting the pieces to a great jigsaw puzzle.

Through *La Gazzetta*, I followed the North American scene. It was a delicious moment when I finally settled at the kitchen table and spread out the pages of the newspaper, suddenly discovering what had happened to the Toronto teams. When the news was good, it made me feel that all was well in the city I'd left behind.

Once I'd scanned the paper, the family and I liked to stroller a familiar route, food shopping with an eye on the clock, because at 1 p.m. the stores shut, streets cleared, and life ceased in our small city for the three-hour siesta.

In general, I was in favour of the siesta, which also saw stores close for the entire afternoon and evening on Thursdays because, you know, once you've put in three consecutive half-days, how can you even get out of bed on the fourth day? If I'd known about this nation-wide timeout while I was a teenager, I might have had more of an

affinity for Italian culture as a whole. But the siesta didn't really work
for us, because neither Cecilia nor Lorenzo slept at these hours. As
a result, while most Italians were lying on their bedspreads weighted
with pasta, Janet and I were busy shredding crayons.

We bought much of our food at the alimentari, the Italian version
of a corner store, only instead of racks of ketchup potato chips and
pornography, there was a glass counter containing everything from
creamy towers of ricotta romana to plugs of bocconcino floating in
salty water; buckets of black and green pesto and fat tubes of fennel-
cured salami as big as Mo Vaughn's hambone. At the same hour
every day, the proprietors brought out wheels of crunchy bread,
which they sold hot.

Beyond the alimentari, on Via Vittorio Veneto, was Cotto e
Crudo, which Norma fancied because of the handsome butcher,
and beyond that, the local frutteria, whose proprietor occasionally
winked at Janet. Once the shopkeepers had won over the women
and then adopted Cecilia and Lorenzo as their own, I was left
without a dance partner. My loneliness hung heavily until I found
companionship at a gazebo bar at the top of the street run by Dino,
a fellow with thinning long hair who almost immediately took to
calling me by my last name. We met across a drink named either
La Bicicletta, Il Motorino, or La Nettunese, depending on the occasion. I first saw him confecting it – half Spumante, half Campari,
served in a champagne flute – one morning on our way to Rome.
Later, I stopped in and asked if he thought it might work for me.
He was sure it would and a few seconds later, I was hammered,
staring at a poster on the wall of a woman naked but for a handful
of white flowers. Before I could say, "Geez, I'd sure like to hoe her
garden!" she walked into the bar, a not unusual event considering
that she was Dino's wife.

One street west from Via Vittorio Veneto was Via Santa Maria,
a boulevard of clothing shops for those Nettunese who required a
caramel leather bustier on demand. In a store called Pool Position
(right beside Coco-Nuda, if you're passing through), I made my
first timid foray into Italo-style: I bought a black leather belt from

a woman who was stuffed into a silver leather bra under a sheer black blouse. While I was happy with the belt, it nearly came back to haunt me. One evening, Cecilia and I were wheeling past Pool Position when I uttered what, I hope, will be the single most tedious phrase that ever passes my lips: "See, honey? That's the place where your father bought his belt!" After taking a few seconds to consider what I'd said, Cecilia shouted, smart as a whip, "Daddy needs a belt!" At which I steered her straight to the gelateria.

South of Via Vittorio Veneto was the Borgo Medievale, Nettuno's old walled city within a city. You entered the Borgo through an arched brick passage that had once housed a twenty-foot iron door. There were a few clothing shops and a restaurant on one side of the vault, and on the other, a sweet shop, Krapfen, which sold what amounted to warm doughnuts filled with the choice of three items: cioccolata, crema, or marmalata.

I was lucky to make the discovery early on that marmalata was a catch-all for anything that wasn't cioccolata (which wasn't really chocolate, either; more on that in a minute). Marmalata was not only marmalade, but every other jam and jelly known to Italians. And they filled everything with it: brioche, cornetto, krapfen, paste, the latter being the confusing name the Italians call the croissant. Which tells you how much they really care about their sweets. Or the French.

Okay: cioccolata. Cioccolata means Nutella, not chocolate. Nutella was everywhere. If you don't know – and if you don't, watch out – Nutella is a chocolate and hazelnut spread that the Italians rank just under holy water as the nation's most essential product. The Italians will put Nutella on anything, most disturbingly pizza. Imagine getting a plain, hot-baked pie from your favourite pizzeria and emptying Pixie Stix over it. That's what it was like to have your pizza with Nutella, the protein equivalent of injecting a Ding Dong with a Ho Ho (now there's a rap act I'd like to see).

Beyond Krapfen (and there's a prog-rock band I'd like to see) was Piazza Colonna. Cecilia and I spent a lot of time in Piazza Colonna, mostly because it had a fountain that she liked in full view

of a chair at the Gabbiano snack bar where I could sit and watch
her play. A snack bar, to me, was a place where hot dogs went to
die, but in Italy the best of them, like the Gabbiano, served a full
complement of wine, liquors, coffee, snacks, and sandwiches. When
I ordered a drink that wasn't coffee, I was served three or four small
china bowls of pistachios, potato chips, olives, nuts, and, occasionally, finger sandwiches, sometimes spread with black and red caviar.

The Gabbiano didn't heed the siesta, so they were open whenever I needed them, which was always. It was one of the great pleas-
ures of being in Italy: sitting on the terrace of a perfect café, just
where the sun married the ocean breeze, and sipping a drink. Some
days it was the cafe macchiato (espresso with a press of warm milk),
other times it was a granita di limone (fresh lemon juice poured
over crushed ice and served in a tall parfait cup), chocolate frappe
(a gelato milkshake with a lightness to equal its ballast, a crown of
bubbles across the top), or crodino (an auburn-tinted, bubbly
bitter). One day, between sipping my crodino and nibbling on a
coconut biscotto, I noticed Lorenzo in his stroller chewing raptur-
ously on a toy rubber hand, his eyes peeled back in his head. The
two of us were on the same level.

In Piazza Colonna I watched the living theatre of Italy. There
wasn't a moment that the locals weren't stopping in at the fountain,
especially on hot days when neck and arm baths were required at
ten-minute intervals. In the space of a few minutes one afternoon,
an old man in a brown suit laid his straw bag against the fountain's
base, stooping to take a drink. Next, three children were hiking each
other up, feet in hands, to reach the water. After them, a pigeon
dipped out of the sky onto the blackened lip of the bowl. Then a
cyclist arrived, pulled off his cap, and held his stubbled head under
the spout before giving way to a young mermaid in a sparkling
green bikini top with long, crimped hair and a body the colour of
molasses, who tipped herself forward to lick the water. Next came a
fellow in a butcher's cloak balancing a tray of blood; an old woman
pointing her bouquet of wildflowers at the cobblestone while leaning
under the spout; the Borgo dog, his coat stuck with bramble and gum

wrappers, two paws over the bowl; more pigeons; Gigi Siggi Siggi, the six-foot-tall local photographer and handyman, cooling himself after repairing a door he'd first broken; a young couple in mirrored sunglasses on a purple glitter motorino; more pigeons; a handful of tourists fresh from a procession to Chiesa Santa Maria Goretti, Nettuno's largest church; a spearfisherman holding a bag of fish; a single, conquering pigeon; and a family of Canadians, attempting to break the spell that held their patriarch to his chair.

Just off Piazza Colonna two narrow streets tipped and swerved like funhouse ramps through the old town towards the sea. I liked the Borgo because of its imperfections: the sloping streets, the centuries of grime, the exposed pipes creeping up walls. The Borgo's charm was in knowing itself, in letting itself be. The Borgo apartments, built hundreds of years ago, were in such close proximity to each other that they were like heads tilting together to get a better view of the street, which, at points, couldn't have been more than ten feet wide. During siesta, the air filled with the clatter of cutlery being drawn from drawers, cupboards rattling open and closed, bowls and plates spinning flat over tablecloths, the grumble of an old man – a percussive symphony that passed through the white lace curtains out of kitchen windows, where families prepared for pranzo. I liked to wander the Borgo at this time, occasionally catching a glimpse of families gathered around their tables. The air would be rich with the perfume of olive oil and garlic kissing a hot pan, in which rhombo, polpo, calamari, or gamberoni – all local fish pulled that day from the sea – were searing.

The Borgo was a perfect, lost place, the best of Nettuno in a pocket of brick and mortar. When the sun dipped on the other side of the sea wall, the alleyways grew dark and cool; at times, I felt like I was escaping from a town to which I'd escaped. Once this sensation took hold, I made my way back through the barrel vault to prevent myself from getting stuck forever in this other world. As soon as I found myself back on Via Resistenza Nettunese, the sting of the salt sea air and the rush of the surf reminded me why I'd come to Nettuno in the first place. Sometimes, before climbing the

three storeys to the apartment, I stood before the sea, imagining
what had once moved across these waters: the countless generations
of Nettunese fishermen, the Saracen pirates, the merchant vessels
sailing from distant gulfs, the "black mountain of ships," as Silvano
Casaldi described it, which brought to the town war – and peace.

And baseball.

10

1985

It was during a stay in Ireland in 1985 that I first dreamed of base-ball. This happened while I slumbered in the foggy aftermath of six or seven pints of Guinness. At the time, I was enrolled in a program of Anglo-Irish Studies at Trinity College, and this much booze in an evening was typical. I don't know if it was the stout or the strange karmic forces that enter one's subconscious when abroad, but when I woke the next morning, I realized that I'd dreamed about Cliff Johnson, the old Blue Jays designated hitter.

He'd emerged from a wall of clouds, asking in a grumbling drawl to be traded back to Toronto. Heathcliff, as he was known to team-mates, looked like himself: dopey, with heavy-lidded eyes, a mottled beard and moustache, and two sprigs of afro sprouting from the sides of his Texas Rangers' cap. Johnson's sporting trademark was the interminable at-bat, which drove opposing teams to fits but delighted home crowds since it almost always resulted in a hit (at one point, Johnson held the record for most home runs by a pinch hitter). Wearing the number 00, if you can call that a number, he'd loiter forever in the on-deck circle before slouching to the plate, where he'd study the bat with suspicion. He would take two wild swings at whatever was thrown at him, then, once he was comfortably behind 0-2, he'd work the pitcher until the count was full, fouling off anything that came near the plate. After about twenty minutes, Johnson would finally connect, and the ball would shoot over the second baseman's head and bounce four or five times before the centre fielder could reach it. Johnson would chug safely to first, where he'd make all the necessary base-running preparations – removing his sliding gloves from his hip pocket, knocking the dirt from his cleats, righting his batting cap – only to be removed for a pinch runner. He would kick the field in protest – "Coach should leave me in. Old Heathcliff can still run!" – but he was just going through the motions. Toronto fans loved him and his act, so when he asked to come home, I said, "Man, I'll see what I can do." As a rule, you don't say no to a ghost carrying a Louisville Slugger.

That summer, I went weekly to the Canadian Embassy, to read old *Globe and Mail* sports sections. The Jays were in the middle of their best season and it was a treat to follow their fortunes from afar. Every week, new players – Tom Filer, Tom Henke, Jimmy Key – were emerging, and the paper was filled with excited stories about the club's climb to the top echelon of the major leagues. One day, not long after my dream, I sat down at the embassy to read a week's worth of sports sections when, there it was, in a great black ribbon across the top of the page: "JOHNSON TRADED BACK TO BLUE JAYS."

It was a sign, none too subtle, that baseball was upon me. When I went back to Toronto in September, the Blue Jays – with Heathcliff batting in the familiar number-five hole, behind George Bell and Jesse Barfield – were in the heat of their first pennant race. One afternoon after Janet got back from Italy, where she'd spent the summer, I waited for her on the common outside the University of Toronto. To pass the time, I was reading an article by W.P. Kinsella about the drama Jays fans could expect, and how some teams, like the Cubs, Phillies, and Angels, had been there before and failed, while others had not been there at all. Janet came out to meet me and we did what we would do almost every week for the next five

Tony Fernandez in flight at Exhibition Stadium, 1985.
(Courtesy of Fred Thornhill)

years: we went to the ballpark. That autumn, the game became a greater part of my life than ever before. Or, rather, *our* lives. Though we'd gone to different European cities in a quest to discover who we were or weren't, baseball was a place the two of us explored together. She had Italy, I had Ireland, but we both had Exhibition Stadium.

Critics called it Exasperation Stadium, but for many baseball fans the Mistake by the Lake had an awkward charm. A Canadian Football League (CFL) stadium with aluminum benches, a pixilated scoreboard, and Astroturf, it was nevertheless unapologetically ours. I remember one extra-inning game on a late-spring evening with snow fluttering from the sky. There were five thousand of us diehards sitting there in toques, blankets, and thick gloves, thwapping our hands together for Tony Fernandez, who grew up in San Pedro de Macoris and had probably never seen a day under 25 Celsius. Fernandez crept rheumatically to the plate wearing a thermal turtleneck beneath his home whites, touched his bat gently to the dish, and moments later struck the ball with the quickness of a viper's lash. Post-hit, Tony stood at second base rubbing his arms as we howled our northern howl. One batter later, George Bell "wallooped" him home, which is what centre fielder Lloyd Moseby used to call Bell's fence-bending doubles. It was pure CanBall.

At the Ex, you could never read the skies. If it wasn't snow or ice or hail moving in off the lake, it was a blizzard of seagulls bursting over the lip of the park. A menace to all visiting teams, they treated the Astroturf as their natural habitat, an attitude that captured all that Canadian baseball fans aspired to be: stubborn, cold-weather creatures undaunted by visiting American teams who had to deal with the snow and screaming birds if they dreamed of stealing a win.

In the late summer, the annual Canadian National Exhibition filled the sky above the outfield with motion and colour: the Zipper, the Flyer, and two ferris wheels carving the air. It was as if the ball-park had been drawn up by a mad creator, who'd decreed, "And there shall be a marvellous carnival just beyond right field!" The diamond's backdrop was an electric theatre where pop-ups and fly balls were painted in a garish light. There was never any need for the kind of post-win fireworks that are standard in today's parks, not when there were masses of kids holding sparklers behind the right-field grille. Before they removed it, you could ride the Alpine Way – the Ex's rickety old cable-car ride – from just inside the Dufferin Gate to the Automotive Building and watch a few at-bats between your feet. After the final hour of business on Labour Day, carnies in greased caps disassembled the ferris wheel, swabbed down streets stuck with gum and paper and toffee, and led the cavalli home from their stables in the Coliseum. The quiet that returned to the grounds signalled that it was time to get to the job at hand: winning the American League East.

The Blue Jays of that era were as young as Janet and I, and in following their fortunes day to day, our lives became webbed with theirs. The 1985–87 teams were about growing up, falling apart, getting it back together, then losing it again, which is the prerogative of all youth. In their penultimate series of the season against the Yanks, they went into the Bronx Zoo for game one and stood along the chalkline as the Canadian national anthem was drowned out by thugs chanting, "Jays suck! Jays suck!" They lost 7–5. At one point, Fernandez and second basemen Damaso Garcia blew an easy double play, Fernandez hitting Garcia in the ribs with his throw. Dave Stieb, the brilliant young pitcher, self-destructed, handing the game to the indomitable New Yorkers. I drove with friends to a restaurant in the suburbs to watch the game via satellite. It felt as if all of the anxiety and uncertainty of my own life was played out on this night. Then, in keeping with the precarious and unpredictable spirit of youth, the Jays stormed back in the next three games, humbling the dumbstruck Bombers. The following week, the *Village Voice* ran the headline, "JAYS JUNK BRONX PUNKS; LEAVE YANKS IN FUNK." I clipped it and pasted it to the dashboard of my car. The Jays' pride was my pride. In a fan's life, there are only a few times that you can point to a team and say, "That's who I am. That's where my heart is." After the Yankees series, every remaining game – there were three weeks left in the season – was a test of the stomach and heart. It was a terrible burden. In the middle of one night, I wheeled my bike into an opening in the Ex's outfield wall and stuck a guitar pick in a seam between the warning track and outfield wall: a talisman for Lloyd Moseby. The games were like the trial of life itself, and in the middle of them all was blossoming love and the awareness that this time – the first time – would not come our way again.

Over that month, Janet and I grew together: boy and girl, boy and team, boy and girl and team. Anyone who's ever come home from a strange and beautiful land knows it's almost impossible at first to relax and feel good about your home and your friends, all of it feels stupid, dull, and suffocating. But the pennant run of 1985 mellowed the blow for me. Just as my summer in Ireland had taken me to a new country, so did the pennant race, which showed me the country of baseball, as Donald Hall has called it. Instead of crawling inward, resentful of home, I leaned on Janet's ear at the ballpark, where we spent all the time we needed getting to know each other, talking about everything. She was nineteen, I was twenty-two. As the Jays took care of New York on the final weekend of the series at the Ex (we were sitting just over George Bell's shoulder as he made the final out), I realized I'd fallen in love with a girl and a team. On the final night of the Jays' post-season, in which they lost the American League Championship Series to the Kansas City Royals on Jim Sundberg's wind-blown home run, Janet and I lay on the couch in my parents' basement, celebrating, in a manner befitting our age, the year the Jays went to the pennant.

II

NETTUNO AT SALERNO

The Peones' next game was against Salerno, but I took a flyer on the 5:00 a.m. bus trip. They lost both ends of the doubleheader. Chencho started game one – a dubious decision by Pietro, one that the boys debated for days afterwards – and was clobbered. Cobra came in and cleaned up, but it was no use; the game was lost. Pompozzi fared a little better in the second game, but his defence sprung a leak. There was no clutch hitting, no energy on the base-paths, and little of the base-to-base aplomb that the boys had shown in their fine victories over Rome.

Pietro was livid. He was upset at the way the team lost, and by how they'd responded to losing. When I called to talk to him he sounded shaken and – for the first time since I'd met him – old. "I not do . . . very good," he said. Later in the conversation, as he opened up, it was all cazzo this and cazzo that, a mad train wreck of cursing. Paolo described this condition as incazzato di nero, Roman slang for feeling anger that is beyond black. Janet asked me to ask Paolo if it was something you'd say in front of your mother.

"No, never," he said.

The next day, in our kitchen, Pietro vented: "The team played like peccorini, little sheep. They looked small and afraid, like they wanted to get on the bus and fanno dormire. It was very, very bad.

"Dave, it is very different from when I played. In my time, we were like lions. Fierce. Con cuore. I wasted nothing in the game. It was thinking, thinking, being ready, in good shape, for every game, every pitch, every inning. But this team, ack," he shouted, "they showed no rispetto. I don't care about losing, but . . . but . . . it was how they lost. Three errors in the first inning. One of their runs was scored from a bunt: an inside-the-park fuoricampo. On a bunt! The ball went here," he said, throwing out his hand, "and they missed. It went here, they missed again. Here, again. Capito? A bunt! After the game, in the pullman, I looked back and they were laughing and joking, caring about nothing. Senza rispetto. Niente."

Pietro talked and talked. Maria Pia, Norma, Janet, and I sat there listening as a light breeze tickled the white curtains. In reconstructing the game, the coach was like a man walking through a ransacked house, tipping things upright that had been knocked over, staring at the cracks in a precious vase. The rest of us strolled a few steps behind, trying to soften the vibe. But it wasn't easy. Pietro sounded flattened. I learned later that, on the bus ride home, he'd sat at the front and stared straight ahead, smoking cigarette after cigarette, saying nothing. In the kitchen, he said, "It was my worst day in baseball. I've been playing for forty-four years, and it was never this bad. After the first game, I felt like leaving the park, coming home. For maybe the only time in my life, I wanted not to see baseball, to put it away."

The first practice after the Caserta debacle was no practice at all. The players arrived at the campo to find their unsmiling coach sitting in a patio chair in his street clothes, throwing his keys in the air, catching them, throwing them again. He wouldn't even look at them. When he needed to know what time it was, he asked me, even though he knew I don't wear a watch. Looking for a distraction, the players ran laps around the field. Solid Gold, who hadn't made the trip to Caserta, arrived and started asking what was happening, why the team wasn't practising. This only exacerbated Pietro's anger and disappointment, which had softened not at all in the two days since the Peones' double beating.

Before I could ask the players what had happened in Caserta, they asked me, "Has Pietro talked to you? What did he say? How angry is he with us?" I told them about his dark mood, and mentioned that he was upset because he didn't think anyone on the team had got enough rest the night before their road trip.

"Oh, I dormito on the field," said Fabio from Milan. "I was late on every swing, and with the fly balls, I look up and only see the sky. I go out on Friday, I go out Saturday . . . I had three hours sleep only! In Caserta, Davide, it was very hot too. And on the night before, I drink and get drunk."

"You got drunk? Why?"

"Davide, it is bad. My girlfriend – five years!" he said, fanning out the fingers on his hand. "She broke up with me. I am twenty-three, so, what could I do? I had to go out and drink."

"We all play like we were drinking," said Mario Simone, shaking his head. "Three errors in the first inning. Then the rest, pffffttt. We were terrible. Very, very bad. Tutta la squadra."

"We were shit," said Fabio from Milan.

Pietro was convinced that there was a discipline problem on the team. When he'd brought up the subject in our kitchen, I told him a story about Casey Stengel. Whenever Stengel suspected that his players were skipping curfew to hit the town, he'd ask the elevator operator in his hotel to get those arriving later that night to sign a baseball, which he'd tell the fellow he would deliver to a sick child the next morning. Then Stengel went to bed. The next morning, he collected the ball from the elevator operator and read the signatures of the late-arriving players, who thought they were helping to put a smile on little Johnny's face, but were actually incriminating themselves. Pietro enjoyed the story, but I could tell what he was thinking from his smirk: "Ya, right, if only it were that easy."

I told him that I thought that staying out late and breaking curfew and basically fucking up was a trademark – sometimes even a badge – of young ballplayers, but this did nothing to convince him that their actions weren't severe. I also offered that, even with no sleep, young athletes think they can rise above fatigue to play their hearts out, and sometimes they can. (It's the same in rock and roll. When you're younger, you go hard from the stage to the band room to the party, and worry about the rebound later.) I wasn't making excuses. I was just trying to paint a picture of his team as being on the right side of normal. He countered by explaining, "In my day, we did four hours of practice for two-hour game. We worked hard all the time and made sure: no mistakes, no mistakes. And also: no drinking, no nothing. If you behave like that and don't respect the game, then you don't care. You have to make a decision. These guys: they have to make a decision."

Even though he was usually charming and magnanimous, Pietro had a fiercely competitive edge that would sometimes fry the more enlightened side of his character. Because he'd been the starting shortstop with the Nettuno Indians at sixteen, held the league's all-time stolen-base record, and was a ten-time champion, competition was in his bones. He'd played all over the world, had attended Cincinnati Reds camp in 1962. His Reds uniform still hung in his closet at home. Whenever I asked if he was hungry and wanted to eat, he'd boast how little food he needed to keep going at full speed. Same with booze: he rarely drank.

Sometimes, I'd arrive at the ballpark for practice to find him alone on the mound under the blazing Mediterranean sun, wearing only his red sweatshorts, grooming the dirt with one of the old clubhouse rakes. Paolo, who sometimes drove me to San Giacomo, would gesture with his chin: "Look. Pietro. He is a big baseball star, yes?" Other times, when there weren't enough players to form a proper infield, Pietro would station himself at second base and have Pitò or Cobra hit endless groundballs to him. In the mid-morning, when the sun was at its fiercest, he'd field more than fifty, sixty groundballs, hinting at the form that had made him one of Italy's greatest ballplayers. Pietro was silent throughout the drills, bearing down with every ball, cursing to himself whenever he missed. Mario Simone, standing beside me at third base, would say, "Dave. Pietro e mal di baseball, no?" quietly enough so that only he and I could hear. Pietro kept working and working – sometimes for twenty minutes, a half an hour – until he'd exhausted himself. Then he'd take off into the outfield and run the perimeter, staying loose. The Emperor would turn to me and sigh, "Pietro, he cannot stop playing."

Once, when I was stationed at third base with Pietro playing second, I caught a floating line drive by sweeping my hand through the air, looking away as I did. The players laughed at my hot-dog move, but Pietro immediately rushed across the diamond and showed me how to catch the ball properly, moving my hips until they were square with my catching hand.

Pietro had noticed what he thought was a flaw in my play, and insisted that I do it right. With him, there couldn't be any other way. He couldn't see that I was sending up baseball's propriety, goofing around, *having fun*. Another time, a young boy and his father brought two lawn chairs out to the field and sat above the dugout, where they watched the Peones practise. The kid wore his glove and shagged phantom hits whenever one of the Peones made a good catch. Near the end of the session, I approached Pietro, who was pitching batting practice, and asked if we might get the kid to come into the outfield and stand with the guys, maybe even shag one of those easy seven-hoppers. Pietro looked at him, then looked at me, and said, "It is not possible. Questo allenamento è formale" (This is a formal practice). Sometimes before the team would run laps, Pietro would tease me as if I were a child. On other occasions, he'd joke about the way I threw the ball or swung the bat. On days I felt particularly tender, I wanted to tell him that I wasn't one of his players, and that he could go fuck himself, but never did. He never cut me any slack regarding my butchering of the language either, though he was harder on Janet, who, because she was better at it, was allowed no room for error. One day, she jokingly lamented the lack of a plural for the Italian word for milk (latte), arguing in front of a group of us, "What if I'm calling for Dave to put both cartons of milk in the fridge, and he thinks I'm just asking to put one away, and the other goes sour?"

"Uh, you'd yell at me?" I offered.

"Yes, but that's beside the point."

"No, it's not. You're not the one being yelled at."

"What I mean is, there's only one word for both meanings."

Pietro, unable to resist the bait, tried to find a similar flaw in the English lexicon. At first he failed, but, despite a very limited grasp of the language – he'd learned his English from a handful of American ballplayers he'd played with in Serie A – he soon had his example. His eyes brightened as he held up a professorial finger: "What about sheep? If I want two sheep, I don't say, bring me the sheeps, do I? I say bring me the sheep!" Janet, no wilting violet in any debate, scrunched her face and conceded the argument. Pietro folded his arms. He'd won.

Even though Pietro was years removed from his days of diamond glory, he carried himself like many retired athletes, moving about as if inside a gilded picture frame, conscious that whenever people saw him, they were reminded of the player in his youth, making city-saving catches and belting clutch home runs. The nature of baseball makes it harder to walk away from than other sports. Because it's a dreamy and chimeric game, it's as unlike the modern world as the Ultimate Fighting Challenge is like it. One of the charms of the game is its dramatic balance – the surprise of action set against the long swim of time – and to a ballplayer whose life, since teenagehood, has been set in this realm, the post-career world must feel oddly flat. It's a mental, physical, and emotional shock that can sometimes happen, in the case of severe injury, in the heart-beat of a single play or moment.

Still, Pietro was by no means the Great Santini. He wasn't a tragic figure, like Denny McLain or Donnie Moore or Doug Harvey, who, on the day he was called to join the Montreal Canadiens' Team of the Century, was living in a twenty-dollar-a-week boarding house without a suit to his name. Pietro was well adjusted, charming, warm, smart, and funny. He gave hours of his life to his team for no salary whatsoever. The players, I think, loved Pietro despite – maybe even because of – these complications, even as they grew weary of his demands. Knowing this, Pietro had to be careful not to let the disciplinarian consume the mensch, and vice versa. At the same time, by showing the anger and despair the Peones' behaviour caused him, he taught his team that, as players, they possessed the ability to turn the tide one way or another. Pietro's dugout silence asked them a question that went beyond winning or losing: it was a question about love, allegiance, and the effect that they had on each other and their coach. In the dugout, as he spoke for fifty unbroken minutes to his silent players, their eyes downcast, the question he put to his charges was simple. It was up to them what kind of team they wanted to be.

The final few days before the Peones jetted to Sardinia – an away date in which Nettuno had to take both ends of the doubleheader if they wanted to keep their hopes of second place, and a playoff berth, alive – things were starting to return to normal. And then Mirko nearly killed someone.

Mirko wore a rakish beard and a sly, mischievous smile, which had given him his boyhood nickname, Sorriso. His solid physique was somewhere between fat and muscle – I thought that his build, combined with his moustache, gave him the look of a strongman who might have hammered a bell at a carnival. This dashing veteran of local ball had been recruited by Pietro to coach first base, play a little infield, and hang around and lighten the mood, that is when he wasn't trying to deplete Nettuno's population one person at a time.

I didn't see the flight of Mirko's death ball, only the sound of it landing in the courtyard of the pink-walled house across the road: glass smashing on pavement, chairs scraping backwards, a door

Mirko.
(Cathy Bidini)

slammed against a fence, and a sudden burst of voices as the family ran out to the road. Their faces were written with shock as they pointed to the batting cage, from where Mirko had hooked his deadly foul. An old woman clutched her head and twisted it back and forth, wailing. Soon, the whole lot were crying. My first thought was, God, he's killed someone.

The ball had fallen out of the sky during cena, the Italians' late-evening dinner. It must have landed like a grenade, something that the elders of the clan had probably experienced first-hand during the war. "Porco Dio! Cazzo Dio! Fuck your game and your base-ball can go to hell!" One old fellow was all over us, howling like a bear. I didn't know what to do. The Emperor went over to talk to them; Pietro followed. The rest of the team walked over to the fence, and then a young girl, nine or ten, ran from the house alongside her father, his arm around her head. They climbed into a van and sped away. The old woman put her palms flat to her face and sobbed. The Emperor put a hand on the shoulder of one of the women, and eventually, he and Pietro calmed the family down. Mirko paced in a circle near the dugout, trying to make himself disappear.

It was a bad scene, but it would get better. When the ball had crashed into the yard, it had rattled around in the trees before giving the girl's noggin a good old knock, nothing worse.

Batting practice was resumed, but we didn't have the heart to keep playing. Paolo and I talked about the perils of sport, and he told me a story. "You know, it happened to me once, when Pietro was coaching me as a boy. I was the catcher, like always, and the runner – il corridore – was coming at me, towards the plate. When he arrived, he hit me funny, you know, at a funny angle?" he said, slapping his hand to the top of his chest. "He hit me and he fell back. I had stopped him from scoring, but he lay there beside the base, shaking. He had swallowed his tongue. It was terrible, terri-ble. I thought he would die, but Pietro, he was there, right away. He knew exactly what to do. He kneeled down beside the boy and removed the tongue from his throat."

"He saved his life?"

"Yes, Pietro saved his life."

A few days after this brush with the unthinkable, the game with Sardinia was upon us. We were scheduled to leave San Giacomo for Fiumicino airport at 6:30 a.m., but Pietro picked me up at 5:15, stealing fifteen minutes from my precious coffee-drinking time because he had to be the first to the park. The poor bugger had probably lain awake the whole night thinking about the game and what he'd said on Tuesday, and how what he'd said on Tuesday would affect the game.

One by one the players rolled into the parking lot at San Giacomo looking groggy, with pressed-pillow faces. But by the time we got to the airport and on the plane, we looked like a team in our matching blue-and-white Peones shirts. I was reminded how remarkable and singular teams are, how they draw together people from every corner of life's chessboard. A move here, a move there, a happenstance meeting, a friend of a friend of a friend, a phone call, a passing word. Teams pull together people who, otherwise, might not ever touch each other's lives. The Peones were no different than countless other teams playing countless other sports in countless other countries.

I saw just how diverse this team was when the family and I went to Chencho's parents' home for cena one night, then to a team party at the Emperor's villa an evening later. Chencho's mother, I learned, was a devil of a baseball fan – she'd been witness to DiMaggio's at-bat at the Villa Borghese and could remember the posture, hair wave, and batter's box tilt of every batter on Nettuno's first teams – and was considered a maestro of the kitchen. When I told Paolo we had a date to eat at the Navaccis', he said, "Oh. You will eat so well," his voice weighted with a kind of gastronomic foreboding. I tried to heed his warning to fast through the day, but it didn't help me at the table. Mrs. Chencho tried to kill us with food.

The meal was a marathon affair: seven courses, served outside in their courtyard by the faint light of the city street, to a soundtrack of zzzing cicadas and kids play-fighting two houses down. Every now and then, friends and neighbours dropped by, lit a smoke, left. The dinner was spectacular: speck-shelled vongole a vivo swimming in vino bianco and olive oil; fresh fettucine served with a modest local fish, cernia (I had two plates and my troubles began); gnocchi, as light as a cloud, with sweet cherry tomatoes and salty salsicce; tacchino (turkey) breast, rolled and stuffed; huge gamberoni (shrimp) thatched with parsley and set alight by tiny spoonfuls of a dark salsa; insalata mista; a whole watermelon cleaved into hunks that spilled across the table; biscotti; grappa; and, by order of the occasion, cacchione frizzante. By the end of the night, I was a dead weight in my seat.

At one point, I mentioned that we were going to the Cancellis the following night. Chencho's dad, already well into the spirits, spat the Cancelli name back at me. "Gianni è . . . politico," said the young Chencho, trying to smooth things over. But it was too late. Already, the old man had barked the names of those Nettunese he considered crooks, including our padrone's late father. Cancelli was at both the top and bottom of his list.

I'd encountered a similar reaction to the Cancelli name – an old blood name, having been around Nettuno for five hundred years – from Silvano Casaldi, who told me, "You and I, we write books. This does well for us, to produce these things. But for Gianni, he wants more. A lot more. People like him want to have the power. His insurance company is the only business that shows his name, but he is involved in many other enterprises here. He is all over town, only you can't see him. He's invisible." When I asked Silvano how the Emperor's dad was able to exude such power so quietly, he told me two things. "One, it isn't always exuded so quietly. And two, because he has people in Rome to watch his back."

The team party at the Cancellis' lush country grounds was held on a terrace next to the thirty-metre swimming pool. We dined by torchlight on pizza and pasta to the sound of the wind whispering through the vines. No neighbours dropped by because the Cancellis had none. My evening couldn't have been more different from the previous night at Chencho's. I'd walked into Chencho's home to the sight of wooden platters of flour-dusted gnochetti pressed not an hour before, over which a calender from a local bakery was opened to Miss August, starfished in all of her womanly splendour on a fur rug. At Gianni's a Dalmatian crept about the property, and after swimming in the big backyard pool, we settled on the terrace for coffee and three kinds of cake.

These stark differences hadn't precluded Chencho and the Emperor from coming together to play for the Peones. Their fathers were polar opposites, but their sons had spent much of their lives on the same ball fields, playing with the same teammates. The rich and the poor, the left and the right, city and country, were all part of the same team.

On the Thursday before our date with Sardinia, our waitress at a team dinner (at Peyote's Mexican restaurant, one of the Peones' sponsors) asked me how many people in our group were ballplayers. "Ten players, and one writer," I told her, but the Big Emilio redid the math: "No, eleven giocatore." I didn't feel the full affect of what he'd said until we boarded the plane together in our blue and whites. Emilio understood that this season was mine too, and that that was my blood and sweat swimming around in there as well as theirs. The summer of 2002 would be unlike any other not only because my wife and I had returned to the land of our grandparents bearing two kids with Italian names, but also because I was spending it on the diamond with these men. I had the sense, for the first time, that we were in the game together.

12

NETTUNO AT SARDINIA

The A.S. Catalana baseball team's field – Campo Via Emilia, in Alghero, Sardinia – was a rutted pentangle of dead sod dusted with grey. Every blade of grass had fought through the packed earth, only to surrender life under the blaze of the sun. Whenever you stamped the ground, a puff of dirt rose. The infield's dry basepaths were littered with bumps and holes and little spires of earth that stabbed the air. Strolling around them was like walking across a dead reef. The outfield was just as wrong, sloping badly towards home plate. Both centre and right field were fenced in by old wire-work that bowed from the top and bottom, and there were two green benches positioned between deep centre and left. I wondered if it was part of the local team's plan to get more people out to the park (future major league promotion: Sit with Barry Bonds in Left-Field Night), but my guess was wrong. A year earlier, Sardinia, like the Peones, had competed in Serie C, which required short fences. For Serie B, they'd had to lengthen them into the adjacent public park. Nobody had bothered to move the benches.

The arid land was the product of two fierce winds – the African sirocco from the south, and the maestrale, which blew in raw from the northwest. These winds, combined with a five-month dry season, made Alghero's ancient soil nearly impossible to till. Waverly Root once wrote of the Sardinian turf, "When God finished making the world, some unpromising material, bare rock and thin soil, was left over. He disposed of it by tossing it into the Mediterranean and pressing it down with his foot."

How could anyone have thought that baseball would thrive on such forbidding terrain? But someone did, and now there are fifteen local teams, divided among men, women, and kids playing both baseball and softball ("In 1974, we were just looking for something to do other than play soccer," said Giovanni Giorgi, one of the region's first players, and assistant coach of the Catalani). On a day when the sun felt hot enough to melt plastic, the Peones and their hosts were living proof that in the world of sports, the impossible is only a challenge.

Both teams changed in aluminum sheds beyond the outfield, which had been baking in the sun since dawn. I poked my head inside and the temperature seemed to be tempting the 40s, so I made my way to right field to inspect the fence, which was tangled in a floral snarl. I noticed two skeins of barbed wire snaking through the blooms; not the kind of padding a player wants to encounter after backpedalling on a skyshot. Under the leaves at the foot of the centre-field fence, I found paving rollers and unused cinder stones, and as I walked around the rest of the park, I realized that there was something hazardous every step of the way. There was ancient scaffolding no more than twenty feet behind third base, and in one section of left field, the metal fencing bordered a yard filled with gutted ambulances, tractor parts, and old piping. Beyond this strange industrial graveyard, I stepped through a hole in the fence and came upon a forest filled with the skreeing of hundreds of heat bugs. They gave me the willies, and I quickly headed back to the comfort of the fried field. The more I thought about it, the more Sardinia seemed like the place where you got your points, then got the frig out.

The Sardinians represented the smallest of small league ball, and for that, they had my support. It couldn't have been easy playing every home game at Campo Via Emilia. The dugouts were fenced in by a roll of chicken wire planted in a dirt floor, and their only amenity was a hose tied to a utility post. To the right of home plate, a plank of wood was propped up on a fence with nails sticking out of ten frames: a scoreboard. At the end of every inning, a friend of Sardinian baseball drew from a stack of small wooden squares stencilled with numbers and pushed them over the nails. At one point I heard a sound like the whinnying of a horse coming from behind the dugout. I went to investigate, to discover, standing in a field of tall grass behind the ballpark, a horse. I shook my head, wondering whether I was part of some wrongway baseball dream.

The Sardinian team were as ragtag as their field. While the Peones wore baseball apparel, most of the Sardinians were dressed only in pants and T-shirts. The first baseman, whose name was Giovanni and who played with a mitt that looked like a piece of old lettuce, was a mountain of a man with an ass as wide as a kettledrum. During the warm-up, he played with his shirt untucked, affecting a beer league slovenliness. His style was in sharp contrast to the Peones, who looked as if their mothers had pressed their shirts and pants and handed them their blocked caps as they walked out the door.

The first baseman's physical opposite was the third baseman, a tiny fellow in pants two sizes too big. He had the unorthodox habit of crouching next to the bag with both hands up, as if waving to the batter. Before every pitch, he collected the fabric that had gathered around his knees and hiked it into his waist, manoeuvring his cup so that it pinched the material in place.

Still, the Sardinian players were full of enthusiasm as they prepared for the game. They lined up along the left-field line and did jumping jacks before breaking for the infield, where they called out to each other with every ball thrown across the diamond. At one point during the warm-up, the burly first baseman pressed his face into his mitt as a ball that had been hit to him bounced straight up in the air, over his head. Pietro stood at the edge of the infield, his arms crossed, body stiff as a mast as he scrutinized the Sardinians' folly. You didn't need a program to tell who was loose and who wasn't, and as the home team took the field behind their pitcher, I wondered whether it wasn't preposterous to imagine the ill-fitted rogues actually winning.

As the first batter, Skunk Bravo, prepared to step into the box, the moment was rich with possibility. The pitcher picked at the rubber with the toe of his cleat, the batter spat into his hands, the ump pulled his mask over his face, and both managers clapped twice to begin the trial of men in this court of sport.

The Peones in the dugout studied the action closely, looking for a sign that would tell them what kind of game it would be. Since the team was feeling fragile after the debacle in Salerno, Pietro's grave lecture, and Mirko's death ball, they needed an indication that would assure them that everything would be fine. Or not. Just imagine, then, what went through their heads when, on the Sardinian hurler's eleventh pitch, the ball ticked off the catcher's glove, spun to the backstop, tore through the diamond's protective netting, and cracked a woman in the mouth. She threw her hands to her face, and blood started seeping through her fingers. The umpires rushed to assist her. While she was led away to a car, I took a look at the green mesh backstop. The ball had torn a hole the size of my fist.

In the Peones dugout, no one said a word, but you could tell what they were thinking: *Porco cane. What the frig else is gonna go wrong?* Over the next few innings, they played well – six runs, to grab the lead – but it wasn't until the stricken woman returned around mid-game, her lip stitched and bandaged, that the Peones started to relax, realizing that, despite these dark forces, they could still play, perhaps even play well.

The game had many heroes, starting with Chicca. His first chance at l'angolo caldo (the hot corner) set the tone for the rest of the day. Pietro had feared that, because of the state of the diamond, anything could happen on balls driven into the ground. It was impossible to read what kind of havoc a groundball might wreak until it had rolled dead. Most hits took a preposterous route before they reached the infielder, prompting Pietro to tell his charges, "Palla alla terra, palla alla terra," instructing them to turn the wrinkled field to their advantage.

On Chicca's play, the ball was hit into a spot about ten feet in front of home plate. From there, it screamed towards Chicca's shoe-tops, only to bound straight up at the bill of his cap. As the ball ripped through his line of vision, his face remained more or less straight, but his body sparked to life. His catching hand shot up faster than a kid at a spelling bee, trapping the pill on its rising arc. As he brought the ball down, those of us on the bench – Paolo, Pitò, Chencho, the Natural, the Emperor, Pompo, and I – rose to cheer the play. The runner thrashed down the first-base line, a sandstorm rising in his wake. Chicca whipped the ball towards Fabio from Milan, who stretched off first base, his mitt snapping like the maw of a Cottonmouth. The ball found Fabio's glove, and the runner was out by a foot. A few feet beyond the bag, he wrenched his batting helmet and strode back to the dugout, holding it at his waist like a man who'd been handed his head. Chicca showed the runner his back, pressing his knuckles into his glove and resuming his blank man's stare, gazing at a point in the dirt that signified nothing.

A few batters later, Skunk Bravo equalled Chicca's play. Unlike the third baseman's crazy-hop, Skunk's ball arrived on a frozen rope hit into the emptiness between short and third, which the little shortstop, by full extension of his body, filled quickly. Skunk leapt at a forty-five-degree angle, he threw his glove across his frame – contro guanto, backhanding it – and the ball slapped in. When Skunk picked himself up, his uniform was scrubbed with the luck of the dirt. He hadn't played great defence in either of the Peones' two previous games, but after Sardinia, he wouldn't misplay a single ball. Nor would he finish a game – let alone the first few innings – without having tasted the dust of the infield.

I watched the game, as was my routine, with the Peones' Black Aces. Each of them had reason to be disappointed with not playing. Pitò still hadn't convinced Pietro that his arm was strong, the

Emperor had been supplanted at first base by his best friend, Fabio from Milan, and Fab Julie and the Natural were stuck as utility players (the Natural, being a natural, was confused and a little hurt that he'd been relegated to such a role). Only Chencho, a reliever, seemed comfortable living on the bench.

For Paolo, things were a little more complicated. The old catcher had trained as hard as anyone in the hope of getting back into the lineup, but Pietro hadn't put him in. When I asked Pietro, he said that, as it stood, Mario Simone, who'd started the season behind the plate, was next in line behind the Big Emilio, who was clearly his number-one ricevitore. I wanted to tell Pietro that I thought he was ignoring a smart, hard-working veteran player and that he was in danger of losing him unless he saw some action. But I didn't, even though Paolo had said to me, "If only I could hit, I think I could get a home run. Really, if I get to hit, I will hit this home run for you. I will try. I think I can." I told him that it couldn't hurt to dream, then grimaced at the cliché.

When we'd boarded the plane that morning, Pietro had handed me the day's lineup card to copy into my scorebook, at which Paolo, sitting next to me, shook his head and gave a despondent laugh. When I asked him why he was laughing, the Black Ace said he couldn't tell me.

"No, not now. It is nothing, really," he said.

"Is it because your name isn't here?" I asked him, pointing at the card.

"No, no. It is not that. Yes, I wish it was there, but I know that I won't start the games. No, it is something else. Don't worry," he said, waving away the card.

"How can I not worry if I don't know what it is?" I told him.

"Dave, please, it is nothing," he said, impatiently pushing away the card. I wondered whether Paolo was starting to work his way through the stages most bench jockeys pass along, moving from "Hey, I'll do anything for the team, whatever it takes!" to "Geez, if only I could get a chance to play," to "Do you think I did something to anger the coach?" to "Coach wouldn't know a good player if he ran over him in his truck," to "The only way I'm going to play is if coach gets hit by a truck," to "Man, I hope somebody runs over coach with a truck."

In the dugout, Paolo at first practised his batting grip, then he killed time by tapping a fungo bat against the dugout screen. Once he'd done that, he busied himself trying to teach me colloquial Italian. I was flattered but also humbled, now knowing that, on his activity list, talking to me ranked just below fidgeting with a bat. But at least I learned what "Eyyy porpo!!" meant. *Porpo* – which is what Nettunese ballplayers yell at a slow-footed, overweight batter – is a corruption of *polipo*, the Italian word for octopus. It's a companion word to *guffo* (owl): those who swing the bat while daft and dull-witted. When Pitò heard Paolo and I playing the game of who was a porpo and who was a guffo, he leapt to his feet and shouted: "Te stacco ste braccette e te ce meno!" When I asked him what it meant – and what it had to do with either a guffo or a porpo – he said that it was a Nettunese taunt about ripping off a person's arm and using it to club them into submission, which he then pretended to do. So I called him a porpo and for the next few minutes, the Aces behaved as if they'd forgotten that they weren't playing, trying to outdo each other with outrageous jeers. Pitò and I resumed our spasmodic dugout wrestling match, and then Chencho walked around the corner of the dugout, coolly peeled a banana, winked at us, and, with Pietro watching him out of the corner of his eye, fellated it.

During Pietro's post-Salerno sermon – and after the games against Roma – he'd stressed the importance of practising, spelling out in no uncertain terms that those who practised would play, and those who didn't would have to suffer on the bench. But even though Paolo had shown up every day to work on his fielding and his swing – which was improving at a steady rate; twice I watched him ding the ball over the left-field fence, dead-pulling consecutive fuori-campi – he had yet to play. Once, after twenty minutes of blocking pitches, he and I sat in the dugout, his shirt swimming in sweat, and he told me, with a tinge of melancholy, "Before, Dave, I was a very good catcher. Very good. When I was sixteen, I could crush the ball. I could throw runners out every time. When I was young, I was good. Maybe the best. The best in all of Italy."

"Well, you're back," I told him.

"No, I am not back. It takes such hard work. Six years is a very long time."

"But that was before. You're starting to crush the ball."

"But this is batting practice. It is not a real game. So, I sit and wait, yes?" he said, smiling and slapping my knee, trying to ignore the anger that waited on his shoulder.

None of the players would say it, but Pietro was flirting with a double standard, leaving those who practised hard but didn't play wondering where they fit in his vision of the team. In previous games, I'd tried to read Pietro's managing habits: when he removed players for pinch-hitters, or made late-inning defensive substitutions, he used his bench. But he didn't use them much. If that didn't make it hard enough for Paolo to see action, Pietro also had an affinity for the Big Emilio, in whom he saw his former self: a resolute, driven stud of a player, gifted and serious, with the whole Italian baseball world in front of him. Once, when Pietro and I were driving to San Giacomo, we saw the Big Emilio walking up the road to the field. When we passed him, Pietro honked and waved at his catcher. It was a small gesture, but it spoke volumes. Though Pietro tried to be an even-handed disciplinarian, this tiny show of affection revealed that even sonsabitches have favourites too.

Now many months later, while Paolo numbingly tapped his fungo bat on the screen, he admitted to me that he imagined that the bat was a pendulum, the nub Pietro's head, and the Old Bugger's face was flattened every time he brought down the bat. He called Pitò over and told him what he was thinking. Pitò giggled and brought Pompo in on the joke, and for the rest of the game, they gestured threateningly towards the diamond, hollering, "Pendolo!" This became the Black Ace curse, which they cast upon any player who refused to bend their way. Paolo never told me whether he'd ever mouthed "Il pendolo!" at the Old Bugger, but you didn't have to be Bill James to see that he had.

The force of the pendolo, it turned out, was even mightier than Paolo imagined, for one minute he was pretending to bash Pietro's face into mush, the next he was fastening the straps of his chest protector, readying himself for his first taste of the dirt in six years. The moment was almost imperceptible, as it should be with white or black magic. In fact, if I hadn't been sitting next to Paolo, I wouldn't have noticed that as Pietro strode past the dugout with his head down he uttered one word – "Paolo" – and pointed at a catcher's mask. The old catcher jumped off the bench, elbowing me as he dug in his kit bag for his spikes.

Since the Peones had stormed out to a comfortable lead – 12-6 – Pietro, noticing that the Big Emilio's right leg was giving him a bit of trouble (and, of course, being powerless against the Pendolo!), had finally decided to give his veteran backstop some work. Early in the game, Emilio had lost himself on consecutive pop flies, pirouetting off his axis under the ball. Neither play had cost the Peones, but Pietro must have thought that the big fellow needed to catch up on some sleep. For his part, the young catcher didn't seem to mind. He grabbed his guantone and warmed up Paolo along the sidelines.

Underneath plugs of mud and dirt, Paolo's catching gear was dark blue. His knee pads – *ginoccheria*, or *scrinieri*, a Nettunese word adopted into Italian baseball lingo – clacked like castanets when he ran. They looked vaguely crustacean, like something H.R. Giger might have dreamed up for one of his aliens. His chest protector was known as a *corazza*, another Nettunese word that alluded to a knight's undergarment, while his mask, his maschera, made it look as if his face had been sentenced to prison while the rest of his body walked free. Once fully outfitted in what former Kansas City Royal catcher Jim Sundberg called "the tools of ignorance," Paolo loomed twice his size. He was no longer the person who, for the past month, had sat slump-shouldered next to me in the dugout. It wasn't Paolo I was seeing.

From the left: Paolo, Skunk, and Chicca. (Cathy Bidini)

It was Sheriff.

Paolo caught Fabio from Milan using his old ciavatta (big slipper, in Nettunese slang). Pietro's Do-Anything kid had relieved Cobra, who'd felt enough of a twinge in the upper muscle of his right arm to be concerned about pitching a full nine. Pietro also pulled the Emperor off the bench to cover for Fabio at first base, bringing the number of Black Aces in the game to two. I got the impression that Pietro almost knew what he was doing.

In his first inning, Paolo threw himself in front of every pitch that hit the dirt, working out six years of inactivity in thirty-four pitches. Even though there was no one on base – and no chance for a runner to advance on a passed ball – Paolo refused to let any ball get past him, throwing a wall behind the batter. It must have felt great for him to be moving in ways other than stretching or jogging, not to mention finding his voice liberated for something other than the jokes and barbs and commiserations of the Aces. With the entire team in front of him, Paolo treated the Peones as if they were an orchestra to be conducted: talking up his young pitcher, obsessively barking the number of outs, directing the outfield with a single swerve of his hand, and speaking, if in monosyllables, to the batter. Paolo was at the heart of the action.

After catching two frames, he led off the seventh inning. I moved from the dugout to sit at my peril on a bench behind home plate. Shorn of his gear, the old catcher looked like himself again. As he walked to the plate with his bat across his shoulder, the guys in the dugout shouted *"Paoloooo!"* and *"Dai sessanta nove!"* and *"Que culo!"* Until his at-bat, I hadn't heard the Peones unanimously support any player. But Paolo had aligned himself with no one on the team and was friendly with everyone.

The first thing he did when he stepped into the batter's box was twist and grind his back foot into the dirt. He put one hand on top of his batting helmet, shimmied the foam tight to his head, then slid one hand against the other, fitting them skin to skin on the bat handle. The Peones continued their cries as Paolooooo! tapped the plate quickly with the bat head before raising it slowly behind his ear. Then he wheeled the wood three times like a man spinning a vault handle, finally bringing it above his shoulder in a frozen lumberjack pose.

The pitcher delivered a fastball. Paolo saw it and hit it. I'd thought that, after six years, he'd have taken a few pitches, savoured the at-bat until it ran deep in the count. But no: he struck the ball. The pitcher turned to watch the ball fly over second base, climb into short centre, piggyback on a slight breeze towards left-centre, climb higher still across the outfield, sail over the warning track, and finally land among the old cable coils and picnic benches and screaming insect trees in Homerland.

The Peones roared from the dugout. It was the first time it had emptied during a game. Paolo rounded first base at a modest clip, head down, shoulders squared, arms and legs chugging neither more slowly nor quickly than was required. When he made the turn around second, then third, I saw the whites of his teeth. As he crossed home and lifted his face in triumph, he was set upon by his delirious teammates, who walked him back to the dugout like a swarm of ants dragging a crumb. I called out to Paolo, but he couldn't hear me. But what I wanted to say really needed no saying.

Sheriff was back.

Paolo – that is, Sheriff – caught the rest of the first game, then was back in the dugout for the second half of the double dip, a 10-2 victory for Pompozzi, who struck out sixteen Sardinians. I like to think that Paolo's homer inspired Pompo's performance, because it affected the team in other ways too. Not only did it give the rest of the Black Aces hope that they too might attain glory, it renewed Pietro's faith in his forlorn bench, revealing, in the process, a prospective pinch-hitter with power. The starting nine were thrilled that someone who'd worked as hard as Paolo was rewarded with a moment of glory, and, for the younger players like Christian and Fabio from Milan and the two Marios, it was a chance to see that their baseball future wasn't all sore gambe and seasons in the dugout. Paolo's hit showed why baseball meant so much to these players, and how, in the sport's fleeting moments of beauty and drama, there is simply no match for it.

After the second game, I sat behind home plate with my arms spread along the back of the bench, considering the theatre of baseball. While athletic heroics come in many different forms – the cross-crease save, the breakaway goal, the leg kick at the back end of a distance race, the long bomb, the buzzer beater – there are few occasions like the home run, where everyone from the fan in the upper deck to the starting shortstop to the guy who hangs the numbers over the nails on the wooden scoreboard is allowed time to swim around in the moment while it happens. In hockey or football, decisive plays occur within the crowd's screams of anguish or triumph, but, in baseball, fans have the opportunity to still themselves during what they expect, or hope, will be the game's salient play. In every sport, there's a moment of breathless suspension that's shared by fan and player with every flight of every final ball thrown or shot with the game on the line, but no sport except baseball has a triumphant play as unrushed or true as the home run.

With the sun falling behind the trees, and the Peones walking back across the campo from their tin sheds – many of the players had opted to change outside, instead of suffer the oppressive heat – I opened my notebook and I noticed something scribbled in someone else's pen. At first, I thought it was Chencho's work, but when I brought the book close to study it, I recognized the writing as Paolo's. It said:

> *Paolo ha mantennuto la promessa*
> *Paolo has kept his promise.*

Later that night, as Skunk, Paolo, Pietro, and I were driving home from the airport, Paolo said, "You know, as soon as I saw the batter's feet, that's when I felt at home. I saw his shoes, watched them move around, and when I looked up, *ahhh*." He opened his arms. "There was the whole field, right in front of me."

"You were diving in front of every ball," I said. "Even without any runners on base!"

"Ah, but, Dave. Six years. I have been waiting a long time," he said, grabbing my arm.

"No, of course. I would have done exactly the same thing," I said, backpedalling. But it was too late, he was already shaking me and shouting, "Six years! Six years! Six years!" his face alight with a great smile.

The traffic thickened as Nettuno came into view, and as we rode over a small hill before hitting the final stretch of road into town, the car was swamped by a cascade of light. Fireworks. They drenched the road with colour, and Skunk, sitting in the front seat, turned to us and smiled, wordlessly thumbing his chest.

"Giampiero says," said Paolo. "Is for us. These fireworks. For us."

"What does Sheriff think?" I said.

Paolo scoffed: "This Sheriff. This is for you, not really for me."

"Whatever it is. It doesn't matter," I said. "All I know is that you hit it out. And that I was there to see it."

A few seconds passed.

"Yes," he said, looking out the window at the sky. "I think maybe, this could be for us."

13

BASEBALL IN THE JAWS OF WAR

Games are usually spread from place to place by two means. They're either passed through the whispers, or exported in a suitcase, as if sport were a newfangled waffle iron. A.G. Spalding's historic 1888 World Baseball Tour was equal parts sale and spore. On one hand, the sporting goods impresario hoped to root his empire abroad, while on the other, he wanted to spread, in his words, "American manliness and virtue" by introducing baseball as played by "representatives of the great Western Republic." These terms paint the truth by granting stateliness to mooks named Rube and Lefty, but there was a certain manifest destiny on the morning of November 17, 1888, when a party of thirty-five men, including twenty ballplayers, embarked on a 35,000-mile journey to the four corners of the world, trailed on their route, no less, by one "Professor" Bartholomew, a famous hot-air balloonist whom Spalding hired to drum up promotion for the tour.

Though Spalding's foray probably wasn't directly responsible for WorldBall as we know it, there's no doubt that his showmanship dented the earth's sporting culture. He certainly cast a wide-enough net. The teams' first stop was Australia, where, according to *Colliers* magazine, "the players' base-stealing never failed to elicit roars of laughter and applause." From there, the athletes weathered a three-week trip across the tumbling ocean to play a five-inning exhibition in Colombo, Ceylon, where, as Spalding said, "the natives looked at us as though we were so many escaped inmates." From Sri Lanka, they travelled to Cairo, where they played in the shadow of the Pyramids for a spare group of curious Bedouins who, according to Spalding, shrieked in horror when the Americans climbed the Sphinx for photographs and soft-tossed over ancient Egyptian tombs. While the rest of the Americans' visit was uneventful, there was one unsavoury incident: the players paraded Clarence Duval, the team's black mascot, in a catcher's mask by tether through the Cairo train station and watched as the locals fled in "abject terror."

Spalding's journey to Africa was not the first sign of baseball in the region. In 1937, an Italian anthropologist, Corrado Gini, travelled to the Libyan desert to investigate a mysterious strain of blondness among the Berber. There, he encountered a game remarkably similar to rudimentary baseball, cricket too. The tribesmen, reportedly, played on a level field with a home base separated from a running base by seventy to ninety feet. The batting team, which hit in order, struck a ball as far as possible while the other members of the team ran back and forth between home and the running base. Fly ball outs and strikes were apparently also part of the game. Gini's research concluded that the Berber game was a legacy from Nordic invaders some eight thousand years earlier. They had also invented longball and northern spell – traditionally played as fertility rites during the spring – both of which were the ancestors of rounders, which became baseball as we know it.

Spalding's first European stop was Gini's homeland, Italy, which promised a better experience than was delivered. Spalding immediately ruffled Roman feathers by insisting, much to the chagrin of local authorities, that his teams compete on the precious grounds of the Coliseum. When he offered $5,000 to ease tensions among the capi, they took offence. The players eventually managed to play a game, attended mostly by American expats, on the grounds of the Villa Borghese. The players met a similar indifference in Florence, Nice, and Paris, where spectators were said to be confused and annoyed by the rules of the game. While the Italians, Germans, and Dutch eventually embraced baseball, the Parisians never quite took to the idea. Perhaps this can be explained by an incident during a 1914 visit to France by the New York Giants and Chicago White Sox. On the day that the two teams were scheduled to play in Paris, there was steady rainfall, enough to cancel the game. While North American fans are used to such digressions, the Parisians, at the time, couldn't understand why, unlike soccer players, the ballplayers wouldn't work in bad weather. They were appalled that there were men who refused to play in case they got wet, and this perhaps forever soured their opinion of the game.

Things improved for Spalding once his party hit England. Their first game was played at London's Kensington Oval in front of eight thousand fans, including the Prince of Wales, his sizable entourage, and, according to *Colliers*, "no end of smaller lordlings." Other successful dates followed in Liverpool, Manchester, Bristol, and Sheffield, and it was in these cities that the players finally felt at home after months on the global fly. They also managed to spend a week in Ireland, where, one player, Jim Manning, visited his ancestral village, in Callon, Kilkenny. There, the entire village came out for his arrival, festooning the streets with photos of Manning in action, and staging a great parade. Manning, naturally, was overwhelmed. He told one reporter, "I had a delightful time. Everything in Callon, even the scores of pretty Irish girls, was mine."

Considering the success of Spalding's teams in the U.K. – to say nothing of its citizens' enthusiasm for two related games, cricket and rounders – many have wondered why baseball has yet to find a home in a country noted for its passionate sporting culture. Some have suggested that an unreasonably wet climate has kept the game from properly taking root, while others have pointed to the Brits' blood allegiance to cricket, speculating that baseball, if embraced by the hoi polloi, might bury the slow, staid game. I have no better theory to offer; however the answer might lie in an incident that occurred during the Giants–White Sox 1914 visit to Chelsea, where trip organizers Comiskey and his fellow mahatmas were sued for damages by the local football club, who were left with a gross of untried tea and crumpets on their hands. Representatives of the local team were irate that the American officials had neglected to provide an intermission during which fans could partake of their traditional tea, thus leaving Chelsea with an enormous unsold stockpile of baked goods. The upside of this, of course, is that the fans were obviously too caught up in the game to leave their seats once the need for a cuppa kicked in. Still, the row between authorities ensured that no future baseball games would be held at the Chelsea Football Grounds, and, as of 2002, none had.

One of the supporters too enthralled by the game to bother with a cup of Darjeeling was none other than King George V, who became as smitten with baseball as anyone in England. The king was so taken that, in 1915, he hired ex-St. Louis Browns star Arlie Latham to teach him how to pitch. Though his Royal Highness never quite mastered the stuff required to fool batters, his affection for the game was such that he convinced the Prince of Wales to try it too, leading to the latter's seventeen-year friendship with Latham, a baseball Zelig who shows up in many of the game's most curious developments. Latham was the first player invited by Spalding to come on his world tour, but couldn't go because of a commitment to perform in a Broadway stage show called *Fashions*, in which he sang, "I'm a daisy on the diamond/I'm a dandy on the stage/ I'd ornament a horsecar/or look pretty in a cage." The Freshest Man on Earth – as Latham was called – was not only baseball's first theatrical performer (step aside, Chuck Connors), he is also credited with inventing baseball chatter, the result of his inability to keep quiet.

Post-Spalding, England experienced surges of interest in baseball during the two World Wars. Historian and author Gary Bedingfield cites 1942 as the beginning of modern baseball in the British Isles, a game played by American and Canadian servicemen stationed in the U.K. Bedingfield estimates that by 1944 there were 1.5 million Americans in Britain, including 340 major leaguers and 3,000 minor leaguers. Since traditional British sports (rugby, cricket, and soccer) were suspended during the war because of the threat of bombing, baseball was the game served to a public eager for athletic spectacle. Bedingfield pinpoints April 25, 1942, in Belfast, as the game's debut. He writes, "Two battalions of the 34th infantry division attracted an inquisitive crowd of more than 1,000 locals who were treated to a play-by-play account on the p.a. system, a concert by the regiment band, and an impromptu jitterbug demonstration on the sidelines." A few months later, two other American teams took to the soccer field at Windsor Park, where baserunners were forced to dodge a goalpost rooted in the path between first and second, and, when running home, had to press their way through the crowd of onlookers horseshoed around the plate. The record shows that it was Private Leo Robinson who hit the first-ever home run by an American serviceman in Second World War Europe. It was also his last, for Robinson later fought at Monte Cassino, just north of Nettuno, and shrapnel shredded his legs, crippling him.

One notable player in this era was Charles Eisenman, who toured his Central Base Section (CBS) Clowns around the U.K., challenging other military teams as they waited to be shipped into battle. Forever disappointed with the state of the fields, Eisenman constructed a travelling pitcher's mound, which Bedingfield describes as "a wooden framework layered with turf," which met the height and width standards of major league ball. The Clowns and their mound-on-wheels were the most visible travelling teams, though it's worth noting that none of this would have come to pass had Eisenman been standing a few feet to his left one summer's day in 1943, when a V1 buzz bomb ripped through his office wall. Not only was Eisenman spared his life, but, as he told Bedingfield, his index finger was badly damaged on his right hand, giving him greater rotation on his pitches and allowing him to throw a breaking ball that was almost unhittable.

Others were not so fortunate. Sandlot or minor league, high school or professional, many ballplaying soldiers were killed or wounded too badly to continue playing the game they loved. Elmer Wright, a prized Browns prospect, died at Omaha Beach just months after writing team vice-president William DeWitt to tell him of winning a handful of games for the 116th Regiment. DeWitt wrote back: "We are mighty glad to hear that your curveball is better. I think you will be ready for some highclass baseball when you get back." Hank Nowak, a St. Louis prospect, was killed fighting in Belgium. Washington's all-star shortstop Cecil Travis spent days in a frozen foxhole during the Battle of the Bulge, which so damaged his feet he could never play well again. Elmer Gedeon, another Senator, and five others died on the French countryside when their plane fell to earth. Harry O'Neill of the Athletics died at Iwo Jima; Toledo's Ardys Keller, of the famous Jewish-American travelling team, the House of David, was killed in combat in France; and Rod Sooth lost his life when his plane was shot down over Germany. Even the wartime leagues took a toll on the players. Gene Stack, who, like Elmer Wright, was on the verge of making his pro team, the White Sox, died suddenly after pitching in an army game, while Creepy Crespi, a young Cardinals outfielder, broke his leg while playing in Europe, broke it again while racing wheelchairs in the army hospital, and never recovered well enough to return to the major leagues. Some players who were lucky enough to resume their careers were still permanently damaged. Phillies star Bob Savage was among those Allied soldiers who liberated the Dachau Concentration Camp, an episode he cannot talk about to this day.

Among the wounded was Bert Shepard, a top minor league prospect, who had his right foot amputated by German doctors after his fighter plane was shot down. A fellow prisoner at a POW camp in Germany built him a wooden foot, allowing Shepard to resume pitching. After being repatriated in an exchange of wounded prisoners, he ended up at Walter Reed Hospital in Washington, where he was noticed by a government official, who convinced Clark Griffith of the Senators to invite him to spring training. Griffith arranged an exhibition in front of three thousand convalescing veterans, where Shepard ably pitched and took batting practice. Shepard worked next in a proper exhibition game, which drew eight thousand fans. Convinced of his talents, Griffith signed Shepard first as a coach, then as pitching coach. Eventually, he threw five innings in a major league game against the Red Sox, before embarking on a successful, nine-year minor league career. In 1949, he signed as player-manager for the Sox's class B team, where he hit .229 and stole five bases.

In baseball lore, two men in particular – Canadian Phil Marchildon and American Lou Brissie – stand out as examples of the courage and resolve of the ballplaying soldier. Marchildon, a tall, thick-necked forkballer from Penetanguishene, Ontario, starred as a member of the 1942 Philadelphia Athletics, winning seventeen games and losing fourteen for Connie Mack's cellar-dwellers. During the war, he manned the rear turret as part of an RCAF squadron that flew twenty-five successful missions, five short of forgiveness from the war. On the evening of August 15, 1944, while preparing to drop battery-powered mines into Kiel harbour in northern Germany, the plane was hit by tracers from a rogue German fighter – an ME110. Marchildon and another crewmate bailed out into the Baltic Sea (the rest of the squadron perished in the blaze). They drifted towards land and were rescued by Dutch fisherman, only to be arrested on shore by Germans and brought to a POW camp near Frankfurt, the venue of the Great Escape, which had occurred just six months earlier. Although Marchildon, in his book *Ace* (written with Brian Kendall), makes a point of remembering the camaraderie of his fellow soldiers and the co-operation of many of the Nazi guards, his experiences were weighted by the bleakness and evil of war. On one occasion, he writes, "Someone missed the ball and it bounced under the warning wire into no-man's land near his post. One of our players, a Canadian, walked to the wire and looked up at the guard. 'Nicht schiessen, Posten!' he called, which meant 'Don't shoot, sentry.' The German waved him in. When the Canadian had no more than a foot over the fence he shot him dead."

After several months in camp, Marchildon and the rest of the prisoners were stirred one winter's morning in early January 1945 and forced at gunpoint to walk on the March of Death. Marchildon says that, on top of the pain and fatigue and hunger and bitter cold suffered on the road, he and his fellow soldiers lived in mortal terror of being strafed by Allied bombers, a common fate for many other marching POWs. What mental resolve must have been needed to cope with the sight of dying men in shredded clothes (Marchildon himself had grown gaunt and sick and had lost thirty pounds) after playing to cheering summer crowds, to have the golden sunlight blotted out by the stench of black smoke that filled the air?

In Italy, Lou Brissie was also suffering. Signed by Connie Mack as a blue-chip member of the A's farm system, the long, gawky left-hander found himself fighting in the Apennine Mountains outside of Bologna, with the hard-slugging 88th Infantry Division. Quoted by Frederick Turner in his fine book *When the Boys Came Back*, war correspondent Ernie Pyle wrote of the Bolognese campaign that, "our troops were living in almost inconceivable misery. The fertile black valleys were knee-deep in mud. Thousands of men had not been dry for weeks. Other thousands lay at night in the high mountains with the temperature below freezing and the thin snow sifting over them. They lived like men of prehistoric times, and a club would have become them more than a machine gun."

On December 7, 1944, Brissie was passing through a ravine, returning to base camp from the front, when he came under a barrage of enemy shells. Once the attack was finished, Brissie's left leg had been blown open from knee to ankle, riddled with more than thirty shell fragments. Rendered unconscious by the blow, he eventually awoke six hours later to a search party sorting through the carnage. No other soldier from Brissie's company had survived. His vision blurred, his voice robbed of sound, the searchers stood over him briefly, then pronounced him dead before moving back to camp. Using all his will to signal that he was still alive, he rustled loudly enough to attract the attention of one party member, who turned back for another look. Brissie was hurried to the battalion's first-aid station, where he was administered the first of forty blood transfusions. When they saw Brissie for the first time, his doctors decided that amputation would be the best, and most immediate, approach, but somehow, as fighting raged over the field hospital, Brissie convinced the surgeons not to take off the leg, saying, "Please send me to somebody who may be able to help me, because I wanna play baseball."

In Naples, he restated his case to Dr. W.K. Brubaker, a devoted Cleveland Indians fan who never smiled or talked unless the subject was baseball. So, even though there was no piece of bone more than four inches long left in Brissie's leg, Brubaker granted Brissie his wish, jigsawing together a construction using wire.

This was the first of twenty-three procedures on Brissie's mangled leg. Once shipped home, the young pitcher moved from hospital to hospital before taking up with a children's orthopedic surgeon, who devised a steel brace and lightweight shinguard to support the leg. After tireless rehabilitation, Brissie phoned Connie Mack and told him that he was ready to climb the mound once again, to test the work that the doctors had performed.

Mack invited him to Shibe Park, where Brissie, donning an A's uniform for the first time, threw to a bullpen catcher. He stumbled with almost every delivery, falling while trying to plant his vulnerable left leg. The eighty-two-year-old Mack convinced Brissie, with fatherly care and advice, to be vigilant in his rehabilitation and to contact him when he was closer. Mack had been just as gracious to Marchildon, who'd returned earlier than Brissie, having been liberated by British soldiers in the German countryside. He and some friends had tracked down among German prisoners the guard who'd killed his POW teammate, and watched as an Allied soldier exacted justice. Mack assured Marchildon that there would be a place in the Athletics starting five for him once the RCAF gunner felt ready to return. But his comeback would not be immediate.

Brissie, refusing to give up, drifted deep into the minors, and Marchildon struggled to regain his composure on the mound, suffering through fits of nervousness and wandering concentration

brought on by his experiences abroad. Back in Canada, he told
Brian Kendall, "My hands shook like I had palsy and I was constantly on edge. My biggest struggle was overcoming the leftover
fear that something terrible was going to happen. [I'd be] on my
way to the ballpark and suddenly something would grab at my
nerves. I wanted to pick up a brick and toss it through a window."
During his comeback attempt, he once wild-pitched ten rows into
the grandstand between third and home. A reporter who interviewed Marchildon in his first year back mentioned the player's
constant scratching, fidgeting, and squirming, while the pitcher
himself admitted to being easily rattled by noise, finding it nearly
impossible to walk down busy streets, the sound and action tightening like a hand at his throat.

Brissie eventually signed on to play textile ball – the lowest level
of the minor leagues – with the Ware Shoal Riegels. In his first
game, he told author Fred Turner, "I don't know how many pitches
I threw, but it couldn't have been too many. I was trying to drive off
the leg, and I couldn't. It just wasn't there." If that wasn't bad
enough, shrapnel fragments in his pitching hand sent shivers of pain
through his arm whenever he tried his curve, and since Brissie suffered from osteomyelitis in his leg, infections set in with even the
slightest bump and bruise. Once, after making a fielding play, he
spotted a red streak colouring the inside of his pant leg, forcing him
to discontinue his comeback for a lengthy program of antibiotics.

Still, remembering Mack's words of encouragement, he persisted.
The pain in his hand forced him to measure the use of his curveball, making him a more well-rounded pitcher, less dependent on
the hook. Brissie moved up, as slow as cold honey, through the minor
leagues. He grew stronger and more confident with each game,
until, in the summer of 1947, he was called up to the Athletics' AAA
team in Savannah. He started the season on the wrong end of three
losses, but in the fourth game, he pitched against Greenville, North
Carolina, a city not far from his home town. That night, busloads
of fans came to see him play. Rewarding their faith in him, he

pitched the best game of his career before reeling off thirteen consecutive victories and finishing the season 23 and 5.

On opening day, 1948, the A's started the season against Boston, a holiday doubleheader. Phil Marchildon, who'd conquered his fears and had returned to the team, winning nineteen games in 1947, took to the hill to start game one, winning 5-4. In the second game, Brissie, making his major league debut after all of those years, won as well, 4-2. Both men, whose lives had been gripped and shaken in the jaws of death, were back. If only for one day, the ghosts of the war had vanished.

It was summer again.

14

The Eye of the Pig

In the fall of 1987, I was on Granville Street in Vancouver when a strange man walked up and poked a finger at my nose.

"Where'd you get that?" he asked.

"Where'd I get what?" I replied.

"The nose, man. Where'd you get the nose?"

"This?" I said, touching the tip of my bugle. "Italy, I guess."

"Italy? Fabulous," he said.

"Fabulous?"

"Yes. Absolutely fabulous."

And then he walked away.

I'm not sure at what point I finally shook off my disappointment at being Italian, but it didn't hurt that a stranger regarded a facial feature that I'd once been as fond of as Grade Eleven functions as "fabulous." That this compliment came during my first tour with the Rheostatics, when I was just starting to get over years of teenage self-consciousness, went a long way towards steeling my self-respect. Afterwards, I started viewing the Italian character a little more for its fabulousness, eventually recognizing the likes of Brando,

Sinatra, DeNiro, Cassavetes, Scorsese, Calvino, Fellini, and Coppola as products of a culture that I'd previously thought capable of producing only opera singers, chefs, and barbers. It was around that time, as well, that I started dating an Italian.

Janet and I both agree that, in our youth, the last person we expected to date – let alone marry – was another Italian. We were both of the mind that, once we gained our independence, we'd train our sights on thin-boned, pasty-skinned Anglo beauties. The first time I met her – and later, as I fell for her faster than a piano pushed out of a window – I couldn't believe that she had anything to do with Italy. She was smart and funny and pretty, with delicate features, the opposite of many of the Italians I'd known in school or who occasionally gathered at my grandparents' place on holiday weekends. When I asked her if she was certain that her family had descended from the Boot, she confessed, "Actually, my mom is one-fifth Austrian," which I thought explained everything.

"But you're Italian on both sides?" she asked, returning the volley.

"Um, ya," I said.

"From where exactly?"

"Tuscany, I think," I said.

"Home of Dante," she said, nodding approvingly. "You've read *The Inferno*?"

"Oh ya. *The Inferno*, ya," I said.

Of course, this was the first time I'd heard of Dante. In hiding my ignorance of this classic of Western literature, my relationship with Janet became haunted by the prospect that she'd somehow find out that I knew more about Dante Bichette than Alighieri, forcing me to steer any conversation that hinted at either art or literature towards the weather. Also knowing who Dante was meant that she was about fifty thousand times more well read and smarter than I. Further complicating matters was her approval of my Italian heritage. With all of this playing on my mind, I was about as charming as a field gnat, and she dumped me a few months later. I paced around town with the sorry dude-who-has-just-lost-his-chick-because-he-hadn't-read-Dante look, though it's not as if I went out and devoured the Great One's collected works. Still, in the back of my mind, a voice told me that maybe it was time to cut the crap and stop running around trying to pretend that my name didn't end in a vowel, and come to terms with all of the life, art, and history that had been poured into my Mediterranean blood.

As you already know, Janet gave me a second chance, despite my limited knowledge of the greater works of Italian literature. From that day forward, I began to make peace with my roots, though it wasn't until Nettuno that I finally learned to love my name. I owe part of this awakening to Bruce Springsteen. After purchasing a copy of *The Rising* at one of Nettuno's two record shops, I spread the CD booklet open, reefed the first track, and decided that "Springsteen" was just about the stupidest name I'd ever heard.

Growing up, I would have killed to have been named Springsteen. I would have even settled for Cougar Mellencamp. But, in contrast to the polysyllabic trampoline by which most Nettunese were known, it seemed like the most ridiculous of titles: a long, closed, shoebox of a word with two beats and a bottle-capped ending. These sentiments, of course, were not an expression of distaste for Springsteen himself. It was more a case of coming across a name – any name – that didn't possess a drumroll of vowels. Springsteen could have been Bob Dylan, John Prine, or Joni Mitchell. Really, anyone except Alfie Zappacosta.

Even though I'd more or less learned to deal with my name before coming to Nettuno – having seen it posted on the occasional marquee, record jacket, and book cover, and clearly liking it enough to give our children names of equal syllabic fancy – I became delighted that it was part of the Italian family of names, an association I'd once been so eager to clip. I'd never valued the beauty of the name Minerva – which is what we called one of my late aunts – until I wandered into Santa Maria Sopra Minerva in Rome and stood beneath Michelangelo's alabaster of Jesus at the front of the church ("and his beautiful, perfect white feet," noted Janet). Even though she was one of my favourite relatives, I'd always associated her – along with the rest of my Italian relations – with black fabric, nylon stockings, rosary beads, and fractured English, not the radiant beauty of one of the world's most celebrated works of art. As a kid, I found no poetry in Italian names – to me, all of those vowels were like holes in the netting – yet it got to the point in Nettuno where, one evening, I raced home thrilled to tell Janet that I'd just met an old man named Archangelo. My newfound appreciation of the Italian handle was such that meeting the Iagos, Lucretias, Domitillas, and Herculeos of my adopted town charmed even the simplest of days. I considered myself lucky to be living among people whose names Cicero might have shouted across a busy street. Even my own Tuscan calling card, when voiced by the Nettunese, conjured the image of a moustachioed figure wearing a cape and waving a sword: "Davide! (Dav-eed!)" Throughout my childhood, my nonna had always pronounced it differently ("David-ay"), dropping the last syllable like a fishing weight hitting the water rather than giving it its delightful Nettunese tail.

With this change in perspective came an altered view of home. Suddenly, the names of my Torontonian friends sounded about as enchanting as the text on a tax form. One day, after pouring over old civic records frilled with Olympios, Valerias, and Valentinas, I decided right then and there that it simply wouldn't do to continue playing in a band with guys named Mike and Tim ("It's no wonder we've never become world famous," I may have complained to my wife. "What we need is a Vasco or Gonfreddo in our lineup to get us going.") Not to disparage the Petes and Sandras and Daves of my Toronto softball team, either, but the Peones players were far more interesting and fun to cheer for, the multitude of vowels in their names allowing me to stretch and twist them around on my tongue as if working a soft plug of Bubblicious. A name like Francesco (or Pompozzi, for that matter) was voiced, for instance, in three beats, two quick, one long, the verbal equivalent of a diver skipping twice across the platform before launching himself into the air. Similarly, whenever the fellows called Fab Julie by his nickname, *Fabiettooooo!*, I was reminded of what one shouts on the downward slide of a roller coaster. No matter how close I felt to Dan or Matty or Sue, their names could never match the melody of those given my Italian baseball brethren.

Since I wasn't required to learn any tongue-clacking or glottal stops to speak Italian, my participation in the music of the dugout came a lot easier than had I chosen to experience sport among the Bantu. One of the first words I favoured was *occhio* (eye), which is what Pietro liked to shout to his hitters after they'd missed a pitch. Once, after listening to Mario Simone sing "Eye of the Tiger" ("Eye of dee Tie-Gare!") while strutting through the dugout, I bestowed a rallying cry upon the Red Tiger – "Occhio di Tigre!" – which caught on, pleasing me to no end. Even better, this phrase passed through a series of mutations until – egged on by Chencho – I found myself shouting "Occhio di Suino!" ("Eye of the Pig!") at pretty much every remaining Peones batter for the rest of the season.

I'd come to the point in my cultural assimilation that I was able to call my teammates pigs in Italian, and be slapped approvingly on the back for doing so, and I felt more relaxed as an Italian than I'd ever been before. There were other suggestions that the whole brood was fitting in just fine too. Cecilia, for one, had mastered Italian tabletalk – "Mama, dammi lo zucchero, per piacere" – while Janet felt comfortable enough that, one afternoon, I came upon her wearing nothing but shorts and a bra, ironing a blouse on the kitchen table while spezzatino burbled on the stove top. Had I been dressed in an undershirt, boxer shirts, black socks, and sandals, we would have made a perfect set. As it was, I was wearing my blue Peones shirt and filthy shorts, waiting for Pietro to take me to the ballpark. There, with one step on the dugout, my cap brim flapping from the force of my voice – "Occhio do Suino!!" – I had found a place that once seemed about as impossible as Oz. In a pig's eye, I'd arrived.

Before coming to Nettuno, I prepared myself for my summer of baseball by putting in extra time at the batting cage. I favoured the baseball bonnets located near Janet's cottage in Wasaga Beach, Ontario, which were part of a go-kart and mini-golf complex. The need to soften my stroke (pardon the term) provided me with an ironclad excuse whenever I needed to escape the madness of a room filled with hollering children and adults. "Gotta go work on my swing!" I'd tell the family, as if I were Cal Ripken descending into his basement. Off I'd go, the car windows rolled down, gravel spraying, glove and bat riding in the passenger seat, bound for forty dollars' worth of yellow grapefruits slung at 50 mph by an arm with more gears in it than Tommy John's wing.

My preparation was just what a middle-aged softball denizen about to join a third-division Italian baseball club needed. After reading a story by *Sports Illustrated*'s Tom Verducci about the off-field batting habits of major leaguers – in which he mentioned nary a go-kart nor a grapefruit – I realized there was absolutely nothing major league about my batting routine. Verducci reported that Edgar Martinez of Seattle routinely "bunts tennis balls blasted from a machine at 150 mph and then completes his twice-daily eye exercises." Alex Rodriguez, he said, takes five batting practice sessions a day; Derek Jeter "uses his team's $350,000 video system to catalogue, analyze, and . . . burn a CD of every first pitch ever thrown to him by the game's starting pitcher (or every second pitch, or every curveball, or whatever subset he chooses)"; and Jim Thome, now of the Phillies, hits against a $150,000 pitching machine that duplicates the "speed, spin and break of the curveball of the opponent's starting pitcher, firing the cloned pitches so they appear to come from the hand of a computer-generated pitcher on a video screen."

These players would have walked into San Giacomo's wonky cage, laughed into their gloves at the sight of such a contraption, and slugged the ball to kingdom come before signing a few autographs and hopping back into their helijet. I doubt they'd be in any hurry to return, since you couldn't have had more spartan equipment than the Peones'. The cage was like a child's Popsicle model, angling badly to the right and barely obeying the rules of gravity. Whenever I helped push it from the side of the field where it slept, I feared the metal struts would collapse on me. It creaked worse than your grandmother's porch and was as brittle as the old lady herself, as if one more screaming pop-up or foul ball sliced sideways might send the whole thing crashing to the ground.

Even when surrounded by nine men, two dugouts, and, in some cases, upwards of seventy thousand fans, batting is a deeply private experience, a journey into the solitude of competition: man against ball, man against pitcher, man against team, man against one's brain. At the plate, hitters fill their heads with words – "Stay back, keep your head down, see the ball, check out the blonde in Section 112" – so that they don't become completely lost in the loneliness of concentration.

When I was at bat, there was nowhere else to direct my attention except straight out at Pietro, who threw batting practice from behind a ratty yellow screen. He must have thrown thousands of pitches over the course of the 2002 season. Of course, he did this shirtless, sweating and with tireless focus, firing the ball like a cannon. There was nothing playful or carefree about it.

Whenever I'd flail at the ball or doink it back at the mound, Pietro used this automatic out as an excuse to tell me what I was doing wrong. I know that, at some level, he thought he was trying to help me, but it wasn't until I told him, "I don't care if my elbow's not high enough. I don't care if my hips aren't turning. I don't care if my legs aren't wide enough. Just throw me the friggin' ball," that he gave up trying to turn me into the second coming of Steve Balboni. The next time I got into the cage, I was encouraged to see that Pietro had abandoned trying to pitch to the Canadian scrub. But then I saw Chicca dipping his hand into the old shopping cart that the team used as a bashed-baseball repository. My first thought, of course, was that the third bagger would bean me instantly but, after a few difficult swings, Chicca generously tapped his front leg and told me, "Keep it back here." He threw me a series of softies, which I thought I'd sprayed around the field pretty well until the Old Bugger passed behind the cage and said, "You're still not making the team, you know." I pointed my bat at him, as if to suggest that he'd best cram it unless he wanted me to portray him as the most miserable sonofagun to ever walk across an Italian ballfield. He jogged away into right field, laughing.

During batting practice, the outfield became a grassy coffee klatch, with small groups of players talking among each other, breaking up as the ball flew, then reforming into another group. There was enough room in esterno campo that nobody had to share a square of turf with anyone they didn't want to. I spent most of my time hanging out in the wide open spaces with Mario Simone.

"Dave, tell me, what is a fat ball?" he asked me one day.

"You mean a fastball?"

"No, a fat ball. It's like a home run. They say it on *Baseball 2000*, Sony PlayStation."

"I have no idea what a fat ball is. I've never heard it used in base-ball terminology."

Whenever Mario didn't understand a word, he'd stare off into space for a second and search for its meaning with a narrowing of the eyes, before conceding. "Termi . . . what?"

"I mean baseball talk, baseball language," I said.

"There is a baseball language?" he asked.

"Yes, yes, exactly."

"You know, a few years ago – ," he said, before shouting, "Aspetta!" and running to chase a ball hit by Chicca to the far reaches of centre field.

"Scusa. I am sorry," he said.

"Niente."

"I was saying that, a few years ago, it was very bad for me in baseball."

"What happened?"

"I had a girlfriend who did not like me playing this game."

"That's not cool," I said.

"Not . . . cool?"

"Not good. Non buono."

"Si, non buono. She wouldn't even come to the games. But, you know, I was young and I loved her, and I wanted to be with her."

"I understand."

"So, you know what I did?"

"Che?"

"I quit."

"Dio!"

"It was a very big error. For two years, I stopped playing. They were the worst years of my life. It made me realize that, without baseball, I was nothing."

"What happened to the girl?"

"I told her that I had to play, and she left."

"How are things now?"

"I have a new girlfriend, Daria. She loves baseball. She is very beautiful and sexy too."

"So it all worked out."

"Yes, yes. Daria comes to every game. She loves to watch me play. But when I think back about those times not playing, I become sad. Angry too. Two years is a very long time, you know."

"Especially when you're not playing a game you love."

"Si, a game we love. You love baseball, yes?"

"Ya, I guess I do."

"Me, too. Without baseball, I think I would be dead," he said, dragging a finger across his neck.

When I wasn't hanging around in the outfield, collecting fat balls hit to my side of the klatch, I was warming up latecomers in front of the dugout, pitching the ball back and forth. At first, this exercise was somewhat of a problem. My shoulder started to hurt, matching the pain in my legs and feet. The game was reminding my body that it was at an age when most players cut back on their practice times, not increase them three hundred per cent.

Whenever I played catch with the Red Tiger and Solid Gold – the two best arms on the team – we started by standing ten feet from each other. I felt a kind of humming reverie on launching the ball into the sky. Baseball is Zen-like at the best of times, and by playing catch I was able to enjoy the motion and rhythm of the game for what it is. There were moments when the Red Tiger – now standing some forty feet away – would scream the ball at me as if gunning down a runner racing for third. It was a treat, from my perspective, to watch the ball coming at me, a single hurrying dot that captured my entire train of thought. I could taste the joy and freedom of baseball, even though, as the Red Tiger's ball slapped into my glove, my fingers and palm thanked me for nothing, eventually bruising like an overripe pesca nuda.

For a few practices each month, I played the position that I'd occupied in my boyhood: a knee-aching crouch behind the plate. Usually, I caught Chencho, though I was occasionally required to work with Cobra. One evening, Chencho and I feigned Ford-Berra for upwards of thirty, forty minutes. At one point, Pietro called out from the top of the gravel driveway, "Okay, enough, raggazi! Basta! I've got to lock the gate!" which I considered an achievement not only because we'd outlasted Signor Baseball himself, but because I'd graduated from il stronzo Canadese to il ragazzo. Chencho shouted to his skipper, "Just a few more," then continued throwing his curve, change, and slider to your Mediterranean Ed Kranepool, who was as keen as the crazy mancino to keep playing.

A symbiotic rhythm and routine often develops within a battery, and Chencho and I had it. There was something about the way he threw, and the way I caught, that the ball liked. You see this happen in tennis all the time, with players whose styles compliment the other. The ball responds to their racket, playing with the air and space rather than against it. It's the same with playmaking hockey forwards, or soccer midfielders and strikers who deftly pass the ball among each other, giving it life. When Chencho told me, afterwards, that it was the best he'd thrown all summer, I wasn't surprised. You could see the movement in the ball, how it was responding well to how it was being treated.

The last time I'd worked behind the plate, Three Dog Night were still selling records. There was a lot about the position I'd forgotten: how the catcher is required to baby the pitcher so that he keeps his head in the game; how he establishes a convivial relationship with the umpire lest he end up with a three-hundred-pound grouch breathing into his ear; how he carries on a running dialogue with the infield and a silent conversation with the manager; and how he manoeuvres the outfield to defend against a batter's tendencies, while engaging the batter in a distracting chatter so that he won't notice the pitcher's 50-mph mistakes. A catcher's life is all thoughts and actions, with nary a respite. Former Negro League star Josh Gibson once told a young Roy Campanella, "A catcher's got to have ten eyes."

Catchers have to be among the most vocal of all the players. It's no surprise that Bob Uecker, Joe Garagiola, Tim McCarver, and Rick Dempsey all had successful broadcasting careers after their long tenures behind the plate. Since their masks conceal their faces, it's hard to get a sense of how animated catchers are unless you sit close to them. It's a requirement of their job, for instance, to holler at an ungodly volume whenever the offensive team is putting on a play – a bunt, sacrifice bunt, hit and run. Baseball is usually such a quiet, poised game that catchers sometimes come across like frathouse louts, their coarse ways belying what is an elevated intellectual position. Barking commands is the catcher's job by default. The infield can't yell because they're too busy fielding the ball, and there's no way the outfield can do it: they're simply too far away. The catcher is left having to play the heavy.

Backstoppers are the housekeepers of baseball. It's their job to pick up loose balls, toss the occasional bat or helmet away from home plate, take or return balls to and from the ump (and to and from the pitcher), and warn the opposing batter of a loose shoelace or unzipped zipper. This is providing, of course, he's not someone like old Connie Mack, who was the first catcher ever to stand directly behind the batter (in the early days, catchers caught the ball on a hop). Mack had a habit of tipping the batter's bat right before he swung, a most unsportsmanlike move. There were moments of recrimination, however, for occasionally, the batter, anticipating Mr. Mack's subterfuge, would bring his lumber down on Connie's wrist as he swung. This must have been the beginning of another catching tradition – broken fingers, toes, and even a speared larynx, which Steve Yeager suffered after a broken bat slivered into his neck, inspiring him to patent a protective throat guard.

During our session, I encouraged Chencho whenever one of his cuciture (sliders) swung out and cruised the lip of the plate, or his sinker dropped just below the phantom hitter's knees, shouting with Paoloesque force. Chencho would respond by nodding his head and glaring at my mitt – actually, it was Paolo's mitt – before thrashing into his windup and grooving the ball. I loved the sound it made shwapping into my glove and even though I knew my palm was turning a deeper shade of purple with every knucklecurve, I resisted the urge to remove the leather and cool my hand. There were also times when, against my better judgment, I'd fall to the dirt, blocking pitches with my bare knees and shoulders even though I knew I was one pebble away from taking a bouncer to the chops. Still, I sacrificed my body without concern, inspiring Chencho to throw the whole of his body into his motion, firing the ball as if some fearsome slugger were looming over the plate, grinding dust with his jaws.

"Bella palla!"

"Grande Kappone!"

I paid the price for my folly. Later that evening, I was in such agony that when I lay flat on the bed, I felt as if I'd gone three rounds with the Headshrinkers. Still, it was worth it, for the next day, Paolo said, "I heard you were Chencho's catcher last night."

"Ya, it was great to get down there again. But, man, I hurt today."

"Well, he said you were a very good catcher."

"Really, he said that?"

"Yes. He said he liked it very, very much."

"A very good catcher . . . ," I repeated.

"Yes, very good."

It had been twenty years since I'd heard those words.

15

MONTEFIASCONE AT NETTUNO

The Peones were blessed with a two-week lull before a pair of weekend games against league-leading Montefiascone, who, after their early-season humbling of the blue and white, continued to pummel teams in Serie B. For the Peones' downtime, Pietro had a notion to drive the team a little harder in practice. He reasoned that, since Nettuno's capacity for loose play seemed limitless, it was their sense of discipline that needed work. This resulted in entire practices spent working on defence, base-stealing, and baserunning, even though the boys would just as soon have spent three hours slugging in the cage. There was lots of running in the outfield too, a sure sign that something important was gathering on the schedule's horizon. If you'd have passed by San Giacomo in the days leading up to the rematch, you might have even mistaken the Peones for a real ball club.

That said, the notion of the blue and white maintaining this sense of discipline and emotional balance was as precarious as a fat man on a tightrope. Tommy Lasorda once said that managing is like holding a small bird in your hand; hold it too hard and you kill it, hold it not hard enough and it flies away. This was the trick that Pietro had to execute were the Peones to find the kind of equilibrium needed to defeat the league's better clubs. Considering that their free-spiritedness and joy of play was their competitive engine, this wouldn't be easy. The Old Bugger couldn't tighten the screws too soon or too hard or the players' spirits would have been destroyed.

Midweek, Paolo told me that Cobra's bicipite was hurting and that he might not be able to pitch. It was an injury that he'd aggravated playing against Sardinia. The only time I saw him at practice, he was telling Pietro that his arm wasn't improving as he'd hoped. It was a strange conversation. Even at the best of times, Cobra rarely said more than five words. So the two men stood there in front of the dugout for twenty minutes, and for long stretches neither of them said anything, as strange an occurrence as you'll find between two Italians. When Cobra had finished, pointing to the exact spot on his throwing arm where his muscle had given out, Pietro told him to get some rest and turned away, walking to the mound where he threw batting practice, chucking pitch after pitch after pitch, each one pronounced with a hard, whipping *awfuckingchrist*.

The bad bulletins didn't end there. Upon collecting me from my apartment later in the week, Pietro broke the news that Fabio from Milan was out with a torn knee ligament, and probably wouldn't return until the playoffs.

"What happened?" I asked.

"He take fly balls," he said. "But he stupido. He no wear his . . . how you say . . . ?" he asked, tapping his knee.

"Oh, shit, his knee brace."

"Ya, he no wear. He wears every day, but not then. He runs and stops to get the ball, and then, bop! È male."

"Man, that's no good," I said, thinking of Fabio's vital role on the team, not to mention his spot on the pitching staff, which had suddenly been whittled down.

"Is Pitò going to pitch?" I asked.

He winced and looked out the window.

"You might have no choice," I advised.

"In Italian baseball, you never have a choice," he said as we drove down the gravel path into the park. "Maybe I pitch," he suggested, folding a stick of gum in his mouth.

"Really?" I asked.

"Maybe I pitch, and not Pitò," he said, looking disgusted.

The morning of the Montefiascone-Nettuno return game was as beautiful as I've ever seen, the sun drenching the city in gold. I woke at dawn to prepare for the day – which involved a highly compli-cated routine of making coffee, trying to remember where I'd left my Peones T-shirt, and not waking the baby – and saw that the town had come to life early. Traffic hummed, and voices carried along the sea wall accompanied by the sound of flip-flops padding to the beach. The pasticcerias on Via Matteotti were especially busy. I sallied across the street to purchase a bag of warm brioche with an eye to surprising Janet and Cecilia, and the scene inside the bakery was all arms and hands as panini and cornetti and pizza bianca were passed over the bar in napkin sleeves before being devoured right there. Outside, the streets were crowded with Nettunese shouting to each other across the traffic, ignoring what-ever distance lay between them. Inside the Borgo, where the ancient walls better contained the sound, there was a rousing chorus of "Oowws!" and "Eyyyyyysss!"

I bought a couple of newspapers and my eyes immediately fell on the front-page photograph in the *International Herald Tribune*, which showed Ted Williams in his 1941 flannels, the year he hit .401, the last time anyone had done that. I read the headline: Williams was dead. I stood in the shade of the edicola's awning absorbed by the shock, and regret, of the moment. Bad news hits you hard no matter where you hear it, but I was grateful, if heart-broken, to learn of the great hitter's demise while in the swim of my season with the Peones. I couldn't help but hope that his spectre had descended upon Nettuno, like Cliff Johnson had visited me in Ireland, to guide the Peones through their difficult time, to help them summon the hard resolve, bravery, and ambition that the Boston slugger had embodied in spades (his recalcitrance, anger, and suspicion of others notwithstanding).

I'd brought up the subject of Williams to the team once before, after a Sunday-night team dinner. I realize that I've painted the Borgo as a picturesque fortress floating across time, but the truth is, after 7 p.m. on weekends, the old town was a little like *My Weekend at Bernie's* Italian-style. Ten years ago, La Commune – Nettuno's town council – decided to open the Borgo for business, edging their city towards becoming a bona fide tropical getaway. When I'd expressed my surprise at the change in scene, Chicca also voiced his displeasure – not at my opinion, but at the Borgo's transformation – saying, "Before, I used to be able to come here with my friends, and it was very peaceful. There was one disco, okay. But why do we need so many discos?" I too preferred the mellow, daytime Borgo – after all, I hadn't crossed an ocean to spend my summer in a medieval town that, beneath its ruddy walls and iron gates, was merely a Fort Lauderdale wannabe – but the setting proved useful after I decided that what the Peones needed to bring them together was a night of drinking, with an eye to loosening a few of the team's tighter screws.

As it turned out, it was yours truly who became a babbling, soul-baring mushball. The melancholy started to set in, I believe, after my eighth gin and tonic. I drank this advanced volume of booze even after realizing, with a shock, that the rest of the fellows were sticking to soda water. I learned, over the course of the summer, that, with the exception of cacchione, the Peones actually drank more spremuta (fresh orange or lemon juice) than booze. Not once did I see anyone dance with a lampshade on their head or try to pick a fight. The Italians were loath to let booze take away their confidence or cool self-control, and really, if you consider alcohol as a means of loosening one's spirits and inhibitions, the Italians needed no help, for they were already rubber souls when stone-cold sober.

I was forced to drink my G&Ts after realizing that, without mass quantities of alcohol, our straight-edged sporting evening might result in a reverse karma. Fearing the havoc this might wreak upon the rest of the season, I kept pace – one soda water for them, one High Karate for me – as if I were partying with the 1986 Mets. By the end of the night, I was tipping back on my heels trying to explain, cross-eyed and intoxicated, how Ted Williams came to hit a home run in his final at-bat.

Forming a horseshoe to protect me from the sound and colour of the Borgo's disco-pubs (the Italians call their bars *pubs* because *bars* were little cafés; they've also adopted another English word to describe a sporting event that matched crosstown rivals, the *derby*), the Peones watched with amusement – and maybe even a touch of pity – as I pantomimed Williams's batting repertoire, ending my drunken playlet by slashing a phantom bat at a phantom ball, sending it high over the Green Monster into the imagined New England night. The Big Emilio – who I'm sure understood not a word of my play-by-play – applauded my performance, and the Emperor said, "Very nice, Dave. Very good story," and put his arm around my shoulder while I leaned against him, exhausted.

I'd like to report that the boys stashed my Ted Williams story away for retelling themselves, but it was not the case. I found this out at San Giacomo on the day of Williams's death when I posted the *Trib* pic in the dugout. Later, I found Mario Mazza staring at it.

"Ti piace questo photograph?" I said.

"Si. Qui?" he said. "Vecchio, si?"

"Si. È Ted Williams," I said.

"Qui?"

"Ted Williams. The guy from the Borgo. Remember I told you his story?"

"Come?"

"Williams. Fato un fuoricampo di l'ultima at-bat."

"Non capito, Dave."

"The story in the Borgo, he hit a home run in his last at-bat," I said, figuring that if I explained it in English, he might suddenly remember.

"Dave, okay . . . ," said Mario, backing off.

"No, no it's not. See, this guy played every day with his heart on his sleeve. He was one of the greatest players ever. He fought in the war, il guerra, flew a fighter plane in Korea, and almost lost his life. Then he came back and hit .390 for the Red Sox. He never backed down at the plate, not for a single pitch. Ma adesso, lui è morto."

"Morto!" he said.

"Si, morto."

"Quando?"

"Oggi."

"Dio. Dave, I am sorry . . ." Pretty soon, Christian, Skunk, and a few of the others came up to find out what had happened. Mario told them what he knew. They seemed truly affected that he'd died, even if they remembered nothing of what I'd told them that night in the Borgo. Sensing an opportunity to work this into a game-day incentive to win one for the Splinter, I glowered like someone about to address his charges, stealing a glance, of course, to make sure that Pietro was well out of range.

"Questa mattina, e pomeriggio . . . ," I said. "Oggi, per lui. Let us win the game for him."

"Did you know this man?" asked Mario.

"Yes, sort of. Well, at least the way a devoted baseball fan knows one of the game's greatest players."

They understood only the first word of my reply.

"Okay, Dave. Oggi, per lui."

"Grazie, ragazzi."

"No, grazie, Dave," they chimed, jumping out of the dugout with vengeance on their minds.

At first, it looked to be a promising day. Despite his sore arm, Cobra started game one. He looked relaxed and focused on the mound, humming his diritto and cuciture with authority while passing his eyes over the Montefiasconians as if they were no more fearsome than a collection of toy soldiers. As he'd done before, he pitched above his stature, nailing the batter with his dark, unmoving eyes while keeping la palla on the ground and painting the corners.

The bottom of the first inning was vintage Peones. Skunk Bravo, showing the impeccable patience of a seasoned lead-off hitter, walked, stole, and was driven home by Chicca, who doubled to the gap. The Big Emilio, hitting cleanup, immediately followed with a single, driving in Chicca. The Peones scored twice and looked like they'd come to the ballpark ready to play. But in the top of the second inning, defeat lowered itself on the Peones. While it was Skunk Bravo who'd suffered an uncharacteristically sloppy day in the field at Montefiascone, this time it was Chicca who lost it at the hot corner. Surprisingly, I wasn't at all happy watching the one Peone who regarded me with suspicion boot and bobble the ball. I'd actually started to warm to the grouch at third base. The ice between us had started to melt, if one drip at a time, after I bumped into him one evening in the Borgo. I'd been startled to see Chicca dressed neatly, looking well rested and clean-shaven. This is to say nothing of how I felt when he took Janet's hand, introduced himself as Danielle, no less, and told me, "You know, your Italian has really improved since you arrived here." My first compulsion was to shout, "You bastard! I know you've had it in for me all along!" but his charm robbed me of the opportunity. He pinched Cecilia on the cheek, fawned over Lorenzo, and asked if he'd see me at the next practice. I told him, "Si, si, sempre per questa stagione," and then he nodded and walked away. Janet, naturally, thought he was sweet and handsome. I told her what I already knew, but she flashed me a look that suggested that if only we would get beyond pissing contests, we might finally see the beauty that each of us possessed, which is to say, Chicca possessed. Of course, the next day at San Giacomo, he acknowledged me by digging his eyes into mine like an eagle on a snow hare's hide. The day before had been a performance for the wife, and in his eyes I still ranked lower than Eddie Gaedel in terms of great figures of the game.

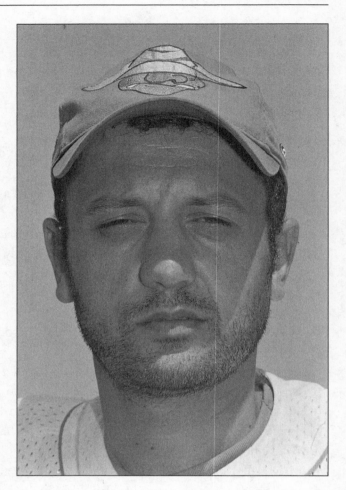

Chicca.
(Cathy Bidini)

Over the course of the season, I'd tried reaching out to Chicca
on the bench. During the game against Roma, I said to him, "Hey,
I talked to Roberta [his sister] yesterday at the Gabbiano. Is she still
going out with that guy Mario?" After I'd said it, I slapped myself
on the forehead, realizing I'd dragged the real world into baseball's
escapist playhouse. If anyone on the bench or in the dugout at home
had said something similar to me, my reaction would have been the
same as Chicca's, which was to make sure that, for the rest of the
game, he sat as far away from the doofus as possible.

Despite all this, I thought that Chicca was the one player who
mirrored my own behaviour on the field. We shared a certain

hardscrabble diamond kinship, based on respect for ballpark propriety, a love of the game, and a desire to play our hearts out for
our team. Like me, Chicca observed tradition and routine. He
always sat at the same place on the bench by himself, warmed up
before games with the same partner (the Big Emilio), and wore the
same clothes to practice. He never argued about soccer or girls
during a game or drew little penises across the pages of my book.
Instead, he played as if being watched from above, understanding,
as any serious athlete does, that running and playing and hitting is
a gift, and that to mock or disrespect it is to deny an awesome
power and force.

Neither of Chicca's errors were hard-hit liners. Both balls were
eminently playable, especially for an infielder of his calibre. Each
time he reached down to grab the ball, it either punched off his
thumb or slipped through his fingers. But it was his unprecedented
third error that was the third baseman's – and the Peones' – undoing.
Cobra, having duly kept the ball on the ground in the early innings,
allowed an easy bouncer up the line. As it danced towards the hot
spot, Chicca focused on the ball's trajectory. Instead of relying on
his instincts, he tried to play it by the book and became entangled in
his own body. He met the ball with his foot, kicking it back towards
the plate. He chased it, picked it up, but just threw it away. The rest
of the Peones' infielders had been nonplussed by Chicca's other
errors, but they now felt a force conspiring against them. Mario
Mazza was the first to show it, swearing at the sky as the runner
dashed across first base. Everybody tightened.

Even Cobra, who needed to stay loose and relaxed for the sake
of his ailing muscle, grew frustrated, shouting at Fab Julie after the
outfielder nearly lost the ball in the sun. Between innings, the
dugout was silent save for the private mutterings of "porca miseria"
(the pig of misery) and variations thereof. I watched Chicca as he
came in from the field. He took off his hat, wiped his brow with his
hand, and lit a smoke. Hauling once, twice, he hung his head and
smiled darkly at the dirt. Then, he laughed. It was the first time I'd
seen Chicca do anything other than scowl, grimace, or stare coldly

into the distance. But it wasn't a joke that was meant to be shared. I looked away before he looked up.

"Che cazzo," said Pietro, grumbling from his patio chair. I did my best to draw attention away from the coach's gathering fury by imploring the blue and white: "Let's get outta this one, boys! Uno fuori, Cobra! Solo uno fuori, Cobra!" But my voice sounded wrong, and only served to emphasize how little cheer there was.

In the fifth inning, Cobra called Pietro to the mound and told him he was done. The rest of the infield joined them on the hill, engulfing Cobra until the small pitcher could no longer be seen. After a minute, he emerged from a door in the panel of blue-and-white bodies, walking wearily across the grass to the dugout. The fans gave him a smattering of applause. He sat on the bench, drew his chin to his chest, and closed his eyes.

Chencho readied himself to enter the game but was met with a sharp look from his coach, which tacked the reliever to his chair. "Aspetta," said Pietro, turning to face centre field. Raising his arm like a flag, he called "Rickaaaa!", gesturing to Solid Gold, whose real name was Ricky Viccaro. The Golden One looked over both shoulders, before realizing he was being ordered into the game. As he dashed in from the outfield, the Black Aces groaned as if gripped by stomach pain. Chencho slumped back on the bench and said, "Don't ask me what he's doing. This move, it is crazy, questo e matto." I looked at Pitò, who gave me a defeated shrug of the shoulders, most likely thinking that if his coach had chosen an outfielder over him, he'd be better off throwing his glove into the surf rather than practise day after day, trying to prove that he still had it. I asked Paolo, "Does Ricky actually know how to pitch?"

"He's tried, yes, a few times, in practice. This player, he has a very good arm."

"Ya, I know. But that doesn't mean he can pitch."

"Ey," said Paolo. "You ask Pietro. He is the manager of this team."

At most points on the field, Solid Gold had enough personality, character, and talent to fill the breadth of one's view. But il monte lent nothing to the Golden One's already impressive aura. Pitching exploited only one of his strengths – his arm – while wasting his speed and power. This is not to say that he didn't have a gift for the position. He threw heat on par with Pompozzi, and he brought to the mound the same kind of conviction with which he prowled the outfield. Still, you could see the M-Birds – led by Zerbini and Cappanella, their tall lead-off hitter – standing on the lip of their dugout, tantalized by the possibility of hitting against a player who'd pitched only twenty innings of baseball in his entire career.

They didn't get much of a chance. After facing his sixth batter over two innings, Solid Gold bent at the waist and swore – "Fack" – his arm hanging limp. Pietro walked to the mound, where the Golden One told him, "My arm . . . is facked."

"Porco madonna."

"Vitello pia nell'culo." (Stick a piece of veal up your ass!)

"Porco Santa Maria Goretti."

Solid Gold walked back to the dugout wincing in pain. Before I could ask Chencho if, considering the luck of the day, he'd rather not go out there, he'd bolted out of the dugout and climbed the mound, eager to throw himself to the lions. After a dozen practice pitches – Chencho had been loose since the fourth inning – he told Pietro, "Sono pronto, I am ready." Pietro passed on a few low words of advice – likely variations on "Just friggin throw the ball and don't put on a show" – before settling back in his chair, where he squinted furiously at the scene.

With a five-run lead (7-2), Montefiascone greeted Chencho by rapping the ball hard, but il matto mancino somehow managed to avoid the death blow of a big inning. It was a little like watching a man standing in the middle of the street with a tornado swirling about him, ducking flying lawn chairs and potted plants. If that wasn't bad enough, il pazzo sinistro was also forced to step to the plate in the Peones' half of the seventh, the result of Pietro's new lineup. Because it was the first time he'd held a bat in years, Chencho waved it with all the sure-handedness of a drunk with a table leg, but the reliever somehow got ahold of the ball, smashing it between centre and right field. When he got to first base, he shouted to me from across the diamond and pantomimed writing into a notebook. He seemed quite pleased with himself, but the gesture soured the rest of the Peones, who were of the mind that the last thing their team needed was any lightheartedness. I flipped Chencho my thumb, then tightened my cap over my head and tried to get small.

In the eighth inning, Chencho gave up a little roller to second base, which bounced weakly between Skunk and Mario Mazza. Upset that the second baseman hadn't been in position to make the play, Chencho swore, then looked into the dugout and rolled his eyes. Mario stepped towards Chencho from second base and told him to worry about the next batter, who, sensing that the Peones were coming apart, waited on the count before doubling hard to the gap. With the hit, Chencho threw his hands into the air. As the ball bounced back to him from the outfield, he swept it into in his glove and kicked the dirt.

Around the field, the players were starting to bubble and spit. After the side was retired, Chencho shouted to no one: "*Porco Dio! Finalmente!*" At third base, Chicca took off his glove and stared at it in disgust. As Chencho passed in front of him, he threw it at the reliever, hitting him hard in the ass and shouting something along the lines of, "You fucking clown! What the fuck was that out there? You don't deserve to play on this team!" Chencho jerked his chin and hurled his own glove against the back of the dugout.

In the Peones' half of the inning, Mario Simone struck out and proceeded to bash his bat against the field like a man clubbing a snake. Everybody was either winging their helmets or throwing their bats, and the game became one protracted argument. Mario Mazza, upon striking out later in the game, returned to the bench saying, "It's impossible to hit this pitcher's high fastball. It's just too good." Both Chencho and Pompozzi immediately pounced on the young infielder, screaming at him, accusing him of throwing in the towel when there was still lots of baseball to play. Mario shouted back, "Eyyy! Listen. Pitchers stick with pitchers. Infielders stay with infielders! Don't talk to me!", which only made Chencho and Pompo argue harder, and at greater volume. Hands were raised and spittle sprayed. I checked to see what kind of action Pietro was going to take, but he remained in his chair, occasionally glancing towards the combatants with the look of a man about to axe a chicken.

Montefiascone strolled to an easy 10-2 victory. After the game, Pietro had two words for his club – "a casa" – pointing to the clubhouse at the back of the field. Once we'd gathered inside, the Old Bugger shot the bolt on the door and, after making sure that no one was missing, exploded in a supernova of anger. Veins popped at his temples and his face flushed. He thrashed about the room shouting, waving his fists, his tenor rattling the lockers and window frames and no doubt ricocheting to where the M-Birds had gathered in the parking lot.

"Lui e lui e lui," him and him and him, he said, pointing around the room. "This is not a team! It is *una cazzo groupo! Fungooolo testa cazzo* . . . It's a *fungooolo* party . . . *Cazzo* telefonino, cazzo brutta . . . from now on, *no fucking cellphones! Niente!* Porco Dio. You show no respect to me, to your players, la famiglia, to the game, no respect at all. *You see the other team? You see them laughing?* They're *laughing* at you, watching you behave like *enemies*, not like una squadra con *amici! Non che cazzo la. You never show up another player! Never!* Did you see the other team? *Cazzo puttana!* Did you see what they did? They laughed, thought it was a *good show!* A good show by the little children. Stupid little children!"

The more he shouted, the smaller the team looked and felt. As the tirade wore on, the room grew foul, the closed door and windows trapping the stink of the drains and toilets. The Peones cowered under the hammer of Pietro's words, their eyes low with shame and fear. Mirko, who was sitting beside me, took my book from my lap. The room paused as he opened it and scratched the page, then held up his words for those around him to see. They read:

> *Uno per tutti, Tutti per uno*
> *Forza Peones.*

It was the right message, but the players acknowledged nothing. Instead, they sat there deaf and dumb, breathing in the hot stink of losing.

16

THE MUSIC OF THE MOUND

After the Peones fled the ballpark, hoping that pranzo might somehow balm their wounded pride, I wandered the field alone, trying to make sense of the day's events. My first stop was the pitcher's mound. I'd always taken the old adage about the pitcher being the King of the Hill as something W.C. Heinz might have invented to colour the dull moments of a midweek Braves-Browns saw-off, but it's true that one's perspective on the rest of the field, and the game, is different at sixty feet, six inches from home plate. It's as if the earth hoists you on a fine dirt point above the rest of the players, whose job, viewed with the self-importance encouraged by the perspective, appears to be simply to catch and then politely return the ball.

Even without a team surrounding me, I felt like I was conducting the field. It was easy to imagine, however, that these journeys up Ego Mountain would be matched by an equally exhilarating descent, for there's simply nowhere to hide on the pitcher's mound. Third and first basemen have the opposing team's base coaches –

and baserunners – to consort with; the outfielders have each other; and the catcher is surrounded by players; but the pitcher is alone. We've all seen pitchers, after allowing a back-breaking home run, hunch down on the mound as if looking for a trap door they might disappear through. Either that or they're burying their faces in their glove, trying to hide their shame and embarrassment. Just as the mound empowers the pitcher, it also showcases his faults.

The pitcher's mound – and the pitcher himself – is the face of the game. It's no wonder that hurlers – and sluggers – are the game's most recognizable figures, considering that they hold the ball more often than any other player. A pitcher is also the most identifiable player on the field because, for the greater part of the game, he is motionless. Our eyes are trained on him because he spends the most time with the ball. We're constantly looking for it, wondering what it's doing. Since it's so often nestled in the oily warmth of the pitcher's glove, we tend to regard him as keeper of the treasured pill. Take a newcomer to the ballpark and, chances are, he'll remember two things: what the pitcher looked like and whether or not he saw a home run.

It's in the pitcher's hand that the ball finds its true home. Only after the pitcher has thrown the ball is the game given life, action, and poetry. The game has all kinds of terms that explain why the pitching mound is the focus of the game's expression: *chin music, a curveball that dances, he let his fastball do the talking, that ball had eyes, a seeing-eye hit, painting the corners, a repertoire of pitches, a sinkerball artist*, a pitch that is *grooved*. All it takes is watching someone for whom throwing a ball is the cause of great deliberation – Juan Guzman of the Jays was a terrible one for this – to know how the life of a game can be slowed, robbed of voice and rhythm and character. While the game has suffered its share of players challenged by the rigours of play – Mackey Sasser, the catcher, got to the point where he had trouble returning the ball to the pitcher, and Chuck Knoblauch suddenly lost all of his ability to hit the first baseman in the glove, habitually throwing it into the stands – I'm still waiting for the pitcher who, in protest, decides not to concede the ball.

There would be grave consequences, of course, for without the ball in play, baseball is just chess with hats and hot dogs.

Though you could draw baseball's formal dimensions on an Etch A Sketch, the rest of the diamond is a vast country, separated into regions that resemble the physiology of a body. Take casa base, home plate. This is the game's head, its intellectual centre. It's here that the catcher and the hitter create the game. The hitter sizes up the game's situation while the catcher designs the order of pitches, both of them working not ten inches from each other on a small patch of red dirt. It's here that the catcher configures the mathematical possibilities of every play – left-handed hitter, runner on, first baseman holding, pitch away; two-out, infield in, runner at second, keep the ball down – while the hitter tries to counter-configure his at-bat. By game's end, home plate is dented and marked as a mechanic's workbench is splattered with oil, or a carpenter's sawhorse is drowned in dust. This is not to suggest that there isn't evidence of thought or labour at other points on the diamond, but home plate is the only area the umpire is required to clean up and constantly keep in order. Second base – the game's other hot point – can remain muddied until the end of the game, but home plate is constantly swept so that both the batter and the catcher are allowed to engage in the game's intellectual banter. Stand at any point on the diamond and you'll notice how all of the field's energy and concentration is focused there, a receptacle for the game's cognitive forces.

Second base, or at least the area encircling it, is the game's heart, the base paths its aortas. It's here where bodies mash, bones crack, and toughness is rewarded. If the middle of a team is soft or lazy or weak, then the heart suffers, especially the high percentage of balls hit within ten feet of second base. With the exception of the catcher, the shortstop and second baseman have to be the most physically capable of any of the players, possessing as much balletic technique to turn the double play as dirt-chewing determination to trap balls sneaking through the hole. The middle infield has to stretch impossibly far to snare escaping liners, to hustle across the dirt to block harried hoppers and backpedal on short fly balls, pulling away from the diamond like a boat sailing from shore.

The outfield is the game's legs. It's no wonder that the team's fastest players are positioned here. The outfield is a runner's domain, a savannah where players gambol, sally, slide, and skip. Whereas the infield – with its parched paths – is hard to the touch, the outfield grass acts like a cushion against the tumbling bone. Even the colour and light of the diamond changes beyond the basepaths, moving from the muted red-pebble infield – where, at its lip, tufts of weeds and small flowers start to appear – to the outfield's green ocean of cool grass. The outfield – which is to say, the San Giacomo outfield – is home to much of the diamond's natural life, sprouting all manner of wildflowers (the Spanish call outfielders "il giardinieri di baseball"). It is as fertile as the infield is fallow. It's here where players stride and jump like butterfly collectors, communing with Nature in this, the most Wordsworthian of all games.

While much of this was a revelation to me, I'm sure it was stale news to Francesco Pompozzi. The nineteen-year-old pitcher was aware of baseball's total game and the character required to reign from the mound. Pompo had been taught the game early by San Giacomo taskmasters, and by his father, a wealthy Nettunese developer whose company had built Nettuno's first superstore, the Inter Marche, at the south end of the American cemetery. (Janet and I had shopped there once, but the experience had left us cold. Many of the Nettunese were actually thrilled at the vastness of the store, having spent much of their lives shopping in places the size of a foot locker. They made me wonder whether the only reason Italians favour fresh produce and fish is because it is all they could get their hands on.)

I liked Pompozzi despite this. He was of the generation that gorged itself on twenty-four-hour cable sports channels, watching hours of major league ball. This exposure to baseball was why

Pompo, like Mario Mazza, affected the look of the pro ballplayer, unlike Mario Simone or the Emperor, whose style, at least at the plate, was what you might expect from someone who'd never seen Joe Morgan's chickenwing, Pete Rose's man-lurking-behind-the-hedgerow act, Tony Bautista's hotel-doorman routine, Craig Counsell's poking-a-balloon-out-of-a-tree stance, or "Pops" Stargell's loop-de-loop. Most of the Peones were unmistakably Italians playing ItaloBall, but Pompo had the look of a young North American pitching for his high-school or college team. His repertoire of tugging his cap, blowing into his hands, leaning in from the mound to look for the sign, and shaking out the tension in his arm had been assembled from watching pro ballplayers on television two or three times a week. Every now and then during practice, Pompo would drop a name – "Jeter, Rodriguez, Soriano" – as if trying to stump me. Once, he did: "Johnny Van Der Wall." Not being up on my fourth outfielders for the New York Yankees trivia, I told him that he must have meant "Johnny Van Der Meer," the only man to have pitched consecutive no-hitters, and former battery mate of Ernie Lombardi. But after checking a Yankees boxscore, I found out that I was wrong. Pompo had shown me what-for, and I was happy for him. Really.

Pompo's understanding of major league baseball was a far cry from what the first Nettuno teams knew about baseball abroad. Back in the 1950s, their knowledge was limited to what the soldiers had brought with them. Silvano Casaldi, quoting Paolo Dinese, said that while the Normandy invasion was the single most important political development of the war, the 5th Army's landing in Italy was its most important sociological event, as it brought the treasures of the West to greater Europe. "We were living in a very provincial way, before the war," Silvano said. "Our region wasn't open to foreign influences, even less so when the fascists were in power." He could remember vividly the arrival of the giubbotto (bomber jacket, or windbreaker), boogie-woogie music, beer in cans, saponetta alla lavanda (laundry soap), American cigarettes, blue jeans, bubblegum, and sweet chocolate. The Allied soldiers were as strange and exotic to the Nettunese as A-Rod and Sammy Sosa were familiar to Pompo. Dinese wrote of seeing his first group of American infantrymen prowl their way north from the beach, their faces, language, dress, and habits utterly different from anything he'd known. He watched as they descended, "comme cavallette" (like locusts), on an onion field, falling to their hands and knees and devouring every plant in the patch. That onion field is now the San Giacomo diamond.

What the Nettunese knew about American baseball was limited to whatever they were told by people like Colonel Trantman – an American fighter pilot based in Germany who flew to Rome, then drove to Nettuno, to play weekend doubleheaders – or what McGarrity, Butte, or others described in long evening sessions gathered around la tavola, cracking talline, drinking cacchione, and retelling the legends of Ruth, Gehrig, and Tyrus Cobb. Sergio Serpe told me one afternoon at a café: "Butte could finish a box of twenty-four beers in one sitting. I would sit here, right by his side, and listen to him talk while he drank, telling me about baseball and all of the great players of the day."

The parochialism of 1950s Nettuno didn't begin and end with baseball. In the early days after the war, the Nettuno team travelled to Milan, where they were fêted, post-game, with bistecca and patates frittes. Not having come across this kind of food before, they sent it back, asking for pasta fagioli instead. I could only imagine what these baseball elders would have thought of Pompozzi – or the Inter Marche, for that matter – who'd travelled the world with all-star junior teams, and who understood pro ball to the point that, during the World Series, he was able to savour every at-bat and second-guess pitch selection like a true continental student of the twenty-first-century game.

I asked my dad to send me packages of baseball cards I could hand out to the Peones and the hordes of cadetti who, occasionally, shared the field at San Giacomo. (With the first carton of cards – Upper Deck Rookie Series – he included a typically Dad-ish note, telling me that he'd got the cards wholesale, from a friend. The

The first Nettuno team at the Vatican, with Pope Pius XII.
(Courtesy of Maria Antonietta Marcucci)

package also included *Globe and Mail* and *Star* sports sections, which I passed around the table at team dinners.) Once I'd torn open the box and laid the decks out, the cards were gone in a matter of minutes. Pompo was always the first at the trough. Once, I saw him come up with a handful of silver sleeves – four or five decks, maybe more. As his eyes caught mine, a ripple of guilt passed across his face, and he walked over to ask, politely, if it was too much.

"No, maybe Johnny Van der Wall's in there," I said.

"Grazie, Dave," he said, tearing them open.

Because Pompo was aware of Greg Maddux, Randy Johnson, and Pedro Martinez, he knew what it meant to be the ace, and carried himself accordingly, with a sense of purpose. On the mound, he affected the look of the hombre, someone who used his fastball like a pistol or tomahawk. His boyish looks tended to belie these efforts – hombres, usually, wear more chin scruff and tobacco spittle, wrinkled pants and mud-splotched spikes – but his attitude nonetheless gave him a star appeal that Cobra lacked. It provided the diamond with a hot point, the apex into which the team poured its energy. With Pompo on the hill, the players worked the field as if they were soldiers defending a citadel.

If Pompo had a weakness, it was typical of most young, fireballing pitchers. He was prone to moments of great stubbornness, when he tried to throw the ball through the wall, even as rival batters caught up to it. His arrogance regarding his heater helped him as much as it hurt him. It was a classic *Bull Durham* condition that Pietro, Paolo, and the Big Emilio had each tried to drum from his skull over the course of the year, steering him towards a more conservative approach to his lower-80s fastball. They also worked on trying to get him to change speeds. Pietro's dream of dreams was for Pompo to throw his curveball more often (initially, he told me that he didn't because it hurt his arm, and that he was terrified of irreparably damaging his meal ticket), but he only flirted with it over the course of the season.

That said, it comforted Pietro – and the whole team, really – to know that he could pencil Pompo's name in the lineup every Sunday. By using him in the second game, he was able to field youthful energy and durability against visiting clubs who tended to fade under the heat of the sun, especially if they'd risen early that day to travel to San Giacomo. And as the boys ran out for the second game versus the M-Birds, the Peones settled down, knowing that their fireballer was leading them from the most important position in baseball.

In ItaloBall, as in the majors, baseball allows for second chances. In the pros, the number of games – 162 – gives players the chance to work themselves out of horrendous batting streaks, and, in Italy, Sunday doubleheaders gave teams who were drubbed in the morning a chance to climb back out of the ditch. Understanding this, Pietro pencilled in the same order as he had in the first game, and once the game began, you could tell that the players were grateful for the chance to atone for their sins of the morning.

Solid Gold, starting as designated hitter, had three singles and a stolen base. The Big Emilio had four RBIs and even the Emperor, from the ninth slot, managed to chop a double into the gap. A typical inning saw Pompo go kappa, kappa, groundball, kappa (K, K, groundball, K). With each strikeout, the Peones cheered him. Mario Simone, who'd hung an o'fer in the first game, accounted for the defensive gem of the day, throwing out from centre field an M-Bird who'd tried stretching a double into a triple. Running in from centre field, Mario raised his hands over his head and yelled, "Forza Peones! Cazzo! Siamo numero uno!" so that the Montefiasconians would be certain that Nettuno had put their mistakes behind them. When I stepped from the dugout to offer my congratulations, he leapt towards me, hugging me with all his strength, sending my pen and notebook flying from my hands.

In the fourth inning, the Big Emilio ended the frame by throwing out a baserunner at second, scotching a potential tying run. After firing the ball, he rose against the play, his face clenched as the runner and Skunk, covering second, converged in a cloud of red dust. The umpire called "Out!" and Emilio, ripping the mask from his face, roared. The Peones had regained their edge. From that moment on, they played with greater fury and determination than they had all season long.

The Peones built a comfortable lead, 9-3, but despite the gap, the M-Birds continued slashing at the ball, forcing Pietro to remind his players, "Piccole cose, piccole cose" (the little things, the little things). There was very little quit in the way Montefiascone played ball. They hustled and advanced runners as if sure that they could still win, nipping ever slightly at the Peones' lead, narrowing it to 9-4, then 9-5, then 9-6.

During the eighth inning, with the M-Birds marching back, everything seemed to fall still at San Giacomo. At the best of times, baseball is a quiet, empty game set to the music of the land – car wheels crunching over gravel, a distant birdsong, the long wail of a child – and at this moment there was only the sound of the players breathing and the ball hitting the catcher's guantone. I was aware of the wind pouring through the row of pines behind first base, making them sway like tired dancers at the end of a long evening. I watched them moving and I wondered whether the Peones had peaked too soon, whether they'd exhausted their will after raging over the better part of eight innings. With the day softening, the sun dipping, and quartet of great white birds – cornacchia – rising and falling over the ravine like rags tossed into the breeze, I wouldn't have begrudged the players had they called it a season right there. I would have agreed if they'd decided that what was truly important to them wasn't winning or losing but the romance of the game as played on an elegant Italian afternoon with the wind talking in your ear. The photo of Ted Williams had come unstuck and was flapping in the breeze. I dwelled for a minute on the silver image of the Splinter, then shut my eyes. When I opened them, it was the bottom of the ninth.

I rubbed away the blur of my sudden sleep and looked up to see that Pompo had loaded the bases with the Peones leading by two runs, 10-8. Chencho and Paolo implored him to finish the game, but, otherwise, the Peones watched with quiet tension, allowing the afternoon to play itself out. As the count ran to 2-2 on Cappanella, Pietro, understanding that his team had reached the fulcrum of the season, hoisted himself out of his patio chair, walked slowly to the mound, and reminded Pompo that the fortunes of his team now rode on his back. The pitcher looked around the diamond – everywhere but at Pietro. Then, he acknowledged the manager's command with a nod before ordering his feet on la pedana, adjusting his cap, and buttoning his heartbeat into his backpocket. Coolly, the ace looked in. The moment hung in the air. The Big Emilio put down one finger – fastball, into the heart of the plate – and Pompo, moving out of his caricamento, came at the batter with his blinding heat.

"Steeeeeeeeerike!"

"Che grande kappone!"

The batter smashed the plate with his bat, then begged the umpire, "Va fungulo! No!"

From the Peones came a rousing, if weary, cheer.

The sound of a team not dead.

17

FATHER BASEBALL

After defeating the best of the league, the Peones had forty-eight hours of joy before things, inevitably, went awry. After a rousing Tuesday-night practice, I looked out the window of our palazzo to find Paolo, Pitò the Stricken, and Pompo standing outside. They called up to me and asked if I'd join them for a drink at Coco Loco, allowing me to indulge in one of my favourite Nettunese pastimes: carrying on a conversation while hanging out of our window. In Toronto, there's very little talk at that height; whenever anyone shouts from their window at home, they're either in distress or the Leafs have just scored an important goal. North American houses don't allow you to use a window the way Rip Taylor used his Hollywood Square, but since most people in Nettuno lived above stores – many of which they owned and ran – and because the temperature inside was sometimes too warm for even the Nettunese to bear, it wasn't uncommon to find people conducting long conversations from sill to sill, rooftop to streetside. The Nettunese loved being on display, and window talk was a good attention-grabber. In

Pietro.
(Cathy Bidini)

the evenings, the windows were stage sets where all human drama was played out, life acted on high for all of the city to see.

The boys shouted that they were in desperate need of a seaside beverage. I told them that it sounded like a good idea, so, throwing Cecilia onto my shoulder, I swept down the marble staircase and headed to the faux Caribbean bar, where I found the boys sitting at a table facing the sea, which, on this night, stretched out like black velvet under a great white moon. By the time I arrived, the two Black Aces – and one ace – were well into it: "Pietro doesn't play me. Pietro favours players. Pietro manages like a dinosaur. Pietro has no clue." What Pompo had to complain about, I wasn't sure, but his presence was a gesture of support to Paolo, who'd helped him with the inside game. The three players had grown pretty tight over the course of the season. Before his start against Montefiascone, Paolo had accompanied Pitò to Pompo's house, where he'd prepared a feast of pasta with tuna that – if you believed Paolo – had alone been responsible for the Peones' most significant victory of the year.

Over the course of the evening, Pompo didn't say much – he was worrying about the argument he'd had with Mario Mazza – and neither did I, for it was Paolo and Pitò who held the table (Cecilia, for her part, busied herself filling a green juice bottle with patio stones), venting indignantly about the injustice they'd suffered under Pietro's reign as manager.

"This is terrible, what is happening on the team," said Paolo. "Look here at Sandro [Pitò]. Every day, he takes a drink with medicine that helps him play."

"Si! Every day!" said the zaftig pitcher, raising a phantom glass to his lips.

"What kind of medicine?" I asked.

"For his arm," replied Paolo, touching his tricep. "It's . . . how do you say? . . . it keeps the pain down."

"An anti-inflammatory?"

"Yes. You put it in water and drink it. Every day he takes it, for the team, for Pietro. And every day, *upfft*, he sits and not pitches."

"Davide, every game," said Pitò, shaking his head.

"Pietro, he doesn't believe," said Paolo.

"Pietro, cazzo," said Pitò, under his breath.

"Pitò takes his medicine to get strong," said Paolo. "He works hard, very hard, as much as any player on the team. He wants to play, to win. To help the Peones."

"Paolo," said Pitò, returning his friend's compliment, "he hits a home run, and still it is not enough. How many players on the Peones can do that?"

"Pietro says that if you don't practise, you don't play, but some players, they come late to every game, or they don't go to San Giacomo for practice. Yet, they play. Andrea Cancelli [the Emperor] plays."

"Porca miseria," added Pitò, on hearing the Emperor's name.

"I like Andrea, I really do," said Paolo. "But why does he play? And every game!"

"You're not saying – ," I interrupted, stopping him before he stated the obvious: that the Emperor came by his job because he ran the team.

"No, but . . . ," said Pietro, raising his eyebrows.

"Upt!" blurted Pitò. "Andrea no practice, but he plays. Why?"

"Why don't you talk to Pietro?" I asked.

Pompozzi laughed.

"What's so funny?"

"Eyy, Dave. Why don't *you* talk to Pietro?"

"Maybe I will."

"No, Dave, no. Please, don't say anything," said Paolo.

"You talk to him a lot?" said Pitò, smiling.

"Yes, we talk."

"About Peones?"

"Yes, about Peones."

"You don't talk," said Pitò. "Okay, you talk, but, you don't *talk*. Nobody talks to Pietro."

The rest of the evening continued in the same vein, the conversation plodding like a tractor ploughing the same muddy trough. I'd been over these issues with Paolo before, but now the other Black Aces were becoming alienated by their coach. It was the first time that anyone had raised the issue of the Emperor's playing time, though I'd occasionally wondered myself why he'd been so entrenched in Pietro's starting lineup. While Pietro showed tough love to the other players, he gave the Emperor a free pass to the ninth hole, game in and game out. Though he competed hard and wore the blue and white with as much pride and dignity as any player, he possessed little of the natural ability the rest of the team had. At the plate, he swung the bat as if closing a rusted gate, standing knock-kneed like Elvis Costello on the cover of *My Aim is True*. He tended to get lost against pitchers who changed speeds, and there were times when he became crossed up covering balls hit to the outfield. Unlike Skunk Bravo or Mario Mazza, the Emperor appeared to have taken up the game rather than been born into it.

That said, the Emperor was beloved by his charges. He was a good guy in the dugout, at practice, and at team dinners (which he organized), and his teammates were loath to use him as an example of where Pietro had gone wrong in his managing of the ball club. Given his privileged background, none of them would have been surprised if he'd farmed out the menial tasks required to run a team, or worse, acted as if such tasks were beneath his caste. Instead, he attacked these duties enthusiastically. He'd often call me on his car-phone from Rome while boxes of balls, bats, uniforms, and score-sheets spilled over from the back seat, obscuring his view. It was the Emperor's ignoble job to make sure there was enough equip-ment for games and practices, that everything was in order with FIBS and their game representatives, that air and bus travel and tickets were properly arranged for away games, and that he got the money from his father to pay for it all. While the other players poured their energies into hitting and fielding, the Emperor's passion was in assembling, guiding, and dreaming the Peones. If he hadn't had the notion to create this team of friends in the first place, the Peones would never have existed.

The Emperor's selfless devotion to the team may well have been in reaction to what his father, Gianni, represented. The differences between Gianni and the Emperor were glaring. Gianni would show up in the dugout, flashing a roll of bills and promising five Euros for a hit. After a victory, he'd wave his money some more while set-tling his debts.

The way the Emperor dealt with his father was similar to the way Pietro's sons did with him. Neither Fabio nor Angelo showed any interest whatsoever in baseball. Angelo was the more flamboy-ant of the two. It was almost as if he was positioning himself so that no one in their right mind would ever associate him with any sport of any kind. A few times when we met him in the Borgo, he was dressed as if he'd just come from an audition for *The Pirates of Penzance*. Other times he'd dress in a frilly shirt, his head wrapped in a Norma Desmond turban. Much of this style, of course, was typical of Nettunese men, but Angelo seemed to push his point just a touch further. Fabio, for his part, was only the second person I'd met from Nettuno who openly spoke about emigrating to the States or Canada. When I asked him why, his face tightened. "Here, it is so small, tight. After a while, you've seen all there is to see," he said.

I saw Fabio Monaco just once at the park, when he came to deliver his dad's lunch (Angelo never made an appearance). When I asked Pietro if it was a sore point that his sons hadn't taken to the game, he said, "Times are different now, in Nettuno, and in the world. When I was growing up, there was only baseball, but today, there are lots of things for a young person to do. They never wanted to play, what can I do? I can't make them play. Besides, the son wants to be different from the father. This is happening everywhere, I think." Pietro seemed to have a pretty good grip on it, but whenever we ran into Angelo at Cafe Volpi, the coach would speak to his son without ever looking at him. I don't know if this was shame or regret or a failure to accept Angelo for who he was, or who he wasn't. Near the end of the trip, I asked Pietro if he could get me an autograph of Bruno Conti, the great Nettuno footballer who'd helped Italy win a World Cup in 1982. What he gave me was an old memento inscribed *To Angelo*, who obviously had no use for it.

The Peones – particularly players like Fabio from Milan and the Emperor – were Pietro's other family. They were the ballplaying sons he'd never had. This, of course, made it even more difficult for players like Paolo to accept being treated the way they were without feeling jilted or neglected. Paolo had once been coached by Pietro as a boy – he'd slept and dined at his house – yet the Old Bugger left his former slugger to languish on the bench, wondering just whathefuck he was doing with his summer. Pitò, for his part, would have loved to have been fussed over the way Pietro guided and taught Pompo, but instead, the coach ignored him.

"I am very angry, very angry at what is going on with Pietro," Paolo told me at Coco Loco, his soft, round face and sympathetic eyes undermining the rage he felt towards his coach. "I feel like I am guilty of something . . . something that I don't know."

"Pietro treats us like it's the big leagues," said Pitò, echoing what Davide Calabro's father had said to Fabio from Milan.

"Eyy. A big baseball star," said Paolo.

"La stella e cazzo," said Pitò.

We drifted in silence for a few minutes as the enormous moon arced over the sea, painting it with wriggles of silver. It was too sweet a night for such stress and concern, but the team had got to a point where something had to give.

Before leaving the boys to put Cecilia to bed, I said, "There's still lots of baseball to play. You just have to believe that Pietro knows what he's doing."

They stared at me, unconvinced.

"Pietro," sighed Paolo, "part of him is very good. The other part . . . I think he has a problem with."

18

THE FIRES OF ROME

Rome is an hour, an hour and a half north of Nettuno, depending on the mood of the train. Before we left Canada, Janet and I decided to visit the Eternal City once a week. We didn't have a goal, other than to take it in with our own eyes. After reading every book I could find about Rome, I gave up the idea that I could grasp a city of such scope over the course of a single summer. So, rather than chase down its cherished landmarks, I decided to let the city just happen. I've been to enough places to know that the most memorable times come accidentally, in places unmarked by guidebooks: a cobwebbed pub, desert gas bar, riverside bookstore, island hummingbird garden.

I made nearly half of my journeys to Rome with only Cecilia, partly to give Janet some space at home, and partly because our chatty little Ewok turned out to be the ideal travelling companion. If I hadn't been required to search for the perfect flat surface upon which to change the babe's diaper, I might never have been led up the Quirinale or to the Museo Nazionale, destinations I hadn't had in mind. They just worked themselves into the serpentine route by which I learned Rome, wandering from one park bench or smooth fountain lip to the next.

Of course, like any parent, I was hoping that Rome might be indelibly imprinted upon her. But there's no rule governing what will or will not stick, and, if my own upbringing is any indication, both Cecilia and Lorenzo might well spend the better part of their adolescence grumbling about holidays abroad. Then again, it took me twenty-two years before I ever travelled anywhere solo, and I often wonder whether having been deprived a Grand Tour in my youth might have fed my teenage desire to stick close to my borough. Still, I hoped that by bringing the kids to Italy, they would get comfortable in a world they would later explore on their own. I imagine Cecilia one day finding herself among the ruins staring at the Roman sun, perplexed why the perspective seems so familiar.

In Rome, Cecilia and I gobbled up the pathways of the city with Palinesque aplomb, pushing on where, had I been travelling with a similarly aged companion, I might have paused. With her, it was always "Forward, ho!" and while she sometimes wore me thin, I was more or less grateful that my pleas for the occasional fountain-side respite were shouted down. Cecilia also proved to be an excellent priority pass in a country obsessed with young ones. Italians love babies. Brutes, businessmen, young women, and even other children clamoured for a chance to cuddle our bambini, sometimes melting at the sight of them from hundreds of feet away. In Rome, Cecilia was showered with gelato, biscuits, juice, candies, and toys. Every trip was a fiesta and I bathed in the glow of this adulation. Were I a Lothario, I could have scored at will.

Cecilia must have felt she'd been swept into a great, caring swarm. Once, on a train ride home from Rome to Nettuno, we were caught in the rush-hour press of three trainloads of passengers rerouted into one, hundreds of commuters packed like Pocky into the sweltering heat of the Campo Leone car. Not wanting to stand holding Cecilia for the better part of two hours (every seat was taken), I sat her in the overhead luggage rack, and held her with one arm. She sat there quite happily, her legs dangling above our heads. The Italians, of course, were horrified. A sudden rush of concern rippled through the carriage and the other commuters scrambled to bring her down. I motioned to them that Cecilia seemed to be enjoying her high perch, but the Italians would have none of it. A nonna with a window seat insisted that I give her the child, so I did. Within a few minutes, Cecilia had fallen asleep against the old woman's bosom. For the next two hours, they were both in commuter heaven.

Rome was, generally, an excellent place for the young one to visit. Because of the city's awesome scale, I can only imagine how its great buildings must have appeared to a two-year-old, often feeling, myself, like a lowly vole in the presence of the Coliseum or the Victor Emmanuel Monument. One minute we'd be strollering happily alongside a steady stream of Roman traffic, the next we'd be cooling ourselves in the shade of a monolithic ruin rearing over the street like a giant with its arms crossed, right there in the middle of a thoroughfare. Cecilia was particularly drawn to the Trevi Fountain, its great swimming horses exploding out the rear wall of the Palazzo Poli, but was delighted with every fountain possessing either twenty-foot tritons or a great pan of swirling water, which was most of them. From Bernini's masterpiece in Piazza Navona – la Fontana dei Quattro Fiumi, which was funded in the 1650s by a city tax on bread – to the cartoon ghouls spitting water outside the Pantheon, each fountain seemed greater and more magnificent than the next. The city possessed countless details that played upon my eye – a red silk scarf waving from the neck of a sunglassed motorinist; a centurian-for-hire lighting a smoke against the gates of the Palatine Hill; a young priest being fitted for his vestments in one of Rome's many ecclesiastical tailors; the wan smile of a painting of Mary captured in an oval frame bolted, offhandedly, to the side of a fourth-century building; the platters of food carried by waiters across rows of busy outdoor terraces fitted into alleyways as wide as your pant cuff. Amid so much life and colour, I half-expected Cecilia to suffer Pokemonian seizures, but instead, she simply lay in the bucket of her stroller, gnawed on a slice of tomato and basil pizza, and watched all that Rome's magnificent theatre had to offer.

After one day in Rome, which we spent at the Rome Zoo in the Villa Borghese, the little girl and I navigated the city at dusk. I was hoping to reach Campo di Fiori by nightfall. Janet, Lorenzo, and Janet's sister, Melanie (who'd flown to Italy to assist in our cause), would meet us there. Promising to reward Cecilia with a granita di limone upon arrival, we set off into town, but not before pausing to watch a group of old men play bocce on a court in the Villa's Parioli park, their blazers hung over the knots of great shade trees. I'd read about them in *Italy Daily* ("Put three of us together and we're older than the Coliseum," one of the bowlers, Carlo Cristoferi, had told the paper), about how they'd grown disenchanted with the slant of their former field and had decided, with the help of workmen tending the Villa's Galleria, to groom a scrub path into a field for themselves. I loosed Cecilia from her stroller so that we might watch the vecchietti bowl a frame, only to have the little scamp make a dash for the dirt. Her enthusiasm had less to do with her bloodlines than with a child's desire to seize all bounceable objects and toss them with great force.

So we moved on, stopping momentarily for a cappuccino and macaroon at a galleria off Piazza della Republica; visiting a busy Feltrinelli's bookshop, where I browsed the Italian-language editions of English titles; and pausing at my favourite alimentari in Rome, just off Via del Corso, where bottles of wine and spirits ran to the top of the store's sixty-foot ceiling in a glittering mosaic of booze. I bought a bottle of limoncella, buried it among the kids' clothes and diapers underneath the stroller, and wheeled back to the street, where we forged through the fading light of Rome at full pre-dusk pelt, the energy and noise lulling Cecilia to sleep.

After nearly half an hour, my shins cried for a rest, but I was able to push on until the Victor Emmanuel Monument finally climbed into view. Built on the most sacred of Rome's seven hills, the VE is often scorned for its glaring whiteness (almost every other monument in Rome is made with the traditional travertine marble) and impossible bulk, which swallowed the downward view of the Campidoglio – including the Capotiline Hill and the Forum Romanum. Its botticino stone, collected into a 500-foot-high, 200-foot-wide mass, has been called everything from "a mountain of sugar" to, in the words of British Second World War soldiers, "the wedding cake monument." I thought it was great, despite its fists-to-chest bluster. As H.V. Morton has noted, its top level, which gives visitors a breathtaking view of the city, makes you want to race to the edge of the terrace and shout "Excelsior!", just the thing a fellow raised on the films of Cecil B. DeMille would dream of before visiting Rome.

As I neared the bottom of Via del Corso, however, I discovered that I wasn't at the monument yet, for the road fell off before it reached the VE, giving way to an Everest of ancient stone stairs descending endlessly. In Rome no street follows a straight line, so I should have known that the route to the Campidoglio wouldn't have been as easy as it had looked from the top of the corso.

I had two options. I could either carry the sleeping girl and her stroller down the stairs, or wheel back and swoop around Via del Corso to Via Nationale, which would have tacked twenty minutes on to my trip. This could mean that I'd miss Janet and company and have to make my way back to Nettuno on my weary lonesome. Unable to fathom the latter scenario, I hefted my precious cargo and started downwards. With each step, I pushed against a tide of bodies surging up the steps from Piazza Venezia, their elbows tipping against mine, legs knocking legs. Cecilia floated through the night at a forty-five-degree angle as if she were a small queen. A quarter of the way down, the crowd – rather than becoming annoyed with me – realized just what I was carrying, and began offering help. But I'd found my balance and rhythm, so I refused their assistance. Besides, the moment held a certain preciousness, for there I was, lowering my daughter into Rome. Climbing down into the deepening blue of the new summer evening, with the VE Monument looming before me in a symphony of white marble, I understood this moment as mine, as a parent. It was one of the first times that I felt like someone's father, and it was okay, not at all like I'd once feared. As I negotiated the last few steps before hitting solid earth, where two small fires burned in golden urns behind the iron gates of the monument, I knew that I was a different person than I'd been at the top of those crumbling steps.

Cecilia opened her eyes for a second, then closed them again. I wondered if Cecilia had felt something too, whether she'd seen anything at all. Then, a few hundred feet up the road, as I pushed her towards Campo di Fiori, she opened her eyes and spoke. I leaned in to hear her better against the torrent of life that moved across the city.

"Dave," she said, pausing to remember her question.

"Yes, dear?"

Her eyes opened wide.

"Did you see those little fires?"

19

1987

Everybody remembers one game. Just one that is frozen perfect. When you return to it, it looks and feels and tastes as fresh as when it happened. You use the memory of it to warm yourself whenever sports or life fails to be what it was on that day that is forever penknifed on your heart.

September 25, 1987.

1987 was a seismic year for me. It was the summer of my first rock 'n' roll tour. The adventure began fifty feet into the trip, when we noticed that we hadn't properly chained the door of the U-Haul and were leaving a trail of clothes and musical equipment in our wake (though not, thankfully, the Strat-O-Matic baseball game that I'd brought along). So we returned, shovelled everything back inside, and started again. Three months later, we dragged ourselves back home across five provinces in a rescuing band's van (our original vehicle, my dad's car, was given a mountain burial in the British Columbia interior). We felt dirty and disconsolate, infected with the fever of a wandering life. This was also the year of the Gretzky-Lemieux Canada Cup (which we followed on our homeward trail across the country) and the Blue Jays–Tigers pennant race, which, for me, produced a series of games as memorable as any of our shows, informed with as many moments of giddiness, despair, and life lessons.

I began following the Blue Jays' pennant quest at the Royal Albert Hotel in Winnipeg – a rummy's last stop. My bandmates and I occupied a room decorated with happy-face wallpaper – five of us sharing a mattress and box spring – where, one night, I listened through the wall to two wasted losers plotting the holdup of a convenience store. This was typical of the nightly theatre at the Albert, at least when the paramedics weren't wheeling away OD jobs or comatose drunks. We did what we could to fight back the misery. I relied on a portable radio to track breeze-blown Blue Jay broadcasts, listening while lying on the carpet dotted with the burn marks of dead cigarettes, and clawing at a bag of raisins. I lived on raisins, having no money to purchase any real food. My clearest memory is listening to the Jays play the Orioles on a warm night by Lake Ontario. Late in the game, an Orioles batter launched a high fly ball to dead centre field, and Lloyd Moseby climbed the wall to bring it down. Moseby led off the next inning and homered deep into the night, giving the Jays a lead they wouldn't relinquish. The next day, I called Janet and asked if she'd seen the game. She said she'd been sitting down the third-base line, twenty feet from where Moseby had performed his heroics. Afterwards, in whatever crummy hotel we'd been sentenced to stay, I listened for her voice in the crowd at every game, and let the sea of noise pull me closer to her shoulder, ear, neck, and mouth.

The pennant race of 1987 was a fantastic world. Listening to it was like being absorbed in a great living novel, chapter by chapter, game by game. All of the game's characters were there, night after night, and since many of the players had been with the Jays since their rookie years, their at-bats were informed by personal history. I knew the Jays' identities from every side. In the case of Tony Fernandez, not only was I aware of every movement at bat, and of how many hits he'd had in what season, I also knew where he

Reading about the pennant race outside the Cattle Prod offices, Vancouver,
while touring with the Rheostatics in 1987. (Janet Morassutti)

shopped in Toronto (Ossington and Dundas, Little Portugal), what
for (yucca, a Dominican staple), and whether he could sing the
Canadian national anthem. (He could. He sang it for author David
Faulkner, who, after quizzing Jesse Barfield in the dressing room
about his knowledge of Canadian culture, or lack thereof, turned
around to hear the little Dominican belting "O Canada!" in full
throat.) The Jays were my connection to home. Letters from Janet
came only a few times a month, but my team was there for me every
night, except on off-days, when I obsessed over them in whatever
newspaper I could find.

I was spending most of my time in the company of five men, all
of us in the neurotic throes of coping with a wild, new touring life,
and baseball became my home. It was a familiar world of manicured
grass, bubbling outfield fountains, grey-and-blue flannels, pine tar,
front-porch musings, Harry Carry, seventh-inning stretches, cotton

candy, teams named after birds, and the prose of Roger Angell. Unlike my journey west, on which I wilfully curled up in the salty palm of the rock 'n' roll gods, and, most of the time, was either lost or had no idea where I was supposed to be, baseball left very little to chance. *A posto*. Everything was where it was supposed to be.

Or so I thought.

In 1987, the Blue Jays destroyed the ball. They set a single-game record for homers by one team (10), averaged 5.2 runs a game, had five players hit twenty or more fuoricampi, and boasted the year's MVP, the recalcitrant Latin slugger George Bell, who became the starting left fielder in the all-star game after a furious write-in campaign by devoted fans. It was Bell who led the Jays into September as the favourites to win the American League East. The antithesis of the sleek, elegant Moseby and the young, lithe Fernandez – whose glove, in Vin Scully's words, was like "a bowl of silk" – Bell played left field like a kid kicking around his toy trucks. If Fernandez – and the sweet-swinging Fred McGriff – effortlessly swept their bats across the plate, Bell worked his bat like a hammer throw, sending balls into the corners of the outfield, many of them dug out of the dirt on a bounce. And while other Jays charmed visiting journalists by singing the Canadian national anthem or posing at Fan Appreciation Day with the mayor, Bell hardened his image by attacking opposing pitchers and crying about bias and bigotry in the major leagues.

Bell was overlooked whenever writers went searching for a local poster boy. Catcher Ernie Whitt posed for milk growth charts, and Moseby scaled local pop charts with "Shaker's Rap" (I own two copies), but Bell curried no favour, choosing, instead, to speak from the heart. One year after they'd made him the Jays' first starting all-star, fans booed Bell for refusing to be a designated hitter, to which he responded by telling the press, "Those fans who boo me . . . they can kiss my purple butt." As with the Jays' other great, misunderstood Latin player, Roberto Alomar, the affection fans had for the player soured, and George was eventually run out of town, to Chicago, where he chased fly balls for the ill-fated Cubs. Still, when he was on song, the Dominican slugger carried the Jays on his back. Moseby used to call Bell "unconscious" at the plate, hitting whatever dreck pitchers wasted on him as if batting was as much demonstration as competition. There was a lot of Pete Rose in Bell. He wasn't fast, but he ran the basepaths as if hurrying from a burning building. And just as Rose was known to hack at balls thrown off the plate if only to test his artistry, Bell also liked to look at a bad pitch, then reach out and club it over the first baseman's head. In 1987, you couldn't get anything past him, at least not until that final week. And even then, it wasn't so much what Bell missed as what he simply couldn't hit.

In 1987, the Jays were still widely ignored by the American sports media, despite being the team with the most wins of the decade. After a while, Canadians started to take it personally. This attitude first came to light in the 1985 post-season, when fans brought signs to the ballpark that read, BASEBALL: THE GREAT AMERICAN PASTIME, with the word *American* crossed out, and the word *Canadian* in its place. It was an unusually bold reaction from the reserved northern sports fan, but we'd grown tired of being ignored by NBC's *Game of the Week* and *Sports Illustrated* and with the U.S. media's idea of the Jays as a backwater team, even though they were first in player development – especially in the Dominican Republic, where, every year, Pat Gillick mined another gem, from Jimmy Key to Fred McGriff, Cecil Fielder to John Olerud. When, in the 1985 American League Championship Series, George Bell said, "Umpires are biased because baseball doesn't want a Canadian team in the World Series," he was only voicing what many of us suspected.

But in 1987, the Jays were simply too good to be overlooked. For the last two weeks of the season, the media finally descended on Toronto, where the American League East's second-place Detroit Tigers were set to challenge the Jays for four games at the Ex, and then another three back at Tiger Stadium. Toronto held a one-and-a-half-game lead over their Great Lakes rival, a cushion that was just thin enough to make me nervous, yet fat enough to let me dream that the team of my youth was about to ascend into the realm of baseball gods, a Big Blue Machine for the 1980s.

With the opening of the first set of games in Toronto, Jays fans saw a chance to prove that they counted. Because the Jays had beaten every team they'd faced that year – mercilessly – fans were swaggering with pride, a characteristic that was the natural result of having a home park – the Ex – where the players – both ours and theirs – were exposed to the joy or terror of the crowd. This was especially true in the bullpens, which lay along the left and right field lines. (One of the most telling features of the SkyDome, by contrast, is its high-walled bullpen stuffed into a dark corner of the outfield; not only can you not reach the athletes with your voice, you can't even see them. You have to rely on the Jumbotron to let you know what's happening inside.) One summer evening at the Ex, my friends and I, tippled on psilocybin, had our sport with Dave "Rags" Righetti, the Yankees' ace reliever. We rode him until he was called in with the bases loaded to face Bell and protect a ninth-inning Yankee lead. Rags threw Bell a pitch that he smoked over the centre-field wall, tying the game at eight. After the ump tossed Rags a new ball, he turned to us, scrunched his face into a tangle of rage, and whipped the ball into the stands, sailing it five feet above my spinning head.

It was from this section of the ballpark that I witnessed the game that I'll remember more than any other. It was September 25, 1987, game two of the four-game series versus the Tigers. Before the match, Janet and I met after work and wandered around the city before making our way to the ballpark. Something about the weight of the long summer was written into our heavy mood, and at nine o'clock – a handful of innings having already slipped away – we found ourselves in McDonald's, barely talking. I don't know why we didn't race to the park (or why we were eating at McDonald's, for that matter). Perhaps it was the heart's way of pausing, sensing somehow that it would spend the next ten days squeezed like a lemon in a vise.

We got to our seats in the bottom of the sixth to find the Tigers leading, 2-0. We'd only just settled when I witnessed the play that has stayed with me more than any other. There wasn't anything obviously heroic about it, yet when it happened, Janet and I both felt as if some great spirit had, at that moment, swooped down upon the field and lifted the darkness. It happened in an instant, and if we hadn't been drawn so deeply into every movement of every play, it might have disappeared like a leaf under a sweeping tide.

It was the quick-handed, pint-sized Manny Lee, the Jays' rookie replacement shortstop, who authored the play. Lee had been pressed into a starting assignment after Tony Fernandez was roll-blocked at second base in the first game of the series by Bill Madlock (known thereafter as "the Maggot" to Blue Jays fans) on a borderline dirty play. Tony had suffered a cracked elbow and was lost for the year. The papers reported that, as the trainers walked the stricken El Cabeza from the turf to the dugout, a brawl erupted in the left-field bleachers, the first time anyone could remember the police being called in to quell violence at a Toronto sporting event.

Fernandez's absence left a chasm at the heart of the Jays' order, and it was all we could do to pray that Lee would, if not fill Fernandez's shoes, then not fuck up. His first few at-bats were inconsequential, and if fans hadn't been watching his efforts so closely, we might have taken his sixth-inning groundout as just another X on the scoresheet. But as the ball hiccuped into the infielder's glove and was delivered assuredly to Darrell Evans, Detroit's forty-year-old first-base totem, there was something about the way Lee got down the line that sugared our hearts with hope. He pumped his legs and thrashed his arms as he ran, a blue-and-white chevron speeding towards first base. Out by two feet, he lunged at the bag, his batting cap ripped away by the force of his stride. He leapt over the base: "*Out!*" Janet and I turned to each other. We saw that Lee – and the rest of the players, their fans, their city, and their adopted country – were trying with all their will to wrench the hammer of fate away from the Tigers.

With Detroit leading by two runs, manager Sparky Anderson, the White Wave, ordered his reliever, former Cy Young award-winner and MVP Willie Hernandez, to warm up in the bullpen. I was out of my seat like a shot. I felt possessed, as if I'd been called to lay my own hands on that hammer and pull it, like an argonaut on an oar, over to our side. The Jays' security force consisted of young women in blue windbreakers, and when they saw me bound, wild-eyed, down the steps to get within spitting distance of the Tigers' ace, they politely stepped aside. I bent over the right-field rail and laid into the shaggy-moustached Hernandez as he threw his warm-up pitches.

"You're going down, Hernandez!"

"*We want you!*"

"You're *going down!*"

Exhausting myself, I ran back to Janet and watched as the Jays nibbled away at the Tigers' starting pitcher, clawing back into the game. Then back at the rail, more venom: "*It's over, Willie!*" "*We want you!*" "*I friggin' want you!*" I was in his ear. The crowd joined in, and a torrent of taunts poured over the fence.

Sparky walked to the mound with all the insouciance of your grandfather going for ice cream and called for Hernandez. We sent him into the game with a horrible roar. It was a biting night, growing colder as the wind picked up from the lake. Janet and I pressed our hands to our mouths as Manny Lee, his blue turtleneck tight to his chin, walked to the plate waving his bat, settling in to face Hernandez with a runner at second base. Hernandez, like Rags before him, tried to push our voices to the edge of his hearing, concentrating on the hitter, the catcher's glove, the growl of his manager's voice as he'd handed him the ball. After wasting a pair of pitches, Hernandez hissed a fastball into the rookie's wheelhouse. Lee swung at the ball and it jumped through the air, sailing over Alan Trammell's glove into an empty swath of centre-right field. The tiny shortstop sped around the bases, stopping at third with a game-tying triple. One batter later, he scored the winning run on Lloyd Moseby's scorcher to short, which Trammell could not tame.

As Manny Lee came home, Janet and I threw ourselves into each other's arms.

The next day, the *Toronto Sun* ran the headline: "BREAK OUT THE BROOMS!" Seven days later, *Sports Illustrated* finally put the Jays on the front cover for the first time: "TORONTO TAKES OFF!"

The Blue Jays won three games of four, but Detroit's thirteen-inning victory in the fourth game left them just alive. Three games remained to be played at Tiger Stadium.

On the day before opening night, I flew with my family to New Brunswick, to visit my stepmother's parents for the first time. They lived in an old house on the banks of Kennebecasis River in Renforth, just south of Ted Williams's favourite fishing spot on the Miramichi River, which I took as a good sign. During my first night there, I listened on a portable radio as the Tigers defeated Baltimore. It was an unsettling experience, not only because the Tigers played flawless ball against the Orioles, but because of my surroundings. Most of us fans prefer to follow our teams in moments of crisis while couched – literally – and cushioned by great, soft arms and an army of pillows, at home. In this unfamiliar Maritime house, I felt that I was orbiting away from the baseball karma that had once been so palpable.

I decided that the best way of righting my personal sporting universe would be to head for a sports bar where I might find a throng of diehard fans. At the back of a nearby bowling alley my sister and I found a tavern festooned with little Blue Jays flags. This was a great relief, and we settled in to watch the opening game, surrounded by tables of rabble-voiced Maritimers, their eyes trained on the small television mounted in the top corner of the wood-panelled room.

After a few minutes, the bowling alley's public-address system called out lane openings. One by one, everyone in the room rose from their tables and left. It was the closest to abandonment I've ever felt as a sports fan. After three innings, we were sitting alone, watching as Manny Lee stroked a three-run homer to propel the Jays into the lead. We cheered and high-fived, but soon fell into an unmoving slump of despair when the Tigers clawed back to tie – then dramatically win – the game in extra innings.

I sought out a different bar for game two. It was a thrilling, table-gripping classic. Mike Flanagan and Jack Morris matched each other pitch for pitch – Flanagan throwing 139 pitches over eleven innings, walking two; Morris hucking 163 over nine, with five bases-on-balls. Finally, in the twelfth inning, Alan Trammell skipped a Mark Eichorn sinker along the dirt, which pinged off a tiny terrestrial sasso and ducked beneath Manny Lee's glove, moving the Tigers into first place by a single game. The loss was the Jays' sixth in a row. I was cloaked in despair. I tried to lift my spirits by going for long walks alone by the river, but I couldn't shake the feeling that a curse had been laid on the Jays and their fans.

For the final game of the year, our family flew home to Toronto. The Jays needed a win to force a tie and a one-game playoff. Before the series, Sparky Anderson, baseball's master gamesman, announced to anyone who'd listen that under no circumstances would he let George Bell – whom he also buttered with hollow praise at every turn – beat him with his bat. As a result, Bell swung his stick like a man beating back shadows, determined to force Anderson's words down his throat. He refused to walk, reaching at pitches three miles outside the strike zone, and missing. The more Sparky talked, the harder Bell worked to prove that he was capable of leading his team back no matter what he was thrown. Every swing was an attempt to hit the chimeric five-run homer. After a while, Sparky ordered his pitchers to toss the occasional heart-of-the-plate fastball if only to taunt the great Latin hitter by offering hittable pitches after so much dirt junk and outside dreck. Anderson remarked after Bell's one-for-three appearance in the second last game of the year, "He missed three pitches that he usually cold cocks," before climbing back on the beam and adding, "But he's starting to swing the bat good again. We've got to remove that bat again tomorrow."

The sorrow of George Bell, Tiger Stadium, 1987.
(Courtesy of Fred Thornhill)

The game was a terrible thing to behold. It was as if a virus had overcome the league's RBI leader and greatest hitter. Every time Bell stepped to the plate, we prayed that he'd find a way to crack Anderson's mad pitching patterns. But he never did, going 2-27 over the last week of the season. "Chester" Proudfoot, the venerable *Toronto Star* columnist, said that Bell was "being fitted for goat horns." The rest of the team reacted poorly to their star hitter's frustrations, overcompensating for his lack of power and production with undisciplined swings and panic on the basepaths. Though the Jays had scored a record 845 runs in the regular season, they managed just five in the last three games against the Tigers, hitting at a .188 clip over their final seven games, each of which they lost. Without Tony Fernandez and an injured Ernie Whitt, the team counted on a young Cecil Fielder – who'd eventually hit fifty-one homers for Detroit – and Manny Lee to pick up the shortfall in runs. Of course, they could not. The season's final crippling play involved both of these players, in a game won 1-0 by Detroit. Fielder singled in the fourth inning, then took off for second on a hit-and-run called by third-base coach John McLaren. A rookie still green to the Jays' inside game, Lee missed the signal and hung Fielder out to dry. On the next pitch, the shortstop tripled to the base of the wall, driving in the phantom run that would have saved the Jays season.

I watched the last game of the year at Janet's parents' house. Nobody said much of anything. At one point, her Uncle Luciano beat his leg with his fist, muttering, "Fuckin' shit, fuckin' shit," which is what we all wanted to say. The season had once been about colour and life and melody, but it was now about the pain and embarrassment and disappointment of knowing that the entire baseball world had watched the team to whom my life was devoted crumple like a Dixie cup. After the game, forty thousand Tigers fans stood cheering their team while George Bell sat like a heavy stone figure at the top of the dugout, his back to the field. In the Jays' dressing room afterwards, Ernie Whitt told the press, "If people want to say we choked, they have every right. If anyone's happy with this season, I think they're losers. This season has been a waste. A total waste." The only consolation for fans was that the nightmare was over, which was no comfort at all.

20

THE ETERNAL GAME

The best part of travelling is being lost. Being lost leaves you standing, your heart jumping like a frog, in the corridor of a railway station, or on an empty street ignored by the cartographers of the map that you're holding up to a fly-splattered light. These are the moments you remember clearest once you've been sucked back into the soft cocoon of home. Many of us take trips on the impulse to visit the great cities and people of the world, but it's in the land of the small shadows that we learn why we left home in the first place: to engage with the lives of strangers.

Before my solo trip to Acilia – a town ten minutes outside of Rome where the local baseball community has, for the last ten years, staged a twenty-four-hour baseball day – I thought it unlikely that I'd happen upon the same thrilling corridors to which I'd been mistakenly directed in other, more exotic countries. Still, being unsure of how to get where I was going allowed me a certain tingle of possibility that, with any luck, I'd fuck things up until I felt, as one does when one is lost, adrift in the world. So, as I boarded the

Rome-bound pullman – which is what Italians call buses, a word that reminded me of the songs of Cole Porter – carrying, among other things, my Pudge Fisk bastone and Raul Mondesi guanto, it was with an eye to getting lost.

I'd travelled via pullman once before, on a return trip with the family from Rome to Nettuno. By that point, we'd traded in Janet's mother – who'd returned to Canada – for her fifteen-year-old cousin, Laura. Within a few days of arriving in Nettuno, Laura publicly declared, "I don't think I could live here, what with all the weird half-cars and wavy streets and everything." She might have added "and those annoying wildcat transit strikes," because that's exactly what we had to deal with as we tried getting home from Rome, a city notorious for mass-transit walkouts.

We'd gone to the opera the previous night: Verdi's *La Traviata*, at the Baths of Diocleziano. As my knowledge of opera consisted of repeated listenings to "Bohemian Rhapsody" by Queen, it was a revelation to watch and listen to the real deal. Of course, that didn't stop us from leaving in the intermission of the two-and-a-half-hour epic tale of consumption, after getting our fill of fat guys in tuxedos and women in long gowns pretending to sound like Freddie Mercury. Still, it was a lovely night: bats dove and slanted through the air, the sky was an ethereal blue, and, just beyond the Michelangelo sculpture garden at the heart of the baths lay Rome. The city possessed such power that there were times when I wished I could stay forever. I must have somehow communicated this sentiment to the transit authorities, for, the next day, they did their best to prevent us from leaving.

The first time we tried boarding the bus – sorry, pullman – we were pushed back to the asphalt by the horde. While waiting for the next departure, I was entertained in a nearby parkette by a small, potato-shaped man in an American bandana with a single front tooth who described, in the kind of Italian that only a man with one front tooth can speak, the nature of every video cassette he owned. Then he ran down the posters that papered his bedroom walls. It was just as he got to his "Ci sono molto CDs!" collection that, luckily for me, the next pullman pullmaned in. I hadn't noticed, but Janet told me that while he was talking to me, the two women with whom he was travelling were twirling their fingers at the sides of their heads, the universal sign for loop job.

When the bus stopped, a crowd rushed towards both sets of doors. Not wanting to get shutout a second time – and needing to be back in Nettuno – I threw my arm across the door frame and dared the Italians to bust through it. I told Laura to hoist Lorenzo over the crowd in his stroller, while Janet brayed, "Let me through! I'm the mother of that child!" Weirdly, it worked, and we all got on, and then stood for two hours in the stunning heat as the bus inched to Nettuno, stopping in every two-bit seaside town.

My pullman ride to Rome on the afternoon of the twenty-four-hour game was less dramatic, though it was not without incident. When I arrived at the metro station, an Italian soldier smoking a cigarette flatly declared that my baseball bat was a weapon, and could not be brought on the subway.

"You obviously haven't seen me hit," I joked.

He didn't laugh.

We argued for a few minutes – I in English, he in Italian – until we reached a compromise: if I tucked the bat into the bag I was carrying, he would allow it, as long as I didn't remove the bat while the train was in motion, which immediately ruled out any chance that I might practise my swing. I promised to keep the bat secured, and stepped on the train bound for Acilia. He reached for my arm and said, "No bringing golf, ever!", which gives you an idea of where the Italians stand on the grey old game.

My next problem was that I really had no idea where Acilia was. An old fellow at the bus stop in Nettuno had suggested that I disembark at the Neapolitano metro stop, but I found out the hard way that no such stop existed. At this point I had to play the "Find out how well Romans know Rome" game; naturally, I was sent in fifteen different directions. After roving around and changing among myriad trains, I finally found myself sitting on a ledge at the San Paolo metro station, waiting, I hoped, for a train to Acilia.

For the past few months, my life had been manic: following the team around town and on the road, trying to patch together some kind of writing routine, and, after ten o'clock, attempting to gather in Cecilia for bedtime, who paid respect to this schedule by running the hallways with all the calm of a shrieking banshee. Her young will had found its wings, and, overwhelmed by the sea of emotions in which she was only now learning to swim, Janet and I often awoke in the morning feeling like we'd spent the night in a bar-room brawl with George Chuvalo, were he a two-foot cherub in pink bear underpants.

So at San Paolo station I relished my independence and sudden freedom, at least until a train pulled in and took me to Acilia. Having reached my destination, I felt confident that I would easily find the diamond. Of course, I promptly became lost again. Naively, I'd assumed that the campo would be kitty-corner to the railyard, as it might be in some Iowan whistle stop. I was wrong, so I wandered around the small town – it was siesta, and there was almost no one about – and asked directions of anyone whose head wasn't buried in a cool pillow. No one knew where the field was, no one knew that a game such as baseball existed in Acilia, or existed at all. After nearly an hour of wandering, hoping that Babe Ruth was steering me from on high with a beer and a hot dog, I stumbled into a bar. Naturally, the padrone had never heard of Campo d'Acilia. It wasn't until a young fellow in beachwear stopped in for a caffeine belt that the connection between the town and Abner Doubleday was evoked. "Ah, yes. Baseball," the man said, staring at the ceiling tiles. "I played a few games of this when I was a boy," he sighed.

A few seconds later this fellow – Alfonso – assumed the role upon which all lost travellers depend: the Samaritan who will drop everything he is doing to make sure that you leave his town with a good impression. Five minutes later, Alfonso opened the passenger door of his car, telling me that he hoped I'd get "one or two double hits" and then deposited me at Campo d'Acilia, the seat of Roman baseball.

The park sat among three apartment buildings, a patch of suburban blight just ten minutes from the Eternal City. Compared to the treacherous Sardinian plain and other less managed Italian parks, however, it was a perfectly respectable dandelion patch. Its only odd feature was a temporary orange fence about twenty feet behind second base, cordoning off the deep part of the outfield. Later, families would pitch tents and stake hammocks here, waking by alarm at intervals through the night to spell off the nocturnal ballplayers and keep the game going.

My host in Acilia was Riccardo Brandi, a sixty-four-year-old grandfather with Coke-bottle glasses and a crackling smile. Riccardo spoke excellent English, which he'd learned as an employee of the local phone company, which, in 1972, was responsible for organizing the first suburban Roman baseball team, having been introduced to the game by visiting American businessmen. For any sporting community to exist – whether it's hockey in Costa Rica, yachting in Saskatchewan, or basketball in southern India – enthusiasts like Riccardo are required to hold it together. When I asked him if he had any literature on the history of Acilian ball, he produced a binder spilling with press clippings from the detritus in the back seat of his Toyota. I was amazed not only by the speed in which Riccardo found the material, but because he dared to drive Italy's dirtiest car.

Riccardo did everything that needed to be done to keep baseball alive in Acilia, from climbing the park's tall light standards to replace burnt-out bulbs and knitting together torn bits of batting cage mesh to spraying bags of red dirt around the infield, harassing the water department so that the outfield was properly irrigated, and making sure there were enough clean balls and unbent bats for every game, or enough dirty balls and bent bats for the twenty-four-hour game. He also maintained a wall in the home team's dugout that featured every newspaper story ever published that mentioned a local ball player. As I studied them floor to ceiling, Riccardo asked me if I was hungry, but I told him that I was eager to hit the dust. After I helped him carry an old table in the dugout to about ten feet behind home plate and roll out a protective batting practice screen in front of the desk, Riccardo sat down with a sigh, drew a sheaf of scoresheets from his binder, and ordered a bunch of older players, "Ragazzi! The Canadian, he would like to play now!"

After taking a few practice swings, the players realized that I was a wandering scrub and not a fading Hall of Famer come to grace their field. My mid-1970s Pudge Fisk special – which weighs in at forty ounces – gave my stroke a laboured reach, but I stayed with it, wanting to use the bat from my childhood in the country of my grandparents. I managed to get only thirteen hits against fifty at-bats over a six-hour period, but it was more than enough to be between the lines again after months of shagging flies and catching Chencho, finally tasting the grit of the dirt with strangers who shared my desperate love for the game.

In the afternoon, the Acilians played softball rather than baseball in mixed teams. My side, la squadra rossa, featured an eight-year-old second baseman and a fortyish left fielder in a brown pinstripe suit among a collection of men, women, and children in all manner of costume. Riccardo's uniform, to his credit, consisted of grand-fatherly black socks and running shoes, shorts, and a shirt with a breast pocket racked with pens.

The calibre and style of play in Acilia was no different than what I was used to at home in the Queen Street league. I was perfectly happy scooping up dinked grounders or homing in on small fly balls that looped above the infield. It was great feeling to occasionally punch the grapefruit over an infielder's head, or dig in on a line drive, trying for an extra base, maybe two. This was pretty much how the day played itself out until, during an at-bat by Riccardo's granddaughter – the third generation of Brandis to play that day – all eyes turned to the far reaches of left field where, through a gap in the fence, Valeri Ginnoso walked in.

As she crossed the field, you could tell that she occupied a place all her own in the annals of local ball. With close-cropped blonde hair, a face like a saucer of cream, and a powerful body that was one part Queen Latifah, one part Hal McRrae, there was some-thing formidable about the way she walked, taking big, slow steps, carrying her head down, her gloved hand hanging heavily at her side. Sporting the blue-and-white uniform of the Italian national women's softball team – Acilia's lone local player on any Italian national team – Val didn't immediately join our game. Instead, she settled in just beyond the first-base line and warmed up, pitching to a girl who I learned was her personal catcher, a thin-legged, gap-toothed kid in glasses and braces named Linda. They were inseparable. Riccardo told me that he'd discovered both of them while visiting one of the local high schools, where he'd lectured on the virtues of the game and had caught the battery's fancy. Linda, it turned out, watched baseball all her young life from a window of an apartment in one of the surrounding buildings. "All she needed was some help, some assistance," he said. After Val had thrown enough pitches, Linda rose from her crouch, picked up a bat, and walked to the plate while the teams were switching over, between innings. She turned around the bill of her baseball cap, bent her scrawny knees, tapped the bat to the dish, and gestured for Valeri to take the mound, which she did, striking out her friend in three pitches.

Watching me watching her, Riccardo said, "Dave. You must see Valeri's spin ball," to which Val, correcting her baseball Yoda, replied, "Not a spin. A rising change." She wheeled her arm and delivered the pill with a mighty whir. Though she called the pitch a rising change, I couldn't tell whether the ball rose or changed, because I couldn't see it. Each pitch buzzed across the air into Linda's glove, and when Val paused to offer me a quick glance over her shoulder, I nodded my head approvingly. "Great, isn't she!" said Riccardo. "Kid's got what it takes," I said, affecting my coolest roving-scout persona. "Like to see her in a real game situation, though, with real players," I added, not leaving well enough alone. Riccardo shouted to one of the local players, a young man: "Mario! Get a bat. Take some swings against Valeri for our Canadian friend!"

And so I watched Valeri pitch her heart out, whipping the ball past a young Acilian shortstop who had played as high as Serie A. There, under the heat of the Italian sun, at Riccardo's twenty-four-hour testament to what he believed was the greatest of all games, Valeri showed us what baseball meant to her: how she'd found a

way out of a typical Italian girl's life and how she'd found a battery-
mate, perhaps a lover (maybe that wasn't important; maybe it was),
who returned the ball to her on a perfect, sighing arc. At this point
I drew my book from under my arm and wrote down what I thought
I could and couldn't see: the parents and their confusion, the other
girls and their catcalls, the boys and their jokes, none of whom
would ever know, as Val and Linda did, what it meant to be an
Italian ballplayer, a female Italian ball player, let alone a butch
female Italian baseball player, let alone a butch Italian female.

Riccardo yelled, "Strike Twenty!" clapping his hands after neither
the young shortstop nor a parade of others had touched the ball.
"Dave? You think she's great now?" he asked.

"Really great," I said.

"You want to try to hit her?" he asked.

"Ah, I don't think so," I said.

Valeri turned and gave me a sharp look.

"Really, it's okay," I said.

Valeri turned and asked Riccardo, "Basta?" her chest heaving,
face flush with blood.

"Basta, e brava," I answered for him, at which Valeri waved Linda
from behind the dish, who followed her to their original position
beside the field, throwing and throwing some more.

Just before dusk, I told Riccardo that the day had provided enough
baseball to last me into the winter. I'd dreamed of experiencing the
marathon through to the end, but these days, as I pace towards my
forties, I have less rebound after hard-fought games, protracted
imbibement, or string of rock shows. I bailed on the game with
barely enough energy left to preserve my status as a mediocre North
American baseball interloper. Riccardo, the consummate host,
tossed his mitt to another player and said, "Now, I will take you,"
escorting me out of the park. I looked back beyond the orange fence

and saw tents sprouting like fungi in the outfield, small families unfolding lawn chairs and lighting barbecues, socking in for their annual long night of the summer game.

Before he drove me to the train station, Riccardo insisted that he show me Rome's first baseball field. "You've seen the Coliseum, the Vatican?" he asked me. "Yes, all of it," I told him. "I'm afraid not all of it," he corrected me. "You've not see the most beautiful of the old ballparks."

We drove about ten minutes outside of Acilia down a service road, where we parked next to a field overgrown with weeds and scrubs. It was bordered by a falling-down corrugated metal fence and an old farmhouse with a small forest in its front yard. Riccardo and I moved through the trees towards an opening in the side of the fence where a sharp metal fin had been partially torn off, revealing even deeper brush on the other side. Riccardo pulled back the fin and climbed through. Sensing my doubt that anything other than crabgrass lay beyond, he said, "Just over here. You must see it. You will not believe your eyes."

On the other side, the weeds were as high as my cap, rough, bristling rushes that whipped me as I followed in Riccardo's footsteps. After a minute or so, he stopped and said, "Look, now," drawing me up by the hand through a clearing in the grass. Straight ahead, on the other side of a ravine, lay Rome, a radiant marble jumble that looked as if it had fallen from the cradle of the sky. My eyes tracked from San Pietro's to the Coliseum to as many of the city's seven hills as I could find, raising my palm to eye level and fitting the entire city across it.

"Beneath your feet, feel it?" Riccardo asked.

"Feel what?"

"Home plate," he said. "When I first started playing, I would stand where you're standing right now and hit into that," he said, pointing at Rome. "I'd take my bat and aim, right there," he told me, gesturing towards San Pietro's gold spire.

"It's so beautiful," I said. "It's all right there."

"Yes, it is. That, that is Rome."

We stared in silence at the view, which was changing, becoming less radiant as the sky dimmed. I tried to take it all in, wanting to store the sight forever.

"Dave, you tell me this," Riccardo said, stepping back a few feet and crossing his arms. "If you played here, how would you feel?"

"Pretty great," I told him.

Riccardo laughed.

"After looking at that view with a bat in your hands, how could you not fall in love with baseball?"

21

NETTUNO AT ROMA

I returned to Campo d'Acilia with the Peones on a damp, warm Sunday in late June, a few weeks after Riccardo's twenty-four-hour marathon game. I was driven there by Pietro with Skunk Bravo and Paolo. Pietro, dressed in his Peones' blues, favoured an Italian pop-lite radio station that he inflicted upon us for the one-hour drive. Judging by his faraway expression and the tension with which he gripped the steering wheel, he was thinking too deeply about the game and how it might shake down to notice either the Italian songstress wailing over drum machines and synthesized strings, or the three of us digging our fingernails into the vinyl arm rests. We might have thought about the day ahead too, had we not been pre-occupied trying to figure out ways to get Pietro to turn off the radio without offending him. At one point, I wondered whether the music was part of Pietro's plan to make us – well, at least Paolo and Skunk – more anxious to get to the ballpark.

As we walked across the outfield, I asked Skunk, "Ti piace la musica di Pietro?" Do you like Pietro's music? The quiet little shortstop raised his eyebrows and said, "I like music, yes, but . . . ," before rolling his eyes and putting his hands over his ears. Skunk never said much, but when he did, it was in a hearty baritone that made people listen. On the rare occasions he swore – usually after a strikeout or flubbed fielding play – the invective flew hard and quick. Even if Skunk hadn't had such a commanding voice, the players would have listened to him anyway; after two months of the season, he'd emerged as the best Peones player and was quietly leading the team. Pietro understood his value too, for when Skunk's work schedule wouldn't let him be at San Giacomo for practice by 5:30 p.m., he arranged the occasional morning session for the shortstop and a handful of others.

Skunk was one of the few Peones with a nickname that described how he played his position: the Wall. That it was an English word showed how highly the team thought of him, and how much like a real ballplayer he was. The name was coined by the Emperor, and while it was meant to reflect the impregnable nature of Skunk's defence, I always thought that he played the ball more like a blanket than a brick wall, softening every hard hop by drawing it calmly into his body. Unlike Chicca, who got rid of the pill as if it were a poisonous frog, Skunk gave each ball a look of reassurance before sending it safely on its flight. While other players fought ground-balls, Skunk Bravo skipped across the dirt with the lightness of a dancer, and whenever he was forced to execute a body-length leap to catch a line drive, it was with an easy, languid grace.

When he wasn't astonishing us with his Flying Squirrel routine, Skunk was uncorking tape-measure home runs and stealing bases unchallenged. Though he stood only five-foot-seven, he had great thighs and a small, square upper body, a bundle of power that was wholly unassuming until he unwound his swing or threw out a runner from deep in the hole. His experience in A ball had instilled in him total focus with every pitch, every batter, and he had the sharpest eye of any of the Peones. A regular turn would see him either singling or taking a walk, stealing second, and scoring within a few minutes of getting on base. He was both the Peones' spark and their kindling. His presence gave Pietro a primary offensive tool with which he could manufacture runs, pencilling his name at the top of every lineup as if by rote. If I hadn't known that Skunk had been struck by the same fate as the rest of the Peones, I would have wondered what business he had slumming it with the scrubs of Nettuno.

The ballpark on the island of Ustica, where Skunk Bravo played at the beginning of his career, was the jewel of all Italian stadiums. The island itself was a tortoise-shaped mass off the northwest coast of Sicily, a fifty-minute boat ride from Palermo. Like San Francisco's Pacific Bell Park, the outfield of the island's campo di gioco backed onto the sea, where local ballplayers dived after games to retrieve lost balls. The owner of the club was a baseball fanatic who owned a popular hotel on the island and let his players stay there during the season. For Skunk Bravo and others, it was as close to a dream life as it gets for an Italian baseball player.

Things changed, however, after the owner decided that he had to rent all of the rooms in his hotel to tourists. He'd been sobered by the economic reality of running an Italian baseball club in a small city, and, soon, the team's best players were lured back to the main-land with offers from other clubs. Skunk stayed on as long as he could, remaining faithful to the person who'd signed him and given him the opportunity to play, but it was only a matter of time before he also left. Eventually, the team folded, leaving the island with a single women's softball club to compete in the FIBS. Skunk ended up in Ancona, in the Marche, where he found himself on a team in disarray. The following year, he bounced to Serie C, but the expe-rience left him cold. Unable to catch a sniff from either of Nettuno's teams, he packed it in, taking a factory job building solar panels at a plant on the other side of Steno Borghese Park, home of the Nettuno Indians, which he passed every morning on his way to work, taunted by what might have been had he been born to an earlier generation of ballplayers.

Whenever I went to see the Nettuno Indians play, I looked out at their infield and thought of who I might have been watching were the circumstances of modern Italian ball different. The starting shortstop for the Serie A club was Ryan Miller, an American. I initially scribbled his name into my bad books, viewing him as someone who was blocking the dreams of young Nettunese ballplayers. But after I got to know him, I realized that it wasn't his fault. In 2001, Ryan had been the starting interbase (shortstop) for the Pawtucket AAA Mets, but like so many other straniere, he'd ended up in Nettuno after realizing that his drive to make it to the major leagues had ended in a cul-de-sac. Not that his heartbreak was written across his face or etched in his behaviour. For the most part, he was a fountain of life, a cartoon rooster with a sharp laugh that crackled the air. Whereas most Nettunese were warm, casual, and loose, Ryan flew at you like a tomahawk, breathlessly telling stories of being coached by Tony Pena, going to Rusty Meacham's wedding, hanging with Lance Berkman. He seemed to know every 2002 major leaguer, in both leagues. I'd sometimes come across him in Piazza Colonna, spitting tobacco juice on the cobblestone with his hands tucked in the pockets of his blue jeans, speaking an even more bizarre Italo-Inglese than yours truly to a beautiful Italian woman he had absolutely no chance of scoring with.

At his farewell party at the Clare de Lune in the Borgo – a narrow, stylish bar with red velvet curtains, lit by candelabra – Janet and I listened as Ryan gave a speech to a handful of his teammates and friends. Raising a glass of "Bravo, Bravo," a confection of Jim Beam and Coke that the proprietors had named in his honour, he shouted, sloshed-faced from behind the bar, "I just wanted to say . . . tutti . . . fuckin' everybody . . . are my buds!"

Ryan was the exception among the Indians' imports – specifically the Dominicans and the Venezuelans – in that he tried to grasp as much local culture as he could (the Latin players were more insular, eating and partying as a group around town). That said, he also consumed bistecca wherever he could find it, and was always renting Hollywood films on DVD. And once the Indians' season had ended – they lost the championship in five games to Rimini, with Ryan committing two costly errors in game two – he was gone within forty-eight hours, returning to California so he could get ready for his winter gig, selling Christmas trees.

When I got to know Ryan I realized how much he and Skunk Bravo were alike, how they'd both been excellent ballplaying prospects whose journey through sport had left them on the penniless side of the chain-link fence. As fans, we're sometimes only aware of the players that we read about in the sports pages. But those who make it to the highest level are among the smallest fraction of athletes, the exception rather than the rule. When I researched the Italian and European leagues – to say nothing of the Pioneer, Northern, Gulf, Mexican, and Latin American circuits – I was astonished to find so many names I recognized: Dave Nilsson, Ed Vosberg, Lenny Randle, Hensley Meulens, Kirk McCaskill, Don August, Chuck Carr, Rusty Meacham, Rick Wise. It's easy to forget that, even though athletes drift beyond the mainstream, players play as painters paint and farmers farm. The bug that sport nurtures isn't something that can be satisfied with a mere taste of big league success. Rather, the opposite happens. The hunger becomes even greater, making the trip down all the more difficult and, at times, tragic.

Paolo's brother, Gonfreddo, had caught for the Indians for many years. He was signed as a backup to Jeff Ransom, the former San Francisco Giants bonus baby who'd been chased from their farm system after becoming involved with the daughter of the team's president. Ransom eventually returned to the States and drifted out of baseball. Around the same time, Mike Miller, an American pitcher, was signed by the Indians to spearhead their staff. But the night before the Indians' first game, Miller decided he couldn't take it any more and left for home. The team's manager was disconsolate when he heard the news. Now he had no import to pitch on the first Friday-night game, traditionally a contest between the competing teams' star import pitchers. One of Gonfreddo's teammates told the coach that he knew someone who could fill in in a pinch, so, as Gonfreddo tells the tale, "The next morning, this strange fellow with sideburns and a guitar, who looked like Elvis, walked into the clubhouse, weighed down by gold jewellery. He said something like, 'Don't worry, boys, your saviour has arrived!' and, sure enough, he went out and won for us. We were glad to have him, even though he was a very strange fellow. I think his name was Doug Cinella.

"Once, in Milan, where the train tracks sit right behind the out-field bullpen, I heard sounds and when I went to investigate, I saw that Doug was drunk and hitting fungoes at the trains going past, the sound coming from the ball hitting empty boxcars. Another time, he asked if I wanted to go along with him to a casino. I did, but left after a few hours when I ran out of money. Doug showed up at the practice the next morning looking terrible; he'd stayed up all night gambling, which I thought, you know, was a pretty foolish thing for him to do. Just as I was about to tell him what I thought, he reached into his pocket and pulled out a bundle of money. It turned out that he was a professional gambler and that he'd won an enormous amount of cash. Within in a few weeks, of course, he was gone. No one ever saw or heard from him again."

Players become nomadic for a variety of reasons. Some wander the realm of WorldBall because they think they might be able to back-door their way to the bigs through Europe (as the Cardinals' Jason Simontacchi did); some want to continue playing a game they love no matter where; some, at the end of their career, yearn to see the world and experience new cultures; others see baseball as a way of returning to, and understanding, their heritage; yet others just need to escape, to travel far enough to erase the memories of a pro life unfulfilled. But wherever the wandering minor league ballplayer plays, he's trapped between the unrequited goal of playing at the highest level and actually playing. Then again, compared to what most North Americans do for a living – and considering the number of players riding in broken-down buses through the American scrub – playing shortstop for a seaside team in one of the most charming parts of the world is an achievement in itself. The worst you could say about what had happened to either Ryan or Skunk was that they'd fallen short of their goal; otherwise, there was no reason to shed any tears for them. In Ryan's case, no other American ballplayer had had a drink named after him in a medieval town where, fifty years earlier, his countrymen had stormed the Italian coast. And that Skunk was doing what he loved was a proud memorial to the sporting dream of his grandfather's generation. It's true that both ballplayers were victims of cruel circumstance, bad luck, and the strange fate of sport, but they were also survivors playing a game they loved.

To his credit, being a top player on a lost team did little to diffuse Skunk's competitiveness. He still played as if the stands were teeming with fans. He once told me, pointing to the veins in his forearm, "Baseball here is . . . how do you say? . . . in the blood of the people." It was obvious that he treasured the opportunity to show his father, his teammates, his manager, and the visiting writer why he occupied his rung on the ladder, and why he deserved to be one step higher. It was written in the way he lifted the bat and squinted at the pitcher, in how his hands smiled when he held the ball. It was because of players like him that Nettuno baseball survived.

The first time I saw them play, the team from Roma left little impression on me. But during the Peones' second set of games against them, I realized they were no different than the many rec-league teams I'd played against in Toronto. They smoked pot, ate constantly, grabbed the occasional snooze, rode each other mercilessly from the bench, and sang and shouted at the top of their lungs whenever the action hinted at a rally, which rarely came. Those among them who could not walk, pitch, or run very well often drew the loudest cheers. The game's defining moment, I think, came when one of their veteran players, an aging, portly jock named Fabrizio who'd just suffered through two knee operations, pinch-hit and nailed a double to the gap. Moving with all the swiftness of a mule with a charley horse, he was easily gunned down by the Red Tiger, but in the dugout, the players were on their feet, waving their panini and pizza squares and crying his name.

Roma's manager resembled Harry Dean Stanton with bad teeth. During the second game, I saw him hoovering on a joint at the far end of the dugout, and as the team started to fall behind badly, you could see the idea "Hey, pitching kinda looks like fun!" dance across the psychedelia of his thoughts. He was in the game a few batters later, tossing taters for the willing Peones bruisers. In game two, Roma used nine lancetore, pulling players from around the diamond to take their turn on the hill. Despite getting hammered by upwards of forty punti, every one of their strikes was cheered by their diehard fans, who sat behind home plate on an old, cracked wooden bench.

The day's blowout came after some pretty competitive ball in the early innings of game one. The game started with Skunk at the plate, singling on the first pitch. The Roma pitcher was a fellow named Massimilliano Picca, a Chaplinesque figure with a thin, rakish moustache whose curveball flew like a sick pigeon. This slow, drooping pitch proved strangely maddening to the Peones hitters, but they still managed to rattle Picca whenever they got a runner on. You could see his confidence sag the instant that Skunk reached base. If Picca had, as I suspected, sampled some Tunisian Gold before the game, it couldn't have been the most buzz-friendly thing to have to worry about this scoring threat.

It was a vital part of Pietro's managing strategy to unsettle the opposition with basepath antics. He saw the runner's lead-off as a way of goading a pitcher, like a child repeatedly sticking his tongue out at another. Whenever Solid Gold or Mario Simone or the Natural got to second, they'd skitter, inch by inch, down the basepath, teasing the pitcher as a cat might stalk its prey. Ricky Henderson, baseball's all-time stolen-base leader, has said that, as a baserunner, he tries to become like a bug in the pitcher's brain, gouging his train of thought so that every decision is made with the creeping base stealer in mind. From the third-base box, Pietro added to the pitcher's anxiety by repeating, in a flat, clipped voice, "Vienni, vienni, vienni." Come, come, come, drawing the baserunner down the line.

Pietro had taught his baserunners to hide in a low crouch with their arms spread like a surfer squeezing under the crest of a wave. "When you're standing straight up, the pitcher sees you when he looks over, but, when you get down, down," he explained, "the pitcher can't see you. He has to look way back, and he gets angry because he can't."

So, Skunk Bravo, his arms reaching out like a small plane, stole. Picca, altogether flustered, threw the ball high and wide to his catcher, who leapt out to make a base-saving catch. Picca tried to turn his concentration to the hitter, Solid Gold, who sensed the pitcher's tension and rapped the ball to centre field, his first of four hits that day. Skunk trotted home before Chicca worked a walk, the Big Emilio grounded out to move the runners over, and Mario Simone, holding his bat high as if about to dust a chandelier, doinked a pitch into centre field. On first, Mario slapped his hands together, pulled the batting helmet low over his head, then crept down the line again.

After scoring twice to jump into the lead, Pompo took to the hill to face the Romans. He had command of his heat early on, but after poorly fielding a sure third-out tapper, he allowed Roma their first baserunner. Two batters later, Vincenzo Giordano stepped to the plate, saw a pitch that he liked, and launched it over the right field fence. The entire Roma dugout spilled on to the field. Giordano's belly jiggled as he chugged around the bases, and leaving home plate, he was mobbed by his teammates, who led him back into the dugout. On the mound, Pompo fired the ball into his mitt and kicked the earth, swearing. Pietro reminded him, "Esterno! Keep it outside!" but Pompo pretended not to hear.

In the Peones' bottom of the second, Picca threw a low strike that the umpire called a ball and Harry Dean Stanton dashed to confront the arbitro. I'm not sure what was said during their argument, but had I been Harry Dean wanting to get the umpire's goat, I would have started with his fashion sense, or lack thereof. Dressed in grey flannels and dark blue shirts, the FIBS umpires were the worst-dressed men in all of Italy, or at least the most uninspired. If it wasn't bad enough that their pants made them look bloated and dumpy, their chest protectors gave the impression of sagging male cleavage. It's no wonder they got very little respect in the world of ItaloBall.

Harry Dean kicked dirt on the ump's shoes before settling down and returning to the dugout, at which point Chicca reached out and clubbed a ball into left, tying the game. In the Roma half of the inning, they put men at second and third with one out, and the next hitter ground a ball to the sleepy-eyed third baseman. As he bent down to grab the ball it hit the bag and was punted in the air over Chicca's head. With the bases loaded, Chicca walked the ball to Pompo and uttered a few strong words. The young pitcher folded into his windup and the Peones bench suddenly screamed, "*Squeeeeeeeze!*"

The Roma batter squared to bunt, and pushed the ball up the line, driving in the go-ahead run: 5-4. There was singing and cheering and more smoking in the Roma dugout; silence in Nettuno's. "Concentrate . . . use your head!" Pietro yelled to Pompo. "*Tanto tempo . . . molto baseball per oggi, va bene?*" One batter later, the Big Emilio, calling for a pitch-out, gunned down the runner at third for the final out. Mirko bounced out of the dugout and stood on the lip of the field, hugging his crotch with his hand and yelling to his teammates to pull it together.

Slowly, things turned the Peones' way. They began timing Picca's slow curve, spraying hits all over the field. A wide throw to first base from the Roma third baseman sent his infielder spinning around like a clockhand as the Emperor, digging from second base, rounded third and came home to score, his chest heaving and his face beet red. The Red Tiger roared, "*Grande cazzo!*" The Peones had bounced back and by the end of the inning, they'd scored six runs, taking the lead, 10-5, before coasting to a victory, 13-7.

After the game, Mirko asked, "Davide, you come with us and eat?" I told him that I would, then spotted Paolo hiking his kit bag over his shoulder, carrying his spikes in his hand.

"You're going to eat?" I asked.

"No, Dave, no."

"Per che?"

"I think I should go home to study."

I looked at him. Tears were tugging at his eyes.

"Oh, Paolo, no . . ."

"Si. I feel very bad. This is very disappointing for me," he said.

"You want me to go talk to Pietro? I've got nothing to lose. I'll go talk to him now," I said.

"Dave, please, no. I must go. It's okay."

"If you go now, you might not play again," I told the veteran catcher. "You'll be sending a message to Pietro that you don't want to be part of the team. You'll make it easy for him to cut you."

"You don't know what it's like, to sit and stare," he said. "I just want one at-bat, one inning in the field."

"Sure, I know. I know what it means to be left out. It friggin' sucks," I said. "But listen, there wasn't any way you were going to play in game one anyway. Pietro, lui è testa dura, vero? He uses the same nine for the start of every game, no matter what. That's that. It's the way it is. If you were ever going to play today, it was going to be in the second game. Don't go, c'mon."

"Dave, really," he said, edging past me.

"I'm telling you," I said, appealing to the sensibilities of the one Peone who'd read a book or two in his life, "you don't want to have to sit down in twenty years and read about how you left the team after the first game against Rome and never returned. Of all the Peones, Paolo, I want to keep you in my story. You're important to it."

Paolo's forehead wrinkled in thought.

"Upht," he said, drawing a deep breath. "For now, I stay. But I hope you are right."

A few hours later, the Peones and I returned to the park after dining in a nearby strip mall, where we put away four roast chickens, a pile of risi e bisi, much salsiccia, a tub of fried eggplant and zucchini, a couple of pizza, a tray of french fries, and a tankard of Fanta Orange. There were coffees and smokes afterwards and a bottle of cacchione, which Chencho and I decided we had to finish. I was rubber-legged coming away from the table, and sitting in Pompo's car listening as he played full blast his favourite CD, the music from *Gladiator*, I felt perfectly zinged, ready for an afternoon of Italian hardball.

I straightened out after an hour under the sobering heat of the sun, but after reviewing my scoresheet later on, I saw that Roma-Nettuno 2 was a blur of black arcs and smudged scrawl. When I first accepted the job of scoring after Peter Calabro's dismissal, I had an "Anything for the team!" attitude towards my task. But after a while, it became kind of a bother. I'd get too wrapped up in the drama of the events to mark down what had happened until many innings later, when I'd have to retrace my steps to make sense of the events. This made for many confused squiggles and arrows shooting across the page, more napkin doodle than scorer's official document.

All told, there wasn't much need for stats-keeping in game two, anyway, won 42-5 by Nettuno. Chencho started and was effective in shutting down the Roman stoners, who were even more slovenly and slow after the feast of pasta and fish that had been prepared for them. Despite the absence of an opposition, Chencho still argued almost every ball called by the umpire. Frustrated at not having his best stuff – he threw every sixth pitch over the Big Emilio's head – he'd come down off the mound and throw his arms out before being ordered back up the hill. This routine elicited roars of laughter from the Romans, which only served to piss off Chencho even more, which, in turn, angered the Big Emilio, who had to chase pitch after pitch. He pulled off his mask more often in this game than the Phantom of the Opera does in a year.

With Nettuno winning by twenty runs, Pietro pulled the Black Aces into the game, much to their delight and my relief. Finally, Paolo was in the game, and even Mirko was subbed at second base, where he promptly lined into a double play, followed by an error at second. His penchant for rally killing, however, didn't seem to

Pitò the Stricken.
(Cathy Bidini)

bother him, nor his teammates. After flubbing his throw, he walked over and put his arm around the Big Emilio, whom Pietro had moved to first base, inserting Paolo to catch for Pitò the Stricken, making his first appearance of the year.

While I felt good for both players, I was more happy for Pitò than Paolo, who'd already found glory in Sardinia. After the Aces' moanfest at Coco Loco, Pitò had come to my house to show me photos from his early baseball days when he was a young, svelte man with a full head of hair, wearing the Tricolori of the Italian national junior team. He had pictures taken all over Europe: photos of him winning great trophies, striking out feared batters, hitting home runs, being carried by his teammates across the field. I couldn't believe it was the same person. The question that I wanted to ask, but couldn't – at least not outright – was, What happened, man? But, without my prompting, he told me.

"I was asked by Nettuno, Serie A, the Indians, to join their team. Of course, it was my dream. They were training me to become a starter, working me mostly in the bullpen. I went to practice every day, worked out, had a locker in the dressing room, got to know the players whom I'd watched all the time as a kid. It was wonderful.

"I got into my first game in relief at Steno Borghese with my whole family there. The field was so beautiful, so green and red, the night sky above . . . perfect. I pitched for two-thirds of the inning, and my heart was jumping through my uniform. But I did okay. When I got back to the dugout, everybody congratulated me. I was eighteen. It was the highlight of my life.

"But a few days later when I was warming up, I heard this *pop* in my shoulder. I thought nothing of it and kept throwing until I couldn't throw any more. I had to stop or else risk further damage up here," he said, running his hand over his rotator cuff. "At first, the Indians were very good about it. They said, 'Just relax for a while, and take your time, you'll be fine.' I thought it would only be a matter of months, but it never went away. Still, I thought that, maybe after the winter, I'd improve and pitch again. I showed up for practice the next year, ready to try to pitch when they told me to give back my uniform. I asked, 'I'm still a part of this team, aren't I?' They said that, yes, I was, but that I could no longer keep my uniform. I don't know why they did this, but I was embarrassed, humiliated. That was the last time I ever stepped through that door."

"How important is it for you to show them that you can still pitch?" I asked.

"Oh, tanto, tanto," he said. "Even more because questo anno, this year . . . is my last."

"Your last?"

"Yes. Baseball, after now, is over for me."

To be honest, Pitò the Stricken flailed rather than pitched. His arm appeared to extend only half as far as it was supposed to. Knowing that Pitò had once been an ace prospect for the Indians made his performance difficult to watch, even though his curveball hummed with authority and his change kept the Romans hopping. But overall, the scene wasn't pretty. Showing the class and grace of a good manager, Pietro never stopped coaching Pitò from the sidelines, but the fallen ace just stared into the dugout as if his coach's advice was a mere nuisance. Pitò affected the same arrogance that he'd used as a weapon in the days he ruled the mound, but here, it came across as posturing and bad attitude. Once, after coming into the dugout, he laid in to Paolo for his pitch selection. After a disappointing inning – disappointing only to Pitò, for the game was well in hand – the pitcher threw his hat on the dugout floor and stared into space. His sulk was his way of telling his teammates that he refused to accept what he'd become, and what his baseball life had delivered. Fortunately for the Peones, Skunk continued to play the game as if every at-bat were his last, Mario Simone was as eager as a hound at a hunt, and Fab Julie competed as if baseball were more an amusement than a contest. Everyone had his own way of dealing with whatever hard-bitten card he'd drawn. Some dealt with the game and its trials better than others.

Paolo had an unrequited day at the plate and in the field. He was twice plonked in the shoulder and ribs by pitches, due spacca denti. In his third at-bat, he crushed the ball towards the left-field wall. It zoomed over the heads of the infielders and appeared headed over the fence, but, all of a sudden, its flight path tugged to the left, just so. The arc was wrong. It was foul.

The slugger swore to himself for the duration of his at-bat, then parroted his frustration over the rest of the afternoon. He brought it up with me after the game, saying, "It was this close. This close."

"It's like what you said before," I reminded him.

"What did I say?"

"You said that you've got to celebrate when good things happen because the difference between a home run and a foul is . . . this," I said, indicating the breadth of fate.

"Yes, I remember," he said.

"You said something else."

"What was that?"

"'That's baseball.'"

"Me, I am so stupid."

"Yes, very stupid."

"Oh, baseball!" he cried, throwing up his hands.

22

MIKE THE DUCK MUST DIE

When we first invited Laura Lunetta, Janet's teenage cousin, to Nettuno to help in the bouncing of Lorenzo and the lariat-roping of Cecilia, Janet and I thought back to our own enchanting experiences as naifs forced into the world. But almost as soon as Laura arrived, she reminded us instead of other things, like how good it feels to lie in bed in the dark at midday wearing headphones and reading *Seventeen*. I'd also forgotten what a lost art form indolence is as you lean into your child-rearing years. Janet and I learned fast that fifteen isn't eighteen – not even with the Internet – and discovered that Laura disliked seafood ("Uh, I don't really like fish") and surf ("Salt water . . . it's gross. I don't think I'll go in the water"). After a few days watching her skulk around the house, the words *You'll eat your fish and damned well like it!* climbed in my throat. But they were trapped by my tongue, which was just as well, otherwise I might have started using phrases like *the rock and the roll* and *they showed it on the television*, growing old in an instant.

Laura arrived with CDs featuring the likes of Jay-Z, Aaliyah, and dozens of other artists I'd never listened to before. I tested most of

Mario Simone.
(Cathy Bidini)

her music, but she held back one disc that, she said, was "only beats.
You probably won't like it." I decided against telling her that she
was talking to a man who'd once sang a vocal track to a skillsaw,
and to let her be. And then she dropped the baby.

Lorenzo was sent flying while Laura tried to navigate the stroller
over the marble lip at the foot of our palazzo. While our padrone
frantically drove Janet and Lorenzo to the hospital – where the
doctor decided it had been a soft bounce, and everything was still
where it should be – Laura locked herself and Cecilia out of the
apartment. Later that evening, as we were all sitting around at the

Gabbiano, she swept her arm across the table, sending a trayload of crystal desert cups shattering to the cobblestone. It was not a good day, not a good start to her visit.

Laura's trip improved the minute Mario Simone arrived on the scene, riding in from the sunset, shirtless, on a motorino. I had expected the team's youngest players – Christian and Francesco – to come buzzing by Nettuno's newest flower, but with the exception of Chencho's pro-forma overtures and Fabio from Milan's invitation to join him on a tour of the Borgo, the team showed little interest, proving that the Peones were even more dysfunctional than I had imagined. When Pitò the Stricken heard me lamenting the state of the Peones' youth, he stepped up to the plate, offering to take Laura out.

"Thanks, but I think she would relate better to the younger players," I told him.

"How old?" he asked.

"You know: between seventeen and twenty-two."

"Ow! How old do you think I am?"

"Hmmm . . . twenty six?"

"Cazzo! I am twenty-two!"

From that moment forward, Pitò constantly petitioned me to let him take Laura out ("He's nice, but . . . ," said Laura. "He's weird!" "Weird, how?" "I dunno. He's old, isn't he?") Finally, one evening Paolo, his girlfriend, Francesca, Laura, Pitò, and I went to Coco Loco for a drink, followed by a tour of the sea wall. Paolo spent much of the evening trying to pair Laura with Pitò. I deflected as much as I could as, a week earlier, I'd seen Pitò at the train station with a pretty girl he'd claimed was his steady girlfriend.

The concept of girlfriend/boyfriend in Nettuno was both loose and tight at the same time. Couples who'd been dating for a few years were seen as being engaged, though this was mostly an excuse to allow them to travel together, which is to say, to fare l'amore without the Pope sending the boys around. Since most people under the age of thirty-five still lived at home, on many nights the streets were filled with necking couples, due to a chronic shortage of love pads. On a train ride from Rome I sat next to a woman who was concerned about leaving her son to entertain his girlfriend while she and her husband spent the night away. Her son was thirty years old.

In contemporary Italy, there's a condition known as *mammismo*, a word for men who still live at home. Both marriage and birth rates in Italy had dropped radically and mammismo was blamed by many for this decline. The Italian male, it seemed, was much too content with his home life to move out, marry, and make bambinos. Even after marriage, many couples opted to live in one of their parents' houses, keeping the family together, and keeping the matriarch cooking and cleaning and cooking some more. Chencho had done this, and Pietro was building a new home that would accommodate both of his kids and their families, should they have them.

Perhaps because most single men and women lived under their parents' roof, Nettuno, like most of Italy, was heavy with sexuality, much of it repressed, but much of it not. This dichotomy of sexual freedom and sexual repression was apparent in small ways too. One afternoon, Janet stopped in at the local tabacchi to buy matches for our stove. The shopkeeper reached under the counter, pondered what might best fit the needs (and, apparently, the desires) of my wife, and handed her a box, which Janet neglected to study closely. It was I who noticed that the box bore a mock-Raphaelite scene featuring six or seven naked maidens. On first glance, they appeared to be cavorting in a swimming hole, but after staring at it intensely – in the interests of research – I realized the painting featured the kind of untoward behaviour that would make even k.d. lang blush. There was much licking and massaging in all the wrong – er, right – places, and behind the maidens sat a figure I took to be Neptune, bending forward on his throne, and, uh, taking the situation into his own hands, or rather, hand.

Before coming to Italy, one preconception I had of Italian men was that they perpetually ogled (some might say harassed) women. But in Nettuno, there was a serious lack of wolf whistling and bum-grabbing. I wondered whether all of those years of, purportedly, melting women with the bat of an eyelid had left the Italian male a little tired, maybe a little bored. So, when Mario started to spritz his cologne around Laura, I wondered whether we were about to see the Italian male behaving as the world portrayed him. As it turned out, Mario almost singlehandedly attempted to compensate for his countrymen's lack of ambition. At the pool party at the Emperor's, he told me that he thought that Laura looked "very lonely, very sad." It wasn't long after that that he flew up our marble staircase in his silver sunglasses, wearing the world's tightest T-shirt and five-shades-of-faded-blue jeans, and liberated the young pup from the viselike grip of her substitute parents. At first, this was all well and good until we discovered that, instead of touring the Borgo, as promised, with his sister, Melania, Mario had taken Laura to a disco in Lavinio where the roof opened to reveal the moon and the stars. Worse, she had the time of her life.

The next morning, Mario called twice, in rapid succession, to talk with Laura. On their second conversation, she carried the phone into an empty room. In the following days, the more she and Mario talked, the less Laura told us. I was under strict instructions from Laura's parents – her father, Sal, a Sicilian, was opposed to his daughter dating until she turned eighteen – to monitor any romantic developments, and I immediately recognized Mario Simone was a speedster in more ways than one.

On the plus side, I was able to learn about Mario's home without going there. Laura was an excellent mole. She told me that Mario shared a room with Melania, who was sixteen, and that, above his bed, there was a big picture of him as a baby with an unlit cigarette sticking out of his mouth. They hung out a few times after their disco date – occasions that also involved Melania and a few of her friends – and when Mario announced that he was going to Rimini with Daria, the woman I'd thought was his steady girlfriend, I was grateful that things were cooling down. But really, they were only heating up.

When Mario got back from his holiday, he called Laura to say that he'd bought something for her on his trip. ("I drove all day, for six hours, but I wanted to see you before I went to sleep.") Janet bet us any money that it would be a bear in sunglasses wearing a T-shirt with the word *Rimini* across it. As it turned out, she was wrong: it was a duck in red shorts, named Mike, or so it said on its chest. "Laura, you like?" asked Mario, presenting it to her in the dim light of our sala d'altesa, Janet and I looming over them like sentries. "Ya, it's cute," said Laura, smiling as if she'd just been poinged by the mallet of teenage love and running her fingers through Mike's lawless yellow mohawk.

After Mario left, Laura trilled, "Guys in Nettuno are so nice!" using the plural, but implying the singular. "Back home, the only time they ever speak to me is to say, 'Hey, don't eat in my car.' Here, they go on trips and buy you gifts and stuff." I reminded her, tenderly, that a plush duck ranks only slightly above a tin of paper clips on the gift scale, but Janet had another take on Mario's token.

"You know what this means, don't you, Laura?"

"No," she said.

"It means you're engaged."

Laura put her face in her hands and laughed the oh-my-god-an-Italian-boy-just-bought-me-an-engagement-duck giggle. Then she excused herself and went to bed.

Being in the position of having to impart a few words of wisdom – or warning – to Laura as she sat perched on the precipice of an international romance was not something I'd bargained for. It's not anything that any parent – surrogate or otherwise – really wants to do. My father, on the eve of my trip to Dublin, pulled me aside and told me not to leave any Irish babies behind, which only served to remind me that there were girls in Ireland, not just dusty rooms with old books where Joyce used to sit and write. Before talking to Laura, I thought I'd run the scenario by the Old Bugger, but he waved it off, saying, "Mario has a fiancée, Daria. They are going to get married. This is a very good couple." After I suggested to Laura that Mario was poised to make his big move, she insisted, "No, he's got a girlfriend. They're going to get married. Don't you trust me? Why doesn't anyone trust me?"

Janet and I let things slide because Laura was, finally, having a great trip. One morning she told us that she could live in Nettuno after all. Later that day, while we were strolling around town, she stopped us, pulled out her camera, and posed for a picture in front of one of those "weird" half-cars. "Aren't they cool?" she exclaimed. But this new cheerfulness came at a price; before we knew it, the romance had spun beyond our control. Later that night, she returned from hanging out with Mario and reported that Daria had been absent because, "Mario told me they're having problems. He said that things have been pretty rough for a while." While walking past the marina, he also had told her, "It is very beautiful by the water. It is even more beautiful with you here." A few days later, it got worse. "It is over between Daria and I," Mario announced to Laura. "We have broken up. I can't be with her any longer. She doesn't like to laugh and have fun, not like you."

After we heard that, Janet and I sat Laura at the kitchen table and told her what we thought the speedster was doing. However carefully my words had been planned (they were, more or less, a variation of the "Don't leave any babies behind" theme), I still sounded like an old walrus as I waved Mike the Duck and yelled, "Engaged! Do you want to be engaged to someone who thinks you'd actually like this?" Laura replied, "I'm tired. I want to go to bed, okay?" That's the last time she talked to me.

A few weeks after Laura returned home, we got a call from her from Toronto. It turned out that Mario had been phoning her almost twice a day. The last time, she said, "He held up the phone to the stereo and played me all of these slow, romantic songs." She asked Janet, "Do you think you could get Dave to ask Mario to stop calling me?" I told her that I'd have to go lie down in a room with the lights off and think about it. What I didn't have the heart to tell her was that, a few days after she'd left, I'd seen Mario lounging at the beach with Daria, and that she'd been present at most Peones games and events. If Laura was to escape her Italian adventure feeling as giddy as she had when she'd left, serious measures had to be taken. It was quite simple.

Mike the Duck would have to die.

23

SALERNO AT NETTUNO

Each home game began for me with Pietro leaning on his horn outside the apartment. He would arrive obsessively early to take me to the park, decked out in his Peones colours. I'd shuffle sleepily down our marble corkscrew staircase in my shorts and Peones shirt, dragging a bag weighed down with my glove, scorebook, tape recorder, notebook, and a green apple, which I never ate. We would head straight to the Cafe Volpi for our morning espressos. We'd find two espressos with a macchiato dollop and a pair of warm brioche waiting for us, because Pietro was an old friend of Cafe Volpi's padrone – Pietro was an old friend of everyone's.

Once we'd finished at Volpi, Pietro and I made our way to San Giacomo, where Pietro busied himself inside the clubhouse while I took my spot either on the bleachers or in the empty dugout. At this time of the morning, the campo was the sole domain of the birds. I'd sit quietly and listen to the light chirping of sparrows, a rooster's cry carrying across the ravine, or watch a swoop of swallows playing in the sky. The day would slowly unfold as if in the hands of a painter. First, the artist laid in the bright green of the field, next the golden sunlight, then the dark, ruddy clay, and finally the blue and white of the players, crossing the grass. Not once did I notice any of the Peones in a pre-game meditation. Instead it was all playful rabble – cazzo this and managia that – as they waltzed around each other while devouring the mandatory pastries and vials of coffee.

On road trips, the fellows passed through airport security armed with foil-wrapped panini made by their mothers, lovingly jammed with combinations of prosciutto, salami, cheese, figs, tomatoes, artichokes, peppers, and basil. And when the boys weren't laying into their sandwiches, they were eating pizza – delicious, flat, hard-crusted squares brushed with olive oil, basil, and slices of pomodoro – which someone's mother had made for the team and their fans. Mind you, this is only what I saw. What I didn't see were the Sunday feasts prepared for them during home dates. After the first game, they'd pile into their cars and race off for a delicious six-course meal, cooked lovingly by their mamas.

On the Friday afternoon before the team's next game against Salerno, Cobra – whose wife had just given birth to their first son, Gabrielle – showed up with two pizzas and half-a-dozen bottles of Fanta Orange. After practice, we destroyed the pizza, which was topped with zucchini flowers and anchovies at one end, black olives and prosciutto at the other. And then we all went home and ate dinner. For other team meals, we dined at Peyotes or at the vineyard of a friend of the team, where Emilio seared bistecca and thick strips of pancetta in a brick oven, while Daria, Mario Simone's girlfriend, served pasta al olio con pepperoncini, as elegant as it was simple. Each time, the Peones followed these meals with excellent Sunday games, so Cobra made sure we had a day of bread-breaking before going to battle against Salerno, the one team that stood in the way of the Peones making the playoffs.

I went one better, wrangling an invitation for the family and I to dine at Mario Mazza's house on the Saturday prior to the game. I did this because, following Nettuno-Roma at San Giacomo, Mario had come up to me and said, excitedly (he only ever said things

Mario Mazza.
(Cathy Bidini)

excitedly): "You want to come over to my house for pranzo? The whole team's going! C'mon, I'll drive you there!" Of course, he said this in Italian, but I got the gist. Well, at least I thought I did. But it turned out that he'd actually only offered to drive me so that I could eat my lunch at home. But eat at Mario's we did, if a month later than I'd expected.

Mario's whole family had gathered for dinner on the balcony of the modest third-floor apartment – Mario, his mom and dad, his aunt, his sister and husband and their five-year-old daughter. After the meal, Mario and his father, 'Nando, brought out their photo albums, and proceeded to walk me through – as Pitò had – the boyhood of a Nettuno baseball prodigy.

They were typical photos; they could have been of any kid who's ever lived to play, his talent and drive and determination accelerating at every stage. Only, of course, the images that we flipped through were of ballfields in Sicily, Sardinia, Rimini, and other points on the Italian baseball map. There were boyhood pictures of Fabio from Milan, the Big Emilio, Pompozzi, Pitò, the Natural, and the Emperor, who had grown up playing baseball together with Mario in San Giacomo. Then, at one point, the photo story made a powerful leap. Suddenly, I was staring at Shea Stadium, at a picture of Mike Piazza walking to the batting cage.

Mario had been picked, at seventeen, to play for the Italian national junior team, and, along with Pompozzi, he'd travelled to the Babe Ruth tournament in Stamford, Connecticut. Mario was the team's starting second baseman and occasional outfielder. The kid could play anywhere; he was a prospect, pure and simple. For Mario, the trip had been a dream. The Mets had invited the boys down to the field, and had let them prowl around the batting cage. Mario had his picture taken with Mike Piazza, but the photographer had been so struck by the presence of the great catcher that only Mario appeared in the frame. The arm that hung around his shoulder could have been anyone's, but the memory of the day was still there. Still, it was the tournament itself that mattered most. The Italians, while still many years behind their American cousins, surprised a lot of fans and scouts (the stadium was filled with them for every game) with their level of play, and in their first match against the hosts, Stamford, they set the tourney on its ear, babying an 8-7 lead going into the ninth.

The Italians, led by Pepe Massanti, who would later be drafted into the Seattle Mariners system, bore down in the ninth, but the hosts rallied and tied the game at 8, pushing it into extra innings. The teams remained even in the tenth, but in the bottom of the eleventh, a Stamford batter cracked a hit to right field, where Mario had been restationed from second base. The ball dropped out of his range, and he chased it. By this time, the batter was barrelling between second and third, and as Mario caught the ball in his bare hand, the runner made his move: he would try to win the game on an inside-the-park home run.

Mario threw what he thought was the perfect throw. He wasn't wrong. The ball screamed midwaist into the catcher's mitt, and the runner arrived a fraction of a second later. The catcher swept his arm behind him, but the runner swivelled his waist and evaded the tag. His body tumbled across the plate: 9-8, Stamford. The next day, a photo of the home team celebrating on the field graced the cover of the local paper. Mario had done his best, but it was not enough. And as we sat there on the balcony wondering how the catcher had missed the tag and why the runner had dared to score and pondering the differences between winning and losing and how it's often an eyelash that separates sporting joy from grief, Mario pulled out the front page of that newspaper and pointed to the photo with pride, as if to say, I was part of this. I was there when it happened. So far, it had been the highlight of Mario's baseball life.

After the tournament in Stamford, he'd been signed by Serie A Anzio, Nettuno's old rivals. It was the same for him as it was for most young Nettunese ballplayers: they dreamed of reaching the highest level of baseball in Italy, Serie A. But it hadn't worked out for Mario. He told me at the dinner table, his smile flatlining, "Sometimes you'd go to practice, and the coach wouldn't even make you part of the drills. Only the starters would practise, nine players. I'd show up at the park and work hard, but it was as if the coach didn't even know who I was. It was awful. I never played, never. It was like they weren't interested in seeing if I could play at the highest level. After the second year, I told my father that I was finished with baseball. I was this low," he told me, chopping his ankle with the side of his hand. "Afterwards, I couldn't even look at my glove," Mario told me, staring into his hand. "And then, the Peones . . . ," he said, opening his arms as if to hug the air. I recalled that the Natural had played with Mario at Anzio, and that his experience had left him sour too. When I asked the Natural to compare their experiences, he said that there was one difference: "Me, I stayed with Anzio and played out the year. But Mario, Mario was asked to leave."

The team from Salerno (known as the Thunder, even though *Granchio* volunteered a couple of extra letters, printing their name as the "Thundhers") were the spitting image of the Peones. Not only were they the only other Serie B team with a nickname (though not the best nickname; that honour went to the Lido Old Rags in Serie A2), but their uniforms might have been ordered from the same garment-maker. The typeface used on their shirts was the same, and so was the design of their vests, which were royal blue and gold. There were no untucked shirts or mismatched socks. Like the Peones, the Thunders were proud and professional. As they strode to the visitors' dugout with their matching blue-and-gold coolers and batting helmets – carried, no less, by a bat boy dressed in blue-and-gold sweats – it struck me that, more than any other team so far, Salerno had the look of a team who'd come to play.

They'd shown up with a guy in shorts carrying a notebook. He hung out in their dugout and wrote feverishly whenever the Thunders were at bat. He also fetched errant balls, slapped players on the behind when they needed encouragement, made jokes, and whispered with the coach. When he strode into the visitors' dugout and helped himself to his team's pastries, I realized that I was staring across the field at my evil twin.

In previous games, I'd tried to manufacture good old-fashioned sporting hatred for the opposition, but it was hard to do with small teams like Sardinia and Acilia. But with Salerno, it was easy. By trying to stop Nettuno from advancing to the playoffs, the Thunders were, in effect, trying to end my season. With this in mind, I wanted nothing more than for the Peones to vanquish them and their scribbler.

There was another reason why I thought they were aligned with the dark side: judging by their track record, they were a group of hotheads. In a game earlier that year against the Peones, one of their pitchers had balked home the winning run. According to Paolo and others, the infraction had been obvious – at least as obvious as an oblique balk can be – but this hadn't stopped the player from taking matters into his own hands. After the call, he charged the home-plate umpire, and the two squashed noses until another Thunder player and the Salerno manager joined the fray, wrestling the umpire to the ground. All three men had been hit with a three-year league suspension, leaving Salerno managerless and with a thin bench for the duration of the 2002 season.

From the very beginning of the campaign, Salerno had carried themselves with great promise, their hopes fuelled by the two Dominican ballplayers they'd hired to help them win Serie B. But, by mid-season, it was clear that their game plan – sign a few ringers and play as if you own the league – was a resounding failure. Neither Dominican player had made the trip to Nettuno. There were whispers about team dissension and unpaid fees.

The last time they'd played, Salerno had handed Nettuno their lunch, stepping all over the nightclubbing Peones. Knowing this, Salerno's confidence must have equalled their hope, though the team they'd beaten had been a mere glimmer of what it was now. That Nettuno knew this, and Salerno didn't, swung the advantage back to the Peones, though there was pressure both ways. If Nettuno lost, they might still advance with some help from other clubs; their Southern Italian rivals needed to win twice to keep their post-season dreams alive. The future of each team's 2002 baseball program would be determined in these two games. As the teams warmed up in opposite corners of the field, maintaining a safe distance from one another, I stopped trying to read where the pressure fell the heaviest. For both teams, it simply fell hard.

Cobra would start the first game. This was good news – and bad news, as the veteran's health was covered in more question marks than the Joker's unitard. He was still bothered by his strained bicep, and during practice, he'd broken open a blister between the second and third finger on his pitching hand. On top of that, Cobra was exhausted from a week of pacing around with his newborn child and it was a sizzling hot day, hot enough to exhaust even the fittest pitcher.

As usual, Solid Gold was nowhere to be found. The day before, Pietro had ordered his team to be at the field by eight to prepare fully for the big game. Solid Gold had told him that was impossible; he couldn't be there before nine-thirty. Pietro relented, but by game time, he hadn't shown. This forced Pietro to tinker with his lineup, and as he stared at his empty lineup card, his thoughts moved towards a player he hadn't started all year:

DANNA, DH.

Paolo was in.

Skunk batted first, followed by the Natural (who was taking a turn at primo base, the Emperor having played himself out of the lineup by missing a week of practices), Chicca, the Big Emilio, the two Marios, the Red Tiger, Fab Julie, and Paolo in the nine hole. In Solid Gold's absence, this was the best lineup the Peones could field.

The day started poorly for Cobra. Before they'd gripped a single bat, the Peones were behind. In the first inning, Salerno's dashingly named Vincenzo D'Addio belted a three-run homer to straight-away centre. The ball had more air time than Larry King. D'Addio had played in Serie A2 for Caserta the previous year and was known to devour small-ball diritti, so when Cobra cruised his pitch a little too deep over the dish, D'Addio made him pay.

Guiseppe Mele, the Salerno pitcher, was Cobra's opposite. He wore red-tinted sunglasses and couldn't stand still for a minute. While staring in for his sign, he held his glove close to his face and all you could see were his sunglasses floating underneath the brim of his hat. Once he started his windup, he was a flash of body parts, displaying a quick, high leg kick – alzare la gamba.

Mele's moves were unsettling – even a little sinister – and they seemed to cast a spell over the Peones. Although he had only two pitches – fastball, curve – and, despite Pietro's admonition that

Mele was nothing more than a batting practice pitcher, he gave the Peones fits. The team answered D'Addio's homer by scoring two runs in the second (3-2, Salerno), but they also hit a lot of balls off the fist. Mele's busy pitching technique – not to mention his sublime curveball – was keeping the Peones' batters off balance, even when the ball hung in front of them like soap on a rope.

The Old Bugger's response was to keep hammering at his team: "*Stop swinging for the fences! These errors are killing us! You see what happens when you leave runners stranded?*" I could have suggested that maybe a little encouragement would have gone a long way in this instance, but it wasn't in Pietro's repertoire. Instead, he harped on the same tune, hoping to give the other team the impression that the Peones were fighting all the way. But it was the Old Bugger who came across as the unbowed warrior, not his team.

The Peones tried to fight through it. Chencho was the first to take matters into his own hands. He soaked a towel in cold water and draped it across his head, put one foot on the dugout ledge and shouted "Occhio di suino!" whenever a Peone was at bat (which, naturally, I echoed). Despite this encouragement, the boys managed only one hit over seven innings. Each player tried to do what he could. Mario Simone was the first to try to bully it out of the Thunder – tirannci in capo, which is what the Nettunese call tactics of intimidation – by knocking legs with their first baseman after running out a groundball. Once he'd sprinted past the bag ("*Out!*" snapped the ump), Mario looked back at the infielder and shouted, "Tu sei uno stronzo!", his face blazing with anger. The infielder stood his ground, but D'Addio, the Salerno slugger, rose to the bait, shouting "Bastardo!" at him from left field.

The heat baked the field and continued to weaken Cobra's effort – he was getting hit up and down the Thunder lineup – and in the third inning, D'Addio again stepped to the plate, waving his bat high over his head like a bully about to smack a birthday piñata.

Two pitches later came the sound of a ball being pasted. It was D'Addio's second consecutive shot to the far reaches of the San Giacomo field. Mario Simone pedalled back on it – the Red Tiger joined him – but neither could get there in time to jump at the ball. However, they were close enough to get a good look at the hit, which proved vital, for as soon as the ball left the yard, the two fielders waved their arms and pointed at the outfield fence.

FIBS had assigned two senior umpires to the game. The plate umpire couldn't have been a day under sixty. As soon as he saw Pietro bound at him from the dugout, he knew that the home run was about to be contested. Pietro met D'Addio at home plate, and once they understood what the Old Bugger was saying, the entire Salerno team, its bat boy and biographer, formed a gold-and-blue horseshoe around the coach, shouting him down.

Then Pietro, a few of the Thunder players, and the two umpires jogged to where the Red Tiger was gesturing at the yellow ribbon that ran along the top of the fence. The ribbon indicated the highest point of the fence; any ball that passed over it was a home run. The Tiger insisted that the ball had dipped below the yellow ribbon and passed through a hole in the fence. After a few minutes staring carefully at the fence, the old umpire walked back to the infield, pointed at D'Addio, who was sitting contentedly in the dugout, and dragged his finger towards second base. He'd ruled it a ground rule double.

The Salerno bench exploded. The entire team raced out to the umpire, shouting.

Pietro stepped back into the shadows. The Thunders argued their case but were shouted down by the umpire, who escorted the Salerno slugger to the diamond's middle bag. A homer would have made the score 5-2 Salerno, but instead, it was still a one-run game, with a runner in scoring position. On the mound, Cobra tossed the ball in and out of his glove and blew out a breath.

The game continued, but Cobra couldn't turn the tide. Salerno, still hitting, got their runs, cashing in D'Addio and another two baserunners to make the score 6-2, Thunder. At the end of the inning, the Big Emilio pushed his catcher's mask back on his head and asked the exiting Salerno batter, Ivano Falcatore, "Hey, you realized that wasn't a homer, right?" It seemed like an innocent thing to say – your basic catcherese – but it infuriated Falcatore.

He stepped towards the catcher, shouted, "Why are you breaking my balls?" and shoved the Big Emilio. The dugouts emptied.

The Thunder were off the bench first (they were better, and had more experience, at this drill than Nettuno). Big Emilio and Falcatore pushed each other, swayed back, bumped chests, and pushed some more, while the other players spun about them. Violence hung in the air, even though the white of the players' uniforms gave the proceedings an air of formality. The brawl was fast becoming more of a dance when a small, plump figure in wrap-around *Terminator* glasses – Salerno's coach – bounded on to the field, heading straight for the Big Emilio. It looked like someone had thrown an angry black bear into the fray.

The Old Bugger stepped in front of him. The coach tried to move past him, but the Old Bugger pressed his palms against the coach's chest with such authority that the man held still, as if his batteries had given out.

"Cazzo duro!"

"Ma va fungooolo!"

"*Pendolo!*"

The players taunted each other even as the umps walked them back to their benches, and gave them all warnings. My attention was distracted by a figure moving along the outside of the fence. It was an old, white-haired man riding a bicycle, a fellow known as Panato, a neighbourhood tifiso who'd been coming to baseball games at San Giacomo for the last forty years. His usual post was under a tree near the third-base line. Panato leaned his bicycle against the fence and walked into the ravine, picking his way through the overgrowth, and was gone. A few minutes later, after both teams had resumed play, he reappeared, holding D'Addio's ball. He tossed it into his bike's basket, then pedalled back to the shade of his tree to watch the game unfold.

In the sixth inning, the Peones got a life. In baseball, it's often the small plays that stand out. Mario Simone's at-bat in the sixth was such a fragment. After running the count to 3-0, he worked Mele for a walk – it was the Peones' first baserunner in four innings – putting him down the line next to Senatore, his recent adversary. It's not often that you find wars won or lost at first base, but, all of a sudden, both teams were focused on that little patch of red to the right of the diamond.

I've always thought of first base as the bar at an exclusive restaurant: you're happy to be there, but it's not where you really want to be. The first baseman is like baseball's maître d', manning the game's most social of all stations, a place for light chat between players. Before the birth of the designated hitter, first base was the ballpark's sofa bed, where beat-up old ballplayers hid during their final years of slugging. It's rare that it ever resembles anything close to the battle zone of home base or second, but as Mario took his lead that's exactly what it became.

On Pietro's command, Mario took off down the basepath. The catcher snatched Mele's pitch – a curveball to Mario Mazza, who jerked the bat back on his shoulder – and threw to second, but was too late. It was the Peones' turn to celebrate as if it was the bottom of the ninth, and as Mario Mazza pointed his bat at the pitcher, they hollered for both players at the top of their lungs: "*Mariooooooo!*"

This did little to rattle the unflappable Mele. With the count 2-2, he gathered into his caricamento and threw the ball. Mario swung and missed. The Peones' groans echoed down the ravine and Mario tossed away his batting helmet in disgust, spitting as many consecutive porco cazzos as I'd ever heard strung together by one human. Still, I thought that something in the game had improved. A bit of light had pooled under the door frame.

The Thunder carried a healthy 6-2 lead going into the bottom of the ninth. While Mele warmed up, Pietro gathered his team around the dugout and told them, "Get your bat on the ball, but take some pitches. This guy is tired and has pitched a lot, so take him deep in the count if you can. He's a batting-practice pitcher, you can hit him. Dai! C'mon! Waste nothing up there. Waste nothing!"

The Red Tiger led off the inning and promptly singled. Even more promptly, he stole second. The side of the door slivered open. Next, Fab Julie belted a pitch solidly into the middle of the diamond, but it found the centre-fielder's glove. Julie, showing more emotion than I'd seen before, tore the batting gloves from his hand and slashed the grass with his spikes. The door sucked shut.

"Porca miseria!"

With one out, Solid Gold, who'd arrived by the second inning, stepped to the plate, his diamond earring blinking in the sun. Ricky had pinch-hit for Paolo after the catcher's second at-bat, a strike-out. (Later, Paolo sighed, "A curve ball. Dave, I haven't seen a curve ball in six years." Paolo had also walked, and the day ended with him studying photocopies of an oceanography text for a forthcoming exam and chipping away at the dugout wall with a stick.) Solid Gold immediately singled and stole second. He was driven home by Skunk Bravo, who singled and also stole: 6-4, Salerno. Bravo's at-bat was a gem. He fought off pitch after pitch, pinning Mele against the horizon. After his hit, you could tell that he'd exhausted the Salerno pitcher, who'd poured everything into narrowing the game to one out. After Skunk's single, the Thunder gathered on the mound to take the pulse of their red-lensed righty. He was, as he told them, stanco, bushed. Without hesitation, they turned to their reliever (they didn't have to turn far: he was also their short-stop), a fellow named Di Patria.

The Natural stepped in to hit. The Natural was the type of player who looks much bigger and more imposing in his uniform than he does on the street. The way he carved his feet into the dirt and pulled his bat behind his ear gave you the impression that he devoured fast-balls like breakfast cereal. Di Patria must have thought this, for he threw no strikes, walking the Natural on four straight pitches.

The Big Emilio hit after Chicca, who'd popped up for the second out, narrowing the Peones' margin of error. The players smoked feverishly. They chanted "Figa la figa!" and "Matadore! and

"Matalo!" at the catcher. Di Patria could not find the plate and walked Emilio on five pitches. After ball four, the Peones' catcher had placed his bat across home plate, looked towards the dugout, and squeezed his hands into two fists, imploring the next batter, Mario Simone, to bring it home:

"*Dai! Mario! Dai!*" The outfielder stood in the batter's box and looked out, holding his bat impossibly high, Di Patria pulled his glove to his chest and looked in. Mario worked the count, then drove an inside fastball into the ground. Mirko, coaching first base, fell on all fours and, blowing out his voice on the play (he'd lose it for the rest of the day), screamed at Mario to get down the line before the ball, which the second baseman had jumped behind the mound to field. He scooped it up and threw it, the ball screaming down a line between his hand and Senatore's glove. Mario bolted to first with such force that we could hear his foot hit the bag, and, a nanosecond later, the snap of the ball in Senatore's mitt.

"*Salvo!*"

Mario, carried by his own momentum, cartwheeled down the line.

6-5, Thunder.

With the bases loaded, two out, Mario Mazza strode to the plate and immediately fell behind in the count, 0-2. I tried to beam encouragement to the young hitter, but the only thing that ran through my head was, Whatever you do, Bidini, don't cry. As I steadied my heart, the bench bellowed "*Mariuuuuucchhh!*", everyone, that is, except Chicca, who sat alone at the far end of the dugout, daring the game's ending to blow him away.

There must have been equal measures of hope and hopelessness in Mario's heart, for the at-bat possessed the potential for both. Two frightening scenarios must have crossed his mind: "If I strike out, I'll try not to let it hurt too much," and "Everything I do for the rest of the year, and maybe beyond, will be judged by this at-bat." Anyone who's ever been in this position knows that the only way to deal with such debilitating nervousness is to play the body's raging spheres against each other and find the place where you can settle the nerves and steady the eye and open the valves so that your blood and energy is moving as it should. But, for me, watching Mario's at-bat was an exercise in total fear.

Mario raised the bat over his head and froze in anticipation of the pitch. Di Patria's curveball swooped through the air, and Mario swung. The ball jumped off the bat, flew over the shortstop's glove, and fell into left field. The runners dashed around the bases: 7-6, Peones. In the dugout, Chencho, Pitò, and I hugged, almost squeezing the life out of each other. The players rushed out to second, where Mario stood, small tears squeezing from his eyes, and buried him in their embrace. 'Nando climbed down from the stands and girlfriends flooded the field.

The sun was at its apex, and the Peones were in the playoffs.

I looked around for Pietro, and spotted him near the dugout, studying his lineup card as if it were the start of the game, not its glorious conclusion. Somewhere inside his baseball heart, he must have felt joy for his player. But if he had, he wasn't showing it.

"That was something, eh?" I asked him, patting his shoulder.

"Yes, but . . . ," he said, rubbing his neck.

"But, what?"

"The ninth inning was good, but not the rest of the game."

"The ninth inning was – ," I said, searching for hyperbole.

"Yes, but that pitcher," he interrupted.

"Doesn't matter. We took care of him."

The Old Bugger laughed.

"What? We won. Aren't you happy?"

"Yes, I'm happy about the ninth. But that pitcher," he said, wagging a finger. "He was a batting practice pitcher!"

24

1992

I have only ever despised two teams: the NHL's 1974-75 Philadelphia Flyers and baseball's Oakland Athletics of the late 1980s, early 1990s. The Flyers drew hockey into darkness for a short period by affecting a street-gang style, icing a team of villainous Swede-beaters and hairy, loathsome thugs, while the A's were a similarly mirthless group, an arrogant, thick-necked hitting machine who, as the defrocked A's slugger Jose Canseco admitted in his retirement, sipped steroids like Lefty Grove downed highballs. The A's played baseball as an NFL game: sullen and tough, favouring elbow-bashing and chest-thumping in a sport that, at its most free, embodies the loose joy and abandon of life. As well as being odious and impossible to cheer for, these two teams had another thing in common: it was their seasonal folly to dominate the Toronto teams. They came for us at the end of each season, like the bad kid crossing the lawn while you hid behind the curtain.

The A's were a Cerberus: the scowl-mouthed Ricky Henderson, who, upon breaking Lou Brock's stolen base record, proclaimed with typical humility, "I can now say I am the greatest base stealer *of all time!*"; Jose Canseco, whose eventual fall from grace was a long, ugly stumble, his body wracked from years of needlework; and Dennis Eckersley, who, dressed in carnival green and gold with his drooping, shaggy moustache and kitten-eating stare, looked like a demented Doug Henning. Some people branded the A's a hard-assed team, but they lacked the play-or-die character of other warrior teams, like the Phillies of 1993, another Blue Jays' rival. Where the Phillies and, to a lesser extent, the Orioles of the late 1970s, were ugly and unkempt, the A's were all angular jaws and grim stares. They played full throttle not because they wanted to defeat the opposition, but because they wanted them to submit. They mirrored the WWF: a squad of impossibly large figures hitting impossibly long home runs. At the time, only Thomas Boswell suggested that Canseco and company were an unnatural creation, but looking back, their team signalled the dawning of baseball's age of science. They were like sporting robots. I both hated and feared them.

In the 1989 post-season, the A's killed the Jays. Toronto's sluggers George Bell and Jesse Barfield were dwarfed in both size and power. Janet and I went to game five of the 1989 American League Championship Series at the SkyDome and watched as Lloyd Moseby, in his final at-bat as a Jay, homered off Eckersley into right field, refusing to let his team die even though the A's were poised above the body, about to administer the death blow. The event was overshadowed by Canseco, who deposited two balls into the upper reaches of the SkyDome, one of them finding the 500 level, the first player to do that. The game ended with a shouting match between the Jays' manager, Cito Gaston, and Dennis Eckersley, whom he called "half a man" before accusing the reliever of doctoring the ball to cheat opposing hitters.

After the disappointments of 1987, my allegiance to the Jays only strengthened. In 1988, Janet and I went to fifty home games at the Ex. My friend David Watts worked the scoreboard at the ballpark, so there were always lots of tickets floating around. After games, we'd climb the grandstand and sit on a deck overlooking the field. I became as familiar with the stadium as any sporting arena I've known, in part because of the hours I spent interviewing Blue Jays and visiting players for *Innings*, Canada's short-lived national baseball newspaper. My first assignment was to interview the Kansas City Royals' sidearming reliever, Dan Quisenberry. The interview itself wasn't nearly as frightening as the quest to find him in the labyrinthine visiting team's quarters. My editor had asked me to deliver a few copies of the paper to Hall of Famer George Brett, doubling my insecurity, and as I made my way down a tunnel to the Royals' clubhouse, my stomach churned with the realization that I was about to enter baseball's inner sanctum for the first time.

At the door, I was met by the Royals' towering catcher, Jamie Quirk, who laid a hand on my shoulder.

"Listen here," he said.

"Uh, sorry," I sputtered. "I'm looking for Mr. Quisenberry."

"Mr. Quisenberry, eh?"

"Yes. For an interview."

"Is that right, kid? Well, I've got a good mind to strap you down and shave that thing off your face!" he roared.

I rubbed my sorry young person's beard and probably looked at him like I was about to cry.

"But since you got a meeting with the Quiz, I won't," he said. "*But next time . . . !*" he growled, punching open the door with his hand.

I pushed my stomach back down my throat and scooted over to where George Brett was sitting.

"These papers, they're for you," I told him, holding up a cover with a picture of Brett in post-swing pose.

"They're not in French, are they?" he asked.

"No, no. English."

"Good. I was never very good at French," he said.

I introduced myself to Quisenberry and we talked for about forty minutes. I couldn't believe how friendly and patient he was, how relaxed he made me feel in spite of my tongue-tied questions read off a sheet of foolscap. My last question was, "What do you want to do after you retire from baseball?"

He paused a second. "You think I should retire?"

"No, no. I just . . ."

"I'm kidding," he said.

"Oh, okay."

"To be honest with you, I'd think I'd like to write books," he told me.

"Me too," I told him.

"I guess that puts us on the same kind of wavelength," he said, smiling. "Hey, if you ever publish anything, send me a copy," he said.

"Okay, I will!" I told him, thrilled at his request. But I never got the chance. Quiz published a collection of poetry in 1998; I wrote *On a Cold Road*. Then a brain tumour pushed the great reliever off the edge of the earth.

I knew the layout of Toronto's new stadium, the SkyDome, less well than Exhibition Stadium when, on a hot summer evening in 1990, I was struck with the urge to spraypaint the ballpark. Its towering grey exterior walls begged for a slash of colour.

I'd spent the night drinking with friends on a downtown patio, and as the evening wore on, we argued whether Cito Gaston's tactics were the cause of the team's current slump.

"Bench Junior Felix! Trade Tom Henke! Fire Cito!" we roared, our brows beaded with the sweat.

After a while, I broke from the debate and walked around the corner of the pub to relieve myself. There, I came upon a Caribana float parked in the alleyway, a can of purple spraypaint sitting on its flatbed. I grabbed the can, hopped on my bike, and sped away. When I reached the stadium, I stalked its circumference, the spraypaint tucked under my shirt, finally deciding to leave my mark on the wall of a pedestrian ramp. I scouted for signs of nighttime security – the Jays were out of town, on a road trip – then started scrawling: HEY CITO! DO THE RIGHT THIN

I would have completed the G had I not felt a cold hand grasp my shoulder.

"Stop it right there!" said the voice behind me.

I turned around to find I was in the grip of a fellow a few years younger than myself dressed in a maintenance worker's jumpsuit, carrying a roll of cable.

"What the fuck do you think you're doing?" he asked.

"I wasn't doing anything!" I protested.

"You were defacing property," he said.

"Awww, c'mon," I pleaded.

He made a phone call to his superiors.

"Listen, I wasn't doing any harm, was I?" I asked him.

"Just sit down and don't move," he ordered.

Once I got a better look at him, I saw that he was half my age. His summer job was to work as an undercover security guard at the SkyDome. I'd held a night-shift job myself, guarding a half-built shopping mall, and I remembered that whenever I encountered another human being – burglars, vandals, drunks – I was thankful that they'd visited.

"What were you trying to prove, anyway?' he asked.

"I'm just a Blue Jay fan," I told him. "I care about my team. That's all."

"But you can't deface private property. It's the law."

"Laws," I said, "were made to protect politicians and business-men, not people like you and me."

From there, the ice melted. We talked about music. He brought up Bachman Turner Overdrive, and since I'd just interviewed Randy Bachman, I had lots of stories to tell. He sat down, lit a smoke, and we talked about the concerts we'd seen, what kind of radio stations we liked. Soon, a CN police cruiser pulled up to the curb and an older man, the security staff's sergeant, walked over and examined my work.

"So what's your beef with the world?" he asked me.

"Awww, I was just, you know, exercising my freedom of speech."

"Is he telling the truth?" he asked the young guard.

"Yah. You could get that paint off pretty easy," he said.

"In that case, son, you're free to go," said the sergeant. He climbed into his car and sped away, but the guard and I stayed a while talking. Just as I was ready to leave, another cruiser arrived. This time, a square-shouldered woman with a brushcut emerged from the car and grilled the guard.

"Well, I'm going to have to write him a ticket," she concluded.

"But, the other guy said – ," I said.

"I don't care about the other guy!" she barked "You have some identification?"

"No."

"All right," she said. "Give me your name."

She looked up, her pencil poised above her pad.

I thought it over for a second.

"Lou Fontinato," I told her.

In 1992, the Jays won the American League East. Once again, they ran into Oakland, the perennial Western Division champions. Just as the Rheostatics had tracked the Jays' 1987 pennant run from the road, we found ourselves touring Canada during the opening series against Oakland. Acknowledging the gravity of the situation, I pasted JAYS! in black gaffer tape along the side of the van. In Western Canada, the three-hour time difference meant that the games fell perfectly between soundcheck and gig, allowing us to take in every game without sacrificing a moment of our repertoire. We were in perfect synch with the post-season until the pivotal game four, when our schedule obliged us to drive through the mountains, from Vancouver to Calgary.

Every sports fan committed to his team knows the sick feeling you get when life, work, destiny, whatever, threatens to deprive you of the moment you've waited years to experience. For our first hour on the road through the Rockies on the morning of game five, we tweaked the radio dial, searching for an orphan signal. We had no luck until just outside of Armstrong, B.C., when Tom Cheek's baritone rang out. Our elation at discovering his voice quickly died when we learned that the Jays were trailing Oakland 6-1. Still, it

Three cornerstones of the Jays' 1992 and 1993 World Championship teams.
From the left: Roberto Alomar, Paul Molitor, John Olerud.
(Courtesy of Fred Thornhill)

was early in the game – I think it was the third inning – and so, until the nervous later innings, we were able to soak in the scene for what it was: the van rambling gamely between the interior's towering, snow-peaked mountains, their great, skyclimbing forests painted gold by the autumn sun. We devoured the view with our eyes, but as the A's seized control of the game through the middle innings, it appeared as if the day, at best, might be all table setting and no champagne.

Listening to baseball on the radio tunes you into the game's rich symphony: the shouting of peanut vendors, the sizzle of scoreboard fanfare, the full-throated ump, the groan of a missed swing, the grumble of a passing jet. You try to read the tone of the game from these sounds, and from the pitch of the announcer's voice; the softer he talks, the slower the action; the deeper the voice, the farther his team is behind. I know a friend who, one evening, was travelling across Canada, spinning the dial trying to find out whether the Montreal Canadiens had won their playoff game against Hartford. Finally, he heard an announcer say, "And the final score was 5-2," and he knew, just from the inflection, that the Habs had won. The next day, he checked the paper. He was right. They had.

It was around the seventh or eighth inning that Tom Cheek's voice took on a certain expectancy, a spike in pitch that told us something had come upon the team. There was a lead-off hit. Then another. A stolen base. A few runs. A few more. Cheek spoke more quickly, with more punch, and, just like that, the Jays rallied to make it 6-4, Oakland. After striking out Ed Sprague to end the inning, Dennis Eckersley, who'd been summoned by manager Tony LaRussa to stamp out the Jays' rally, spun on the mound, glared into the Blue Jays dugout, and shook his fist. The crowd climbed to its feet and cheered. "It was pure Little League shit," said the Jays' Jack Morris after the game. "Once he did that, it was 'get even' time for our guys."

In the ninth, Cheek's words snapped off a little harder, as if he was laying his chin against the microphone, going to work for the first time all afternoon. We got the sense that a victory was peeking over the horizon as our van climbed and fell down the mountain pathways, whirling in and out of pockets of sonic darkness. When we came upon a patch of flat highway, we decided it would be best to wait out the inning, so we pulled the van to the shoulder of the road and listened.

Well, most of us did. Two of my bandmates – Dave and Martin, neither of them baseball fans – chose instead to take a walk along the nearby river. Roberto Alomar, the Jays' acrobatic second baseman, approached the white triangle, cocked his Cooper once, twice, then peered out at the pitcher, drawing Eckersley into his sights.

The Oakland crowd groaned with the tension of the moment, and we could hear it through the dashboard. Eckersley, his glove pressed to his uniform, gazed at Alomar from under the bill of his cap as my bandmates strolled up the river towards the forest. Eckersley threw once, twice. Alomar hacked through his at-bat until the count drew full, 3-2. My bandmates stopped and kneeled before a huge, luminous elk, which had suddenly made its way out of the bush. As Alomar jerked his bat and the elk sniffed the air, time seemed to pause. Then Eckersley threw the ball, and it exploded.

At first, Tom Cheek held his tongue before announcing, "He's hit it a ton . . ." The ball jumped into the Californian sky as the elk inched closer to Dave and Martin. "*It could be . . .*" There was no more than ten feet between my friends and the animal as Alomar stepped up the line, dropped his bat, then raised his arms above his head. "*It's gone! Home run Roberto Alomar!*" Inside the van, we grabbed our heads, crazy with joy. We punched the windows and thrashed about on the benches, rocking the beast back and forth on its wheels. Cheek, in *The Road to Glory*, wrote that, with Alomar's hit, the entire Blue Jays team bounded onto the top step of the dugout, and "an unrestrained barrage of obscenities rocketed towards Eckersley."

With Alomar's hit, millions of fans across Canada felt the weight of twenty years of losing lifted from their shoulders. The world became suddenly light and free. As I screamed the scream of retribution, I leaned on the horn to let my bandmates know that the Jays had finally laid the killing blow on the team who'd come to represent all of the dark forces that had conspired to keep them from ever tasting victory. The sound of the horn shot through the mountain pass; the elk's eyes flared as he reared up and then sped away. Dave and Martin turned around and gave me the "What the heck was that for?" kind of look, but I stayed on the horn. I leaned into it with all of my force. Birds burst from the trees; animals leapt out of deep, dark lairs.

But I couldn't see them through the tears.

25

THE ITALIAN

And just like that, summer ended. September arrived, the last sun-bather capped his bottle of tanning butter, the grille came down on Señor Frog, ombrelloni were plucked out of the sand, the soccer nets were unhooked, the children's playground was hoisted onto a flatbed and driven away, and after a sweeping rain that lasted four days, Nettuno returned to what it had been when we'd first arrived – a graceful seaside town of golden light and stone. The temperature ducked so low, Janet and I were forced to pull the blankets up to our chins. The Nettunese apologized for the cold weather, warning us that, if we stayed past Labour Day, we'd see the city stilled by winter. But we had no intention of leaving soon, for the nip in the daylight and the chill of the moon meant only one thing to me: the playoffs.

One afternoon, I stood in the dugout with Chencho, the Big Emilio, the Natural, Pietro, and Mario Simone and watched as rain sliced across the field, turning the diamond's ruts and depressions into a quagmire of muck. Every now and then, the rain would reverse direction, sending us flying to the opposite end of the bench. I was thrilled by the drama of the downpour, so when Pietro commented, "Che brutta pioggia! It's the fault of the Canadese!" I strode proudly into the storm (the players hugged their stomachs in laughter and disbelief at the water washing down the back of my neck, and pouring through my soaked shorts and out my shoetops), all the while staring at the Old Bugger, who smiled and wagged a finger at me, his eyes showing me that I had him. "Che Pazzo! Che Matto! Che stronzo Canadese!" So the Canadian had hung in there after all.

A few days later, we made another futile attempt to practise between tropical storms. We were forced into the dugout, and waited for the weather to abate. Once the skies brightened, Mario Simone asked if I needed a drive home, and I hopped aboard his motorino.

There are many different ways to navigate a new city, but there's nothing quite like viewing it at 60 mph from the back of a motorbike. It's Tourism at 78 rpm: all of the sounds and colours and faces of the city compressed into one thrilling experience. Mario swept us expertly and at great speed through the narrowest of passageways, and as the wind roared in my ears, it made all of the hours I'd spent in Nettuno seem so earthbound, when, all the while, I could have been moving through baseballissimo like a low-flying bird.

I've never been particularly fussy when it comes to getting from point A to point B. I've wandered through Transylvania on a horse and buggy, ridden a camel into the Omani mountains, dragged my hockey bag over pyramids of snow on the Gobi desert, travelled by taxi across the Canadian prairie, and sailed by dhow across the mouth of the Persian Gulf. Once, Janet and I toured Beijing on a little wooden hut strapped to the back of a bicycle driven by a two-hundred-year-old man with asthma. I inventory the above not to boast, but to suggest that the best moments of travel happen after you've been swept from your feet. In Ireland in 1987, the Rheostatics – racked with dissent, poverty, and homesickness at the time – travelled to Cork by train, in a carriage packed with small men in furry hats, hurling fans travelling to an away match. As soon as they spotted our drums and guitars, they demanded, "Play us a song, boys!!"

"Uh, we're actually kinda tired," we said.

"Nonsense," said one of the men. "What do you need, food?" he asked, and produced a wheel of cheese and a handful of fruit that he offered to us in his hurling cap.

"Um, we're not really hungry," we said.

"What do you need, drink?" he asked and pulled out a jug of clear whiskey – pochine – which he poured into little plastic cups. He did everything short of grab the backs of our heads to get us to drink it.

"Um, we're not really thirsty," we told him.

"*Let's hear it now!*" he commanded.

We had no choice. We gave them Stompin' Tom. We played for hours, fuelled by the hot white liquid. At one point I looked out the window at the lush Irish countryside peeling past us and realized where the rhythm of train songs comes from. Our tour had been a muddled disaster from the beginning, but this journey had made our spirits climb (if only to come crashing down again, but that's another story). My point is that sometimes it takes an outside force to sweep you along the road, to show you something about a place or a people that you can't find by foot.

As the motorino wound through the city, it started to rain. "Oh, no, Dave! Dio!" Mario said, turning his head sideways, showing me the beads of water hanging off his magnificent nose. Then, the skies burst. I watched the Nettunese scramble through the streets, throwing every manner of handbag, newspaper, seat cushion, and pizza box over their heads. Every now and then, Mario would come upon an enormous pool in the middle of the road and slice through it, throwing up two waves in his wake. He moaned, "Oh, Dave! This is no good!" I shouted back, "This is friggin' great!", but he didn't hear me. The rain was so thick I could barely see anything. My clothes were waterlogged, even my armpits, the band of my underwear, the back of my knees. Finally, we turned off the main road and made our way north to where Mario lived with his sister and mom and dad. We leapt off the bike and dashed inside his house, our arms aloft and legs bowed in an effort to distance the soggy clothes from our skin.

Mario's mom immediately started making espresso. Then she fetched clothes for the bedraggled Canadian, who, for reasons unknown to the Nettunese, was actually grinning the I've-been-caught-in-a-thrilling-rainstorm grin. I changed in Mario's room, and returned to the world in sandals, a tight yellow T-shirt sporting the name of an Italian designer, red-and-black track pants that buttoned up the side, and a Ferrari baseball cap. Sitting in the Simones' kitchen nook sipping hot sweet coffee, I caught my reflection in the coffee pot. The transformation was total. Finally, I looked like the Italian I'd always been.

The weather gave us one good day before the start of the Nettuno-Palermo best-of-five semifinal. The guys used the time solely for batting practice, readying themselves for the Sicilian pitcher – Giampiero Novara. An allegedly titanic figure, Novara starred for the island team with two of his brothers – Umberto and Carlos – all born in Venezuela, where they'd played semi-pro ball before settling in Palermo. Chencho, trying to rally the club, announced that the upcoming series was *Novara contro Navacci!* Mario Simone spoke for everybody when he said, "Dave, I wish we could play the game *right now*."

The coach was the only one too busy in thought to give in to the tension. On our drive to San Giacomo for the pre-playoff practice, Pietro had settled into a long monologue about the complications of his lineup and how he might field the strongest nine without comprising the team's health over what could be a five-game run.

"Pompozzi is the only one who will pitch for sure. The rest, pfffffttt," he said. "Cobra, I don't know. He says he is okay, but he looks funny, tight. Still, he throws, he throws, so what can I say? Eyyy, this is baseball in Italy. I have to let the players decide if they can or can't play. Fabio Sena [from Milan] e stupido, you remember?"

"Yes, I remember."

"Is very bad, because I only have three, maybe four pitchers. What do I do with Pitò? Chencho, okay. Chencho è stronzo, ma lui è forte, capito?"

"Capito," I said.

"Maybe Fabio Julie. Maybe he pitch."

"Fab Julie?" I was startled.

"Chicca tells me that, a long time ago, he was a pitcher."

"But he hasn't pitched all year."

"Ey. I take any pitcher, I don't care! We'll see today. Maybe he throws and I can see. If Cobra and Fabio Sena can't pitch, what do I do? I'll play Fab Julie, it's fine. If this team plays smart, easy, and no panic, maybe we'll be okay. But Giampiero Novara, eh, this is a real player."

After batting practice, Pietro gathered the team in front of the dugout. He talked about the need for them to be calm and confident and smart, about stealing bases and putting pressure on their defence – "*Scivolo! Scivolo!*", and about the threat of debilitating panic – senza confusione, solo tranquillo, okay? He spoke for twenty minutes, maybe twenty-five, filibustering baseball wisdom until, having run out of ideas of his own, he touched on the Canadian's concept of team unity, of working together – "Siamo una squadra, si?" – opening his hand, then closing it as we had during that car ride through Piazza Mercato.

Pietro spoke until darkness fell. After a while, I could no longer see the faces of the players sitting opposite me, only their fingers fanning out, then drawing in – cinque dita, ma una mano. It was one of the few times where it was obvious how much the Peones looked up to Pietro, how much they needed him to show them the way. You could see how all of his years of baseball – the innumerable at-bats, runs scored, base hits, and stolen bases – comforted his charges, who'd tried visualizing clutch hits and catches and series-winning home runs of their own, only to have them swallowed by doubt. Pietro was the one athlete among them who'd thrashed in the sea of uncertainty, and had risen above it like

Neptune himself. With the most important series of their baseball
lives on the horizon, one was enough.

The next morning, the Palermo Athletics stepped from their bus
and strode onto the San Giacomo field. I hadn't slept much the
night before, and my blurry-headedness tricked me into believing
that the Athletics were impossibly big. But after pressing my fists
into my eyes to clear the sleep, I saw that it was no illusion at all.
They were, indeed, huge. The other thing that struck me about
Palermo was their colours: gold and green. Oakland colours.

Whenever players get a first glance of the opposition, it's impossible for them not to affect the posture of a hood leaning against a
brick wall, pretending to comb an imagined ducktail. So as soon as
the Athletics arrived, the Peones, who were tilling, weeding, and
prettying the field, started to till and weed with a home-turf toughness, scowling with every stroke of the hoe. I could feel their
anxious energy gather, their intensity start to harden. I started
acting tough myself, while I raked the field. Chencho had started
the job of scraping ragged piles of grass to various points around
the diamond, but the Canadian in me decided he wasn't up to the
task. I seized the implement from il strano lancetore, and showed
him what-for. I might not have been able to hit a ball effectively
over the centre (or right or left) field fence, but I was king among
the Peones in a skill that was essential to baseball.

In 2002, I led the team in raking.

Before taking to the field together, each team had been nothing but
a rumour to the other. But every player on both sides had constructed a mental image of what the opposition would be like
without ever having laid eyes on them, making them more phan-
tasmagoric and fearsome. This rarely happens in modern pro sport.

With the exception of, say, the Belarussian hockey team in the 2002 Winter Olympics who, after stunning Sweden in the knockout round, sent hockey writers scrambling for an atlas, or the Senegalese soccer team, who announced their global presence later that year in similarly shocking fashion by defeating defending champion France 1-0 in the opening game of the World Cup, we have to work pretty hard to remain ignorant of what the rest of the sports world is doing. In modern baseball, thanks to the Internet and a deluge of print, television, and radio news, it's possible to scout the opposition from your bedside. But ItaloBall was more like pre-1950s baseball, relying on word of mouth and the stories of returning sports wanderers. Giampiero Novara – whom his teammates called the Wild Thing – had an intimidating profile assembled by friends of the Peones who'd played against him, and from a conversation yours truly had had one evening in the Borgo with an A division team from Messina. They'd told me, "When his slider is on, he's almost unhittable. It's not a nice experience to be standing there facing him. But he's also pazzo, and if you can get to him, he can lose it. We've seen him have games where he just walks off the field, disgusted with himself. You have to find his weaknesses, and make it hard on him."

Giampiero Novara was a mountainous man, standing six-foot-two. Everything about him was big, from his chin to his tree-trunk torso. When he reared back from the mound to deliver the ball, he was like Hercules chucking stone finials (some players called his fastball la bomba mano, a hand bomb). At the plate, he dwarfed the catcher, umpire, and the bleacher. The only thing that stopped Novara from being a Bunyonesque figure on the diamond was the way he peered out at the world, a long, dark stare that seemed to have hardened like cold lead across his mug, with crushed flower eyes and a mouth that had yet to taste candy. There was one other thing that the players from Messina had told me about the Sicilian pitcher: "Giampiero Novara hates North Americans. He hates them very much."

Giampiero's brothers – Umberto, who pitched and played first base, and Carlos, who pitched and caught – were also huge, but nothing compared to their older brother, who'd played in Serie A before dusting his manager in a dressing-room brawl, effectively walking away from high-level ItaloBall. Umberto and Carlos were more affable than Giampiero, but not by much. When I walked over, after batting practice, to ask Umberto for a short history of their team, he held up his hand and told me, brusquely, in English, "Later. This game is too important to talk now." I returned to the Peones' side of the field, where Mirko scolded me: "Why did you go over there, talking to the enemy?" The Big Emilio, striding past us, stopped too, and said, in halting English, "You Peone, okay?" Of course, they were both right. I'd been stupid to put my journalist's curiosity ahead of respecting the Peones' need for total unity. But my encounter with Umberto had fuelled my desire to see my team vanquish the Southern behemoths.

The game began, and the Peones were delirious as Pompozzi retired the Athletics in order in the top of the first. Paolo had told me before the game, "I worry a little about Francesco. He just throws fastball, fastball, fastball, and if it's true that these players were once in Serie A . . ."

But Pompo was fine. Still, you would have thought it was the bottom of the ninth the way the Peones greeted each other after escaping the first inning. That the lid had been lifted off the game without any kind of evil serpent rushing at the players, their fans, and a hopelessly devoted Canadian writer gave them cause to rejoice. They were in it now.

They were playing for keeps.

26

PALERMO AT NETTUNO

Cue the rain.

It was as if the heavens themselves could not suffer the tension of the affair, and something had had to give. Both teams were forced back into their dugouts, where they peered at each other through the downpour. After a thirty-minute delay, the skies finally cleared, and a great rainbow arced gloriously across the ravine. But all we saw were the enormous pools of water that had gathered between the basepaths. No amount of hubcap-scooping or metal-rod drainage would drain them. Both Pietro and Carlos Novara – the Athletics' player-coach and captain – had to do something that neither man wanted: they met at home plate and pretended to be nice, discussing whether any baseball could be played on this day.

Pietro came back to tell us that, because of the field conditions, the teams would play three games the following day. It was a small victory for the Peones. Novara had argued that it would be best to schedule two matches instead and play three back in Palermo, but Pietro had pointed out that since three home games had been nego-tiated prior to the series, it would be wrong to switch now, having already been through that process, en formale. He might have also considered that since the Peones were considerably younger and more durable than the Sicilian team, they could manage a three-game baseball day, whereas the Athletics (Giampiero was thirty-six, Carlos was thirty-nine, and Umberto was thirty-five) might wilt.

The other question was where to play the game, as it would take days for San Giacomo to dry. What a change of venue would do to the series' karma – which is to say, Nettuno's karma – was anyone's guess. Home-field advantage, after all, is supposed to be exactly that. With the games held elsewhere, the knowledge of how the ball hiccups off the dirt, the personality of the outfield, the manner in which the light bounces off the bleachers, would all be for naught, at least it would in most Italian baseball cities. But Nettuno wasn't just any other baseball city, and since the players had been born into the game on a number of local ballfields, when it was announced that a field at Santa Barbara was available, the players took the news in stride.

Almost all of the Peones had competed at Santa Barbara, in games big and small. Even though a player had almost died in a game Paolo had played there, he insisted, "No, I like to play there. It is a good field." But the thought of playing there again brought back memories for him.

"Our team was losing by two runs in the bottom of the ninth. It was my turn to bat, but I was very upset, very upset. When I walked up to the plate, I looked down to see the place where the player had been rolling around, holding his throat. I started to cry. I was in tears for the entire at-bat. You can ask Pietro. It was very hard for me, I was so upset. I was crying when I swung and hit the ball and I was crying as I watched it go, go, go, hitting the wall in right field. Two runners came around and scored and we won the game. I always think about this game, so, yes, it is a special place for me."

When I asked Mario Simone what he thought about playing at Santa Barbara, he said, "I think it is a good opportunity for me, because I have not had such good experiences there. I played very well there as a boy, but never had good luck, non buona fortuna. Once, I played in a boys tournament and led my team – every team,

I think – in hitting the ball. It felt great. Our team won and I played very well. At the end of the tournament, they brought all of the teams onto the diamond and started giving out the awards – best pitcher, MVP, this kind of thing. But when it came time to announce the MVP for our team, I knew, just as the name was about to be said, that it would be this other boy's name, not mine. It was the name of the tournament organizer's son. People were confused, some were upset. Everybody looked at me, but I was smiling. What could I do? He was the tournament organizer's son, and this is Italy, so . . ."

"So you want to play at Santa Barbara to even the score."

"No, no," he said. "That is over. All of that is finished."

"Whatever happened to that player?"

"He plays for Serie A2, with the Leones."

"Oh, I see."

"Yes. This player also took my job on the Italian junior team too."

"The same player?"

"Yes. His father was also our coach. On the day of the tryouts for the national team, he told me he would pick me up and take me to the field. I waited and waited, but he never came."

"That's terrible."

"Because I didn't go, they watched his son play and he became the starting shortstop."

"Do you ever see this guy around town?"

"Yes, sometimes."

"Do you wanna punch his lights out?"

"His lights?"

"Do you ever want to, um, even the score?"

"No, no," he replied, laughing.

"Why are you laughing?"

"Because this is just baseball," he said.

"But you told me that without baseball you'd be dead."

"Yes, but I have baseball. I am alive."

The Santa Barbara athletic complex was built on a table above the city, a Nettunese plateau with three fields lying flat under the open sky. Santa Barbara also boasted an Olympic-sized piscina, a gymnasium where, a few weeks prior, hundreds of cadetti from Trieste to Verona to Liguria had slept on air mattresses between tournament days (an event won by Nettuno 1, with Nettuno 2 coming in second), and a grey building with racquetball courts that looked like it had been built in the days of Mussolini's Rationalist designworks. There was a snack trailer in the middle of the three fields where batting statistics and out-of-town results of touring Nettuno teams were posted. Everything about the grounds seemed more monied and cared for than at San Giacomo. The Peones' regular field gave way to an overgrown ravine of sheep and its whistling orchestra of insects, but Santa Barbara's bordered a subdivision of new homes with terracotta rooftops, which had been built to accommodate those Romans for whom the Eternal City had become prohibitively expensive. These houses lent an air of Ring Road affluence to the grounds, which, as I walked the basepaths, felt truer to the step than at the old onion field. The outfield had been groomed symmetrically, possibly by a mower that, unlike San Giacomo's, had been bought well after the rise of disco.

The next day I arrived at Santa Barbara and watched as the stands behind home plate filled with a great press of bodies, more people than had watched a Peones game all year, including Panato, who'd broken his rule of only watching games at San Giacomo to throw his support behind the fellows. Solid Gold showed up late for the game (of course, making Pietro shout, "Porco Dio! You can't even be on time for the playoffs!", before writing his name near the top of the order). Fabio from Milan read the players' names aloud to the Emperor, who wrote them on the official scoresheet, then paused when he came to the box for massage therapist. He made up his mind: "Bidini, Davide: Massaggiatore."

I was in the game.

I did what I had to do to make certain that the dugout felt just so. I was never sure whether the photo of Ted Williams I'd put up at San Giacomo had had a positive effect against Montefiascone, since the Peones' fortunes that day had moved from the depths of embarrassment to the heights of retribution. But perhaps Ole Splinty hadn't hurt the cause – the Peones had made it this far, after all – so I tugged the Salerno-Nettuno scoresheet from my binder, circled Mario Mazza's GWRBI in black ink, and pasted it to the wall just above the water fountain where the players could look up and be reminded that there had once been magic among them, that they possessed the power to govern their own sporting destiny.

Like Tony Gwynn's waistline, the Palermo lineup was imposing through the middle. The Novara brothers hit two through four (the Wild Thing batted third), and were followed by Carmello Maglio – who looked like a lost Soprano, full-cheeked with dark, piercing eyes – and Giovanni Leone, who also swung a big bat. The team's seven, eight, and nine hitters were as unassuming as the top of their order wasn't. It was hard to notice Fillippo Madonia, Joe Acquaviva, or Manny Manno in the dugout for all of the real estate taken up by the Novaras and the others. The Athletics' bench players were as small as their bottom hitters. Besides carrying a senior Novara who rarely played, they had a player named Jose Mosca (the Fly), who wore his hair in a grey ponytail and was even older than I was.

As Pietro and Carlos Novara exchanged lineups at home plate, I saw that the umpires had dressed for the occasion in light blue tops, black pants, and smart blue-and-red FIBS caps. They must have recognized, as the athletes themselves had, that this was no ordinary Sunday in the park: it was the post-season. Their nod to style added further shine to the event, which began in earnest with the Big Emilio behind home plate wishing Palermo's lead-off hitter, Carmelo Ferraro, "Buon gioco," before putting away the niceties for what would end up being a thrilling day of Italian hardball.

The first inning was almost sick with silence. It wasn't until the second inning that the players from both sides lost themselves in the game. After Pompo retired the side, the Wild Thing took to the hill, looming over the game like an elephant on a soapbox. He immediately announced his authority by striking out Solid Gold on three sliders, the pitch that the players from Messina had warned me about. It so dazzled the usually sure-eyed Golden One that he swung like he were blindfolded. The ball had sailed true towards him, then dropped into the corner of the plate.

Roger Kahn, in his book *The Head Game*, credits the slider – which became integrated into the pro game in the 1930s and 1940s – with saving baseball from "becoming extended batting practice." It was a pitch that vexed – and continues to vex – hitters because of its resemblance to a fastball, with the exception of those deadly, final few feet. When a slider is thrown hard – as Dave Steib or Steve Carlton did for decades – it can make hitters look silly, swinging at a ball that lands a foot wide of their kitchen. When I first asked Cobra to show me how to throw the pitch (Chencho could toss a slider too, and while Paolo said it was very good, the reliever was afraid to use it in key situations, instead relying on his curveball, which was not as good), he brought out a practice ball with colour-coded thumb- and fingerprints over the seams. The slider's grip, I discovered, was almost identical to the fastball only the pitcher rolls his wrist clockwise at the moment of release, giving the ball its fatal spin. I tried it a few times, but my elbow – or rather, a point on the inside of my elbow – seized with pain. I winced, and Cobra put his finger on the spot where it had hurt. "Striking out the batter with the slider feels good. But throwing a slider does not," he said.

It wasn't until Chicca – hitting in the third hole – got his bat on Novara's bread-and-butter pitch that the Peones realized that even giants have blind spots. Fighting off the slider in a protracted at-bat that saw him hack the ball into every square inch of the backstop, he made solid contact on Novara's twelfth pitch of the series, singling it to straightaway centre field to start a rally that he would see through to the end. The at-bat was something to behold: Novara's death-mask staring into Chicca's snake eyes, their jaws tightening. While I sometimes thought that it wouldn't have killed Chicca to mix a little bit of Brooks Robinson's gentle genius or Graig Nettles's honest gamesmanship into his game, in this situation, as the ball spanked off the end of his bat, putting him at first, from where he promptly stole second, then third, then scored on the Big Emilio's RBI, I was grateful that he was ours, not theirs, and that the Wild Thing's ill temper had met its match in old Bitter Face.

The Peones scored two runs, jumping into a lead that the Sicilians matched almost immediately with a passel of singles dashed about the field. In the fourth inning, Solid Gold, reaching for another slider, dinged a weak fly ball into left field, which the Athletics' player – the Fly – settled under but then dropped. With his cap springing from his head to reveal a forest of spiked gold-black hair, the Golden One ran like a fox with its tail on fire before sliding into third. The Fly's throw back to the infield revealed a weak arm, which showed the Peones that they were free to take the extra base on balls hit to the veteran fielder. Picking up such details was essential for either team to get the upper hand. Considering that it was a short series, the final result could be determined by how quickly one team learned how to exploit the opposition's weaknesses and mistakes.

As soon as Solid Gold got on base, Pietro called for the double steal, pouncing on what he hoped would be the Athletics' lack of focus in light of the Fly's costly error. It was a thrilling play, and it worked. Solid Gold barrelled home, putting the Peones in front 4-2. Sometimes the movement of players on a diamond is achingly static – base to base to base – but this was like watching the waking of a beehive, a sudden shiver of movement that reminded me that baseball can be as much allegro as adagio.

In the fourth inning, Gianni Cancelli arrived with a Peroni bottle filled with espresso, which the guys drained in an instant. Mirko, who'd proclaimed himself Dr. Zucchero, passed out sugar packets to his teammates, and someone's mother came down from the stands to hand them la busta di dolce, filled with cornetti and paste. I was concentrating on an important Peone at-bat when I felt a tap on my shoulder. It was the Emperor, waving a raisin and crema brioche and telling me, "Davide, you eat this, it is very, very good!" as if we were picnicking at the Villa Borghese. When I said, "Thanks, but Mario's at bat," he replied, "Okay. But we also have cornetti too, you know?"

Chicca singled to start the sixth inning, his second hit of the day. He advanced to second, but the Wild Thing retired the next two batters. Straining to keep the inning alive, Mario Simone – the other Peone for whom Novara's slider was too deadly to hit – fought off a fastball, awkwardly doinking the ball into left field. Noticing that the Fly was about to field the ball, Pietro wheeled Chicca home with a swooping right arm and skip-stepping backwards as the third baseman ran past the bag. Any manager would have sent the runner, and by the baseball book, it was absolutely the right play. But because the Athletics had noticed how much the Peones liked to run, the Fly knew that there was absolutely no way the Peones would not try for the extra base. Once the ball had left the bat, the Fly readied himself for a play at the plate. Chicca roared towards home, the ball caught up to his shoulder, flew past his head, and dropped at Carlos's feet. The old catcher got his glove on it and touched Chicca's leg.

"*Out!*"

The next inning, there was more excitement. Carlos Novara doubled down the line, igniting a rally that put Palermo within a run, 5-4. After the play, the Red Tiger, arguing that Carlos's ball had fallen on the other side of the chalk line, made a two-hundred-foot beeline towards the umpire, running at great speed from his place in the outfield to push his face into the arbitro's, jumping up and down on his heels and yelling, "Porco Madonnaaaa! Why do you fucking do this to us? Why are you trying to ruin this game?" It was as fierce a display of ump-baiting as I've seen, and because the Red Tiger was on him so fast, the umpire froze, his hands on his hips as the player jumped in the air.

"What's up with the Tiger?" I asked Paolo as we walked on to the field with the rest of the team.

"He is funny," he said. "He takes this drink, it makes him crazy."

"A drink?"

"Yes, a vegetable drink. It has something in it," he said, snapping an imaginary twig with his hands. "It makes Sandro go like that . . ."

After the confrontation ended, Paolo and Fabio from Milan held the Tiger by the shoulders and pointed him back to his position in right field, attempting to calm him down. I timed the outfielder's shitfit at eight minutes, a spectacular episode of hotheadedness. There are occasions when this kind of release can suddenly free a team, but as it turned out the Red Tiger's eruption did the Peones – and Pompozzi – no favours. Once things settled down, Carlos Novara widened his lead at second as the Wild Thing stepped to the plate. Earlier in the year, Pompozzi would have welcomed the scenario with all the eagerness of a man about to be strapped into a dentist's chair. But now, he gave Novara a tall, straight-shouldered stare.

As it turned out, the coda was actually longer than the song itself. The at-bat lasted three pitches, and, in the end, both players achieved what they'd set out to do. The Wild Thing struck the ball hard but hit it straight to Mario Mazza, whom Pietro had positioned perfectly. It was a small triumph for Pompozzi, but if the ball had been hit a few feet the other way, there's no telling how long the Athletics might have kept on swinging.

In Palermo's seventh, Carmello Maglio, the Athletics' stubble-chinned number-five hitter – and quietly the most formidable banger in the Sicilians' order – homered to tie the game at five. Maglio had a great, round face, which he shadowed by wearing his cap low, hiding a set of murderously deep, dark eyes. The ball that he hit took off like cannonfire, disappearing into the blue-white sky. No sooner had the Peones stomached Maglio's long bomb than Manny Manno, the skinny kid with the science-class lenses, plinked the ball over second base, driving in a go-ahead run.

The Big Emilio tried to stay the team's disappointment by seizing the game by the throat. He was also egged on by a group of Serie A2 players – who'd arrived to play at another of Santa Barbara's fields and had gathered behind home plate. They talked about Palermo's strengths, how they'd risen from the mat to take over the contest, how the Peones were good, but, after all, it was Serie B, and what could you expect from a team of players not good enough to make it to A2 or A1? This made the Big Emilio's nerves pop after a close call at first base. With the umpire's wail, "*Salvo!*", the big catcher turned around – facing the crowd as well as the arbitro – and, through his mask, unleashed a torrent of anger at the umpire. He tore off his mask, his face afire, his jaw snapping the air, and squeezed his fingers into a duck beak, which he waved under the umpire's chin. Carlos Novara jumped out of the Athletics' dugout and Pietro bounded onto the field to confront him. Pompo hustled in from the mound, and the Emperor, frozen at first base, bellowed, "This umpire is a criminal!" Pietro called the man in grey a pucinello (clown) while Emilio thrust his chest at the arbitro, then at Carlos Novara, then at the Emperor, who'd run in to calm him down. Once the catcher wandered away to the edge of the field, Pietro spoke in a low, even tone to the umpire, who replied that he was certain that the ball had landed fair, and that if he didn't get his charges in line, he'd start throwing them out one by one. Pietro told him, yes, of course, there'd be no other incidents, but as he walked towards the dugout, his face crumpled in disgust, I heard him mutter, "Go fuck you and your mother."

For the next few innings, the hitters tried desperately to get on base. They hacked and slashed at the ball, but neither the Wild Thing nor Pompo would let the game get too far from their reach. Novara continued to throw sliders for strikes while Pompo played with the speeds of his fastball, keeping the hitters high on their arches. After a particularly long, stirring at-bat, the Natural shot the ball down the line and dove into first. The umpire called him out.

I'm a great fan of diving in any sport. Diving shows great spirit and sacrifice to leap through the air without worrying what's going to happen to your face. I can support diving in any sport: diving to knock the puck away from a player on a breakaway, diving in the outfield to catch a fly ball, diving in the infield to snare a line drive; diving headfirst to punch the soccer ball into the goal; diving to make a through-the-air catch in the endzone; diving for a rugby try across the goal line (one of the reasons I've never been drawn to golf is because, really, there's very little diving). I can also get behind diving to save a human heart flung from a passing ambulance, to push a small child out of the way of a rumbling automobile, to close the front door before the house pet makes a run for it. But I've yet to get behind the sport of the same name. I much prefer a certain non-sanctioned sport invented by a tippled friend, who, upon coming across a barrel of cooking oil while wandering home one warm summer's night, coated his stomach, loins, and legs with the liquid, and, yup, dived all the way home.

As the Natural pulled himself off the ground with dirt scrubbed into his uniform, I was struck with the urge to express the same kind of spirit that he'd shown getting down the line. I leapt out of my seat, pointed at the speedy outfielder, then shouted at the players, *"Qui! Qui è il grande coure di Peones!"* Here! Here is the great heart of the Peones!

The boys were startled by my outburst. For a second, they said nothing. And then Chicca climbed to his feet. He walked towards me, pressed his face into a fiery red point, and turning back towards his teammates, punched his chest and howled, *"Che grande coure di Peones!"*

Still smouldering from the umpire's bad call, at his next turn at-bat, the Big Emilio met our wave of emotion, stepping to the plate against the Wild Thing with the game tied at six. Novara looked at him dead-eyed and impassive, and the Palermo infielders shuffled expectantly, as if the heat had been turned up under their feet. The Peones in the dugout stood in a line along the edge and, led by the Emperor, yelled, *"Non molliamo mai!"* We will never lose our nerve!

The Wild Thing, trying to staunch our song, stepped off the mound and wiped the back of his neck. Of course, this only made us sing louder. Chencho found a metal pipe and clanged it against the side of the dugout. Then Novara tucked himself into his windup, reared back, and shot a fastball that the Big Emilio was able to pull squarely into his sites. He throttled the pill, driving it into the far reaches of centre field. As the ball left the park, we leapt three feet off the ground. The Big Emilio punched his fist into the air, then shook it as he rounded first. The crowd – including the players from Serie A2 – went crazy. The Peones ran out to home plate, where they watched Emilio come down the line roaring, his tight face having exploded into a thousand arrows of light: "Forza! Forza! Let's put these devils into the ground!" Turning back to the dugout, I found Pietro standing near the bat rack, where he clapped his hands, then nodded confidently to himself. I walked over to him: "There's still lots of time, eh coach?" But Pietro was way ahead of me.

"No. Too much time," he said, correcting me.

The Athletics began the next inning in typically defiant fashion, pushing along a runner to third before flying him home: 7-7. Neither team had any quit in them. The two teams were evenly matched, I started to consider the intangibles – how long could either starting pitcher last? When would the heat start to take its toll? Would the Peones' addiction to speed be their downfall? Would Palermo's lack of speed be theirs? Was the fate of the game – the fate of all games, really – in hands greater than their own?

In the bottom of the ninth, a Peones victory felt within reach. They loaded the bases for Chicca, who'd been at the heart of the action the entire day. What happened next might not have meant anything during a mid-season game against a lesser team, but, in the post-season, every little detail – every managerial move, or non-move – matters. Having executed a successful squeeze earlier in the game, Pietro called for Chicca to lay down a bunt with the Natural sneaking in the Peone crouch down the line at third. It was the obvious play to call, but perhaps Chicca thought it too obvious. He gave Pietro a slight wag of the chin to signal that he understood the command, collected himself in the batter's box, and, shockingly, swung away.

He popped out.

Pietro rocked back on his heels like he'd been shot. The players grabbed their heads, as if they couldn't believe what they'd seen. Chicca, walking back to the dugout, swore a spitstream of invective, hurling his batting helmet against the fence. For the next two innings, Pietro berated his third baseman. When he wasn't on the field, he stood over Chicca in the dugout, trying to get him to say why he'd done what he'd done. And when Christian the rookie came to the plate with the bases loaded in the eleventh, I wondered if Pietro wasn't too distracted to notice that both Paolo and Fab Julie, each of them seasoned players, were sitting on the bench waiting to be called in to pinch-hit.

I thought it was only right to bring this to the skipper's attention.

"Hey, Paolo and Fabio aren't gonna become heroes just by sitting on the bench," I told him.

"Che?" he said.

"Fabio and Paolo. Shouldn't they pinch-hit for Christian?"

"*Che?*" he snapped, shooting me the fierce look that I'd expected all summer.

Christian lashed heroically at the first pitch, but the ball landed in the glove of the Athletics' second baseman. The inning ended with nothing having been decided. Then, in the top of the twelfth, the Wild Thing strode to the dish, dropped the bat head to the plate, balled himself up into his batting stance, and clubbed a three-run homer over the centre-field wall. The Athletics greeted him at home plate en masse, with some of the smaller players climbing on top of his shoulders. The slugger shook them off and high-fived his brothers, who'd gathered in the dugout among themselves, vowing to pin it down for good.

The Peones bowed out in the next inning, losing the game 11-7. With the final out, the blue and white collapsed against the grass. For what seemed like forever, they lay pinned to the warm field, staring achingly into the empty sky.

27

IF THEY DON'T WIN, IT'S A SHAME

W hat's the toughest part of being a writer? Oh, hearing the sound of your own voice prattling in your head for twenty-four consecutive months when you'd rather be stuffing your face into a bass bin at a Rocket from the Crypt show, for one. Another drawback is all the pen lids ingested while lost in a writerly trance, convinced that you're scribbling poetry to tease the gods when what you've actually written is, "And then, like a blue-and-white pigeon, Paolo perched atop the Borgo wall." There are the many fists-upon-the-forehead searchings for the perfect metaphor that isn't; the I-shoulda-been-a-crane-operator humblings of spending four days on a chapter that not even the editor of *Penthouse* letters would find sturdy enough to print; convincing yourself that the best thing you could do for your book would be to take a break and not write, thereby loosing the rodent of guilt to chew a cruller-sized hole in your brain; and the cold sweat of worry that comes from journeying into the mansion of storytelling, where, if one of the walls isn't built right, the whole house caves in, exposing the writer – adrift in a dream of hoisting highballs with the literary lions of his time –

as nothing but a crumpled figure on a cement floor, chewing on his hand.

In the case of this writer and this book, however, I'd have to say that the toughest part of the creative process was having to report that game two was a game for the dumpster. The score – 15-8, Palermo – left the Peones one game away from elimination in front of their home crowd.

Cobra started the game. He threw one pitch, then felt a hot, seizing pain in his bicep. He raised his arm to stretch out its tendons, but the injured muscle just tightened harder. It was a shocking turnabout for the Peones' hopes. After taking the longest twenty-foot stroll of his career from the top of the hill to the bottom of the bench, the small pitcher spent the afternoon sitting alone, staring at his unscuffed spikes. Later, he moved to a place nearer to the dugout's exit, behind a few overturned tubs and an old card table, his shoulders slumped in defeat.

The Peones were divided among the angry and the disappointed. Some of them – including Pietro – were upset because they suspected that Cobra had known all along that he wouldn't be able to pitch, and that his stubborn pride and vanity had fooled him into believing that he could. They thought he hadn't listened to his arm, hadn't thought of the team. The Palermo lineup unloaded against Chencho, who was forced to enter the game early and cold, and who deserved better considering how badly he wanted to beat Palermo and how hard he'd worked to prepare himself in practice. Watching il matto sinistro pitch against the Southern clubbers was like seeing a man hugging a swaying flagpole in a windstorm. When balls weren't being pelted past him, they were falling into gaps or popping in and out of his teammates' gloves. One high pop fly dropped above the Emperor's head. He looked like Gene Kelly in a rainstorm, spinning into a blue-and-white blur until he could no longer reach out far enough to pull the ball in. Even though both Solid Gold and Chicca walloped the ball around the field, pulling the team from trailing 9-1, to within four runs, the Athletics were confident enough to tear off their jerseys and cool themselves as if playing at a summer picnic, somewhere between the roast pig lunch and the three-legged race.

Feeling helpless against Palermo's tornado of power, the Peones lay down in the face of imminent defeat. Mirko stretched out on the bench and fell asleep, while others, like Fabio from Milan and Paolo, sat with their backs pinned to the fence, their faces long and drawn. Mario Simone and the Big Emilio were loath to sit in the dugout – which, because it was above-ground and in full view of the fans and the opposition, offered no dark shadows in which to escape – choosing instead to pace behind the bench. Even Pietro, who usually held form against whatever fate his team had been dished, sought refuge among the garbage cans and discarded furniture that seemed to be a feature of every dugout in Italy.

Then 'Nando came to the rescue. Around the seventh inning, he walked into the dugout carrying a large tub of freshly harvested purple grapes, immediately rousing the players from their sad slumber. The boys picked over the ripe fruit glumly, then reached in with both hands. "Oggi, è il primo giorno per questa uva," said 'Nando as he crammed his cheeks. The players' faces lit up as the tart juice hit their throats. It was the perfect tonic for the bitter grit of losing, and we devoured the contents of the tub, leaving only a pool of water and some spat seeds at the bottom.

I noticed an immediate change in the team's mood. Despite the misery of the score – the three Novara brothers had each hit home runs, and Umberto had pitched with as much command and confidence as his big brother – the glory of the season's first-plucked fruit seemed to be enough to blot out the sadness of the game.

Do or die. The Italians call it *spareggio*. The term is actually a bit of a misnomer in sport considering that, in certain cases, with loss also comes life. In the instance of Olympic boxers fighting in a semifinal, the losers end up sharing a bronze, while both baseball and football allow passes into the post-season for "wild card" teams, rewarded for their ability not to win their division. Similarly, I can't imagine that any team who loses the championship of anything feels close to death on the morning after. Hungover, maybe, but dead? Tumbling at the start of a sprint, forgetting one's shot putt, or having your trousers drop while bowling ten frames at the local lanes: that's more like it. But this is not to suggest that the do-or-die games aren't cause for great concern among those who play them. I'm usually as calm and composed as the San Diego Chicken whenever I find my shoulder blades pressed to the wall. One minute I'll be swimming in hot, rising sweat, the next I'm encased in cold fear, a pneumonia of the spirit, at least before the game. No one can touch me, let alone talk to me. I'm a walking mass of nerves and frightened eyes.

Over the course of my softball team's existence, playing among the overweight, underweight, gammy-legged, near-sighted, drug-addled, booze-slurping rubber-armed minions of inner-city scrub ball, we've made it to three league finals, winning once and losing twice. While our victory – against the godless terror that is Squirrely's restaurant – was indeed sweet and life-affirming and memorable, I can't say that I actually enjoyed winning, since most of the time I was tensed for whatever horrible turn of events might make us lose. After the final out of the championship game, there was no post-victory lollapalooza. We simply shook each other's hands. We're much better suited to losing. The first loss was the most heartbreaking of all baseball varieties: a bottom-of-the-ninth defeat to a team that we hadn't beaten in the seven-year history of our club. Our undoing came after we'd taken the lead in the top of the ninth, making the loss all the more sickening and vivid.

With the Peones preparing to face their gravest moment of the 2002 season, I sat down in the dugout and tried to stay out of their hair by doing what I'd done best that summer: I wrote. I slashed at the pages, digging my pen into the rough paper. I wrote about my time among the Peones. I wrote about how experiencing sport in another place is like walking down a dark country road that's familiar in the way the trees look, the tint of the night sky, and the call of the evening birds, even though it's different from any road you've ever walked down before. I worked over the pages, knowing that the crisp flavour of September meant that it would soon be time to return to friends with one syllable names and a cold game played under pounds of heavy equipment, and that, upon sinking back into my life in Canada, my time in Italy would become just a dream. As I raised my pen from the book, the top of my forearm aching, I realized that the only thing that remained of the season was its end, which might come in a matter of hours, maybe minutes, even seconds.

Then I remembered that Janet and the kids were coming to meet me at the ballpark. Looking up to see if they were in the bleachers, I saw Mirko standing over me, munching on a tart and pointing at my formerly scribbling hand, exclaiming: "Che cosa scrivi? What are you writing?" he wanted to know. "Che scrivi forte?"

Game three: I settled in to watch the Peones face their executioner, hoping with all my heart that they'd steel themselves for the baseball battle of their lives. But they couldn't have been less steeled. Instead, they were as loose as a Cubs fan in the seventh inning of dollar Bud night, bounding about the diamond like it was the first time their feet had touched grass. The energy that had abandoned them in game two had returned at twice the strength. It was remarkable. There was singing, laughter, joking. With Mario Simone's first at-bat, a voice called from beside our dugout – "Hey, Mario. '*Pia la palanca!*'" (Get your plank!) It was the Big Emilio, of all people, swinging a piece of wood the size of a cellar door and laughing. The Emperor strode across the dugout with a strudel held aloft, which the players ripped apart and shoved into their mouths. Paolo, whom Pietro had inserted into the lineup to catch, was pestering the Wild Thing from behind the plate, asking him, "Are you the oldest Novara? Or are you younger? When were you born? Where did you play baseball growing up?" Paolo told me later, "He kept telling me to shut up, but I kept saying, 'Oh, that's not a nice thing to say! Why do you have such a bad mouth?'"

Pietro stayed on the edge of the action, letting his players goof

Fab Julie.
(Cathy Bidini)

around. His two significant moves had been to start Fab Julie – as he'd suggested in the car – and insert Paolo, the veteran, into the lineup to catch him. As the infielder-turned-pitcher threw strike after looping strike to the befuddled Athletic hitters, I thought he looked a little like a baseball angel, his soft face and quick smile reminding me of David Cone or Greg Maddux on a midweek job in July. Pietro told me later that he'd had no choice but to start Julie, but I knew that the Old Bugger was trying to put one over on me. He could've cashed Julie in game two, and saved Chencho for the final game, but it was clear what he was thinking: because Julie was liked by everyone, the team would rally behind him. Since they needed a player to focus their prayers upon, Julie was a better option than Chencho, about whom there was very little that was angelic.

Even though Julie hadn't started in seven years, Paolo worked him just right. He mixed his curveball and change of speeds expertly, so that the Athletics – Pietro's hunch that they'd lose their edge after the second game was dead-on – were off balance the entire time. They had no answer for the Peones' high spirits either. They'd come into the game prepared to squeeze the throats of the young Nettunese; that their would-be victims were laughing and gorging themselves on pie and grapes and pots of espresso was too bewildering for the behemoths from the south, too weird and unsettling. And when Carlos Novara threw a shitfit of his own – sarcastically applauding the umpire for what he thought was a questionable call – I relaxed for the first time in three days, looking ahead to the following weekend, when games four and five would be played in Palermo. If this team of clowns from the ancestral home of Italian baseball could make it through a day when they'd once seemed as dead as da Vinci, anything was possible.

28

THE NIGHT OF THE WOLVES

Earlier in the summer I'd been surprised to find the Nettunese almost completely indifferent to the World Cup. I'd thought that all Italians were crazy about soccer. But it wasn't until autumn that that game took hold, even of the Peones. Then Mario Simone invited me to accompany him and his friends to Lazio-Milan, the fourth game of that year's Serie A schedule, to be contested at Olympic Stadium in Rome. Whenever I mentioned to anyone where I was going, they told me how lucky I was. Marco Calligaro, Janet's cousin in Rome, said it would be a dream game – Milan had one of Italy's best (and most expensive) sides, while Lazio always played with the fight of tigers – and that tickets were very hard to find. "You sure you are going?" he asked. I told him that Daria – who'd remained on the scene despite the fact that Mario continued to romance Laura long-distance – had an uncle who ran a Nettuno ticket agency. When Mario handed me my ticket, I wondered whether her uncle was, in fact, the tie that bound these two together. After all, love is love, but soccer is soccer.

Nettunese kids loved baseball, but in early August their minds turned to soccer. I watched as ten- and eleven-year-olds at a temporary pitch constructed at Vittoria Bagne worked the ball with more dexterity than I could ever dream of. For two weeks, they played games twice a day, ending in a championship draw. On the train ride to Rome, I spotted young and old playing calcietto, a seven-man version of soccer played on a pitch the size of a small hockey rink. Greater Lazio was painted with these patches of green and brown the way Toronto is dabbed with ovals of ice. Calcietto – or calciotto, which uses eight men – was a relatively new sport, developed because it proved too difficult to find twenty-two men with the time for a proper game of footie. Calcietto was street ball gone legit. In Nettuno, games sprouted up like fungi, and it seemed that the whole of Italy flip-flopped from a country unsmitten by the World Cup into one that lived to play soccer.

Even the Peones took to playing soccer after practice, a pastime I felt obliged – if not goaded – to join in. I might not possess anything like the sweet steps of Mario Simone or the Red Tiger, both of whom were considered blue-chip prospects in their cadetti days (Mario continued to play high-level, competitive soccer), but still, I tried not to suck. As it turned out, I only barely sucked. The ball, when kicked to me, would more or less bounce off my shin, and the one time I lashed at the fruit with my head, it shot straight up, landing in a backwards arc somewhere near our goal. This was the first and last time I tried a header, which felt like being struck on the forehead with a brick. It left me dizzy, which I cunningly parlayed into a personal advantage, acting shell-shocked in order to avoid the burden shared by all lazy soccerists – the backcheck – in which one is required, if you can fathom such a thing, to dash to the deep end of the field to take away the ball from the other team. Soccer, I learned quickly, is not a game for the indolent; and thus, not one for me. Give me a sport where you either stand in one place for a really long time, like baseball, or cry "Wheee!!" when you're making a dash up the rink, like hockey.

Mario and I were among a group of twelve fans – our allegiances split between both teams – who made our way to Stadio Olimpico. We walked through the busy grounds, which were ringed by a circle of marble statues symbolizing the world of sports, though baseball, represented by a figure in short pants with a bat hiked over its shoulder, was not part of the ring, but rather squired away near one of the exits. It was also the only figure without a city name on its plinth. When I'd asked Giulio Glorioso about it, he told me, "I kind of like it that it's alone. Somehow it tells the story. It's still wearing short pants, just like our game."

Mario led us to a green door just off Curva Sud, through which a few thousand Milan fans were streaming. Once behind the door, Mario pulled off his coat. Now he was properly dressed for the game in a Milan jersey, official Milan ball cap, and a red-and-black team scarf. We found our way to our seats, which weren't seats at all but blue plastic pans we were meant to stand on. I gazed out towards the inviting field (real grass), considering for a dreamy second what I'd need to do to elude the riot police and their guard dogs and take a champion's dash across the turf. I was about to scribble something to that effect when I realized, with a start, that I'd left my notebook in the car. Then Mario started jumping up and down like a piston, shouting *"Lazio is shit! Lazio is shit!"* His target was the Lazio supporters, who sat on the other side of a ten-foot Plexiglas wall. The whole stadium rumbled with such taunts, a beast coming to life.

Minutes later the skies opened. The Lazio fans, goaded by the Milanese' cries of *"Back to Serie B!"* climbed to their feet and, within an instant, it was raining fruit. The Milanese supporters – many of whom had unfurled great red-and-black banners, some with stylized monster heads stitched in the middle – were deluged by oranges, tomatoes, lemons, shoes, bottles of Coke and water, and the occasional Euro, one of which hit me on the arm. A cordon of riot police rattled down the steps to separate the warring fans, their helmets providing an alternative target for both sides. The police stood in a twenty-foot swath of seats left empty because it was within range of any scrub with a decent arm. Critics have often compared sport to war, which I never really got – scoffing at the thought that the Anaheim Angels versus the Milwaukee Brewers was anything more than the gleeful play of overpaid fat guys – until this night. Only Lazio-Milan wasn't *like* war.

It was war.

The citrus blitzkrieg came at us in waves. Lazio would sing a disparaging song, Milan would answer with one of their own, and the fruit would fly. To my left, an older man feigned outrage whenever a fruit or battery or lighter landed in our section – shouting as if the fans from Lazio had evolved just one rung above the feral ape – before hoisting the offending mandarino back over the wall, thus returning both the bullet and the gun. I threw my hands over my head and peered out at the field, where the players were warming up, Lazio in powder blue, Milan in matte black and red. I stole a look at the stadium clock as Mario Simone waved his fist and screamed, "*Take my shit, Lazio!*"

It was 7:30.

One hour until game time.

Forty minutes later, eighty thousand people had filled the stadium: a sea of humanity, locked in song and the threat of revolt. And this was only the fourth weekend of play in Serie A. Both teams had yet to settle into their positions near either the top or bottom of the table. For five hours, the game's pitch approached Stanley Cup Final or World Series intensity.

There's an enormous difference between how sporting events are presented in Europe and on the other side of the Atlantic. In North America, fans are assaulted by stage-directed sound and light, but at Stadio Olimpico, most of the voices I heard were the fans'. The public-address announcer spoke only to inform Milan supporters that they were required to stay in the park one hour after game time to allow authorities time to clear a path safe from the Lazio Ultras, some of the most dreaded villains in Italian football.

Back home, great importance is placed on the availability and range of concessions (although never the affordability), but in our section, I found only one drink stand. A single roving soda and salt salesman was constantly ridiculed by fans, and, at times, was pelted with detritus. I don't think he sold a peanut all night. Supporters munched on panini and pizza that they'd brought into the park. None of it was used as ammunition, further proof that Italians value eating over all else. The other big difference was the price of the event – twenty-two Euros – which, these days, won't get you in to see the Minnesota Wild play the Nashville Predators.

Before kickoff, the players were introduced on two small, CFL-quality video screens at either end of the pitch, followed by a short film depicting the flight of an eagle – l'aquila, Lazio's symbol – sailing high over Rome, to which Lazio fans sang their fight song – "*Vai mogliamo mai.*" Milan answered with a war cry of their own – "*Sandro Nesta lei!*" – at which point I felt a rush of heat behind me and turned to find a dozen Milanese fans waving flares with their bare hands, showering the crowd with hot light. At the far end of the pitch – in the Curva Nord – sat the Ultras, fans so notorious that the Milanese were seated at the opposite end of the stadium, beyond their reach. From their section, the Ultras launched bomb after bomb at the field, leaving trails of blue and white smoke, and as the eagle sailed across the screen, the largest bandiera I've ever seen was unfurled – of an eagle, no less – which dwarfed entire sections of supporters and was met with cries of "Lazio is shit! Back to Serie B" from the Milanese. Suddenly, Lazian flares started coming over the Plexiglas barrier into our section, one of them landing in the first few rows. People in the surrounding seats started motioning for a stretcher: someone had been hit. I looked back and saw the other Milanese fans – at least those who weren't waving banners depicting Lazio players in various states of distress, one of them stuck bleeding at the end of a pitchfork – just shrug. After a few minutes, a stretcher finally appeared, but as much as I'd wanted to follow this subplot to the end, I could not: the smoke from the bombs was too thick. All I could make out was the blur of the players' jerseys against the brilliant green of the field.

I was grateful that the bitter autumn wind finally managed to disperse the acrid smoke. After a spell, the game was suddenly in front of me, if not around, beside, and on top me. Mario bit his lip and, fists clenched, watched the frenzied action. At the five-minute mark, Rivaldo, Milan's prized off-season signing, lifted the ball near the goal-mouth, and Paolo Maldini clubbed it into the mesh with the flat of his head. Our section exploded. Mario was so happy, he was crying. A family that sat behind me were crying too, and, at one point, the matriarch, taking me for one of hers, threw her arms over my shoulders and planted a wet one on my cheek. A small green tomato fell from the sky and landed at my feet. I picked it up and held it in my hand until, twenty minutes later, Lazio evened the score, sending their charges screaming and leaping against the Plexiglas. Mario grabbed my arm, the veins of his neck protruding like a bicycle chain. I was left with no choice.

I chucked the fucker.

29

COMING HOME

Palermo.

It's my mother's name. My grandparents' name. Their grandparents' name. Their grandparents' grandparents' name. While I'm not at all certain how the Sicilian capital managed to hook its moniker to mine, I fancy that, when my ancestor first hit the mainland, his fun-loving antics, broad humour, and espresso-bar wisdom made others ask, "Where does Giovanni get such charm? Palermo? Veramente? Hey, Johnny Palermo! Over here, Johnny Palermo! Come sit with us!" On my way to Palermo, I felt I was travelling to the place the original Me had come from, the nest of all nests.

A day ahead of the rest of the team, I flew to Palermo, and as my plane descended into the Madonie mountains – a rough and beautiful stand of rock, their brown-sugar slopes giving way to turquoise waters and golden beaches – my heart was racing, my blood high. Beyond the search for self, there was, of course, the practical purpose for coming here: to watch the Peones roar at the face of elimination like a dog howling into the mouth of a lion. Were the Peones a touring musical act, I would have been the advance guy. Not that I papered utility poles or passed out handbills (BEWARE! CHENCHO IS COMING), but, in a way, I was there to straighten the occasion's karma, a quiet salvo against the Athletics themselves. I wandered the streets in my Nettuno colours, a fifth columnist working to corrupt the energy that ostensibly gives the home team the upper hand (not that it had done the Peones much good at Santa Barbara).

It wasn't until I'd wandered into the heart of the city that I realized what I was up against. In Nettuno, a visiting team would be immediately recognized – and its presence reported – after a short stroll through the Borgo, but Palermo's crowds and action and busyness was such that I could have stood at the gates of Teatro Massimo – Europe's first concert hall – with a GIAMPIERO NOVARA IS A BUM-LICKING WOZZLEHEAD sign and no one would have given me a second glance.

Palermo reminded me of Hong Kong, especially with its great fist of rock – Mount Pellegrino – punching the sky above the city. The centre of town was as wild a tumble as the former British colony, only with the occasional Arabesque, gold-mosaic church rising like an enormous sand castle in the middle of the city's markets. They, like Wanchai and Sham Shui Po in Hong Kong, were places of furious sound and energy and writhed like snakes that, if you looked over enough market stalls, you'd surely find for sale, twenty Euros a crate.

In parts of Palermo, there are as many magicians as doctors, more puppeteers than soccer players. It's a city where the culture of North Africa (Tunisia lies just twenty hours away, by boat) bumps into Mafia protocol, and where Baroque and Norse art adorns churches as tall and magnificent as Rome's. In the endlessly winding Vucciria market, many of the merchant stalls were built into the stone door frames and wall niches of old, decrepit palaces. The market offered a cornucopia of goods and produce. I passed a high-rise of small, cardboard boxes filled entirely with dark chocolate biscuits; the most enormous orange squash I've ever seen; a circle of young Arab men in robes and fezzes doing sword tricks; and a hairy-browed fruit seller in an undershirt sweating onto his tomatoes, which were covered in a black crust of flies. I devoured un panino di trippa (shredded, fatty beef, crushed sea salt, and lime, served on a warm sesame seed bun); sampled il formaggio di cavallo (horse cheese), one of the rarest of all Italian cheeses; and bartered mildly with a small man who sold beautiful old black-and-white soccer posters and other paraphernalia from a fine wooden bookcase that belonged in a Victorian drawing room. It was easy to become entranced with the sights, smells, and tastes of the market, but I had to keep my head up for the motorinos that roared down the alleyways at highway speeds, many of them driven by boys who couldn't have been older than twelve.

Seduced by the charm and life of the city, I realized, as I lay on my bed at the end of the day, that my attempts to penetrate Nettuno's enemy state had been for naught. It hadn't helped matters, either, that in a record shop/bookstore I'd stopped on the way home, I'd found my band's name staring back at me from a wall rack featuring imported CDs. Later that night at a restaurant just outside the Santa Catarina temple, I overheard two elderly Floridians trying, in worse-than-broken Italian, to ask one of their long-lost cousins the name of his wife. After five months on the Boot, I thought, What the frig? and gave it a shot, not only drawing out the name of the wife, but also his brother's name, what he did for a living, and the name of the town where he was born. The grateful Yanks offered to buy me a drink and asked what part of Italy I was from. "Nettuno," I told them. With the word, my stomach jumped.

The game.

It felt strange to be separated not only from my family, but also from the team. The great thing about being part of a team is that you belong. Even those times when the coach is on your case, when you can't find your game, or when you feel disenchanted, if momentarily, with the sport, you belong. Even after you boot a ball or lose a batter or strike out with the bases loaded in the ninth inning of a championship game, you still belong. Teams comfort and cloud. They throw an arm around the vulnerable, shy, and self-doubting. When they work – as the Peones did – they stretch as vast and wide as the breadth of the sun to warm whatever fear or pain the player may suffer in life or in sport. Teams are more essential than ever in a world pushed apart by technology (though not, I gathered, the timeless Sicilian world), where it's easy to fall victim to doubt and fear and isolation. By bringing together people with different realities – not by videophone or chat rooms, either, but by a shared effort – teams unify the disparate, even if it's to pitch horseshoes or shoot darts or swat shuttlecocks, to say nothing of chasing flies under the broad smile of the Roman sun. Teams – like bands – show the world the ability of people to get along. They are a pronouncement to the world that people want to be together, that they need each other, that, despite nasty falls and bitter words and cruel fortunes, people can persist and occasionally triumph together in spite of a society – at least in North America – that tries to wedge us apart, to compartmentalize and cross-market and demographicize us. On the ice or grass, you're encouraged – at least at an amateur level – to be who you want to be. Teams teach us to listen to our hearts, and worry about the consequences later. They draw on a player's naked emotion, rather than cloak it for fear of embarrassment or reprisal. Families do this too, but at home, you're born naked. Home is where you implode, or explode, for the first time. A team is where you do it the *next* time.

Sometimes it takes leaving to realize what a team really is. During my first night in Palermo, I wandered downtown in my Peones shirt to the beat of the cafés and open-walled bars swinging full blast, places like the Aboriginal Internet Café flooding the streets with young life. I saw one kid – maybe the first drunk Italian I'd seen the entire summer – lean over and puke from the back seat of his friend's motorino, a glass-eyed man pouring dusty chestnuts into a paper cone – one Euro per sleeve – and a bride and groom who crossed Via Masquero, stopped at a café, shot back two espresso hits, then dashed out again, their heads tipped back in laughter, the bride's train grimy from the street. I should have felt free and alive. But I was lost without my team.

The next morning, I came across two signs that suggested how the afternoon might play itself out. The first sign occurred in the Vucciria market, where my meander was stopped by a strange sound. Behind a table crowded with socks and underwear, I spotted a little boy holding an empty plastic soft drink bottle and a rock. He threw the rock in the air and hit it with the bottle, swatting it into an alley. From what I could tell, he was playing baseball. Likely he wouldn't have known baseball from Tai Bo, but it didn't matter. While Nettunese kids flooded the ballfields with upwards of thirty local junior teams, I hadn't yet come across any of them playing baseball with a found object. Seeing him do his thing, I got the sense of how games are born on their own among kids using rocks, bottles, or whatever else might be at hand, with nary a soldier nor a marketing campaign to bring it to them.

I left the boy to his game, but something made me turn around and watch him some more, further considering this point. The boy froze, eyeing me suspiciously. I moved ahead, then turned back again. He stood still, holding the rock in one hand, his bat in the other, waiting to strike the ball the moment I disappeared from view. Understanding that a game had come upon us, we stared each other down for a few moments, right there in the teeming Babel of Sicily.

On the way to the airport, I mused over what I'd seen, fearing that the birth-of-the-game tableau might be a harbinger of the day's events, to say nothing of the fact that the young boy had clearly won our game. Just as I wondered whether my attempt to ready the Peones' karma had managed to spin the tables all wrong, I looked to the sky for an answer and saw the second sign: a plane, only three hundred feet above my head, coming in from Rome.

Fenway Park may have Il Grande Verde, glorious for making left fielders appear as if they're about to be flattened by a giant Ping Pong paddle. Chavez Ravine, I'm told, is the setting for some of the most beautiful Pacific sunsets in all of sport. The park where the Houston Astros play – I've forgotten its name, but why anyone would want to give up calling it the Astrodome is beyond me – has a small train in which revellers can ride, putting a whole new spin on why serving alcohol at a sporting event is not the greatest idea. San Francisco has its bayside homer pond, Chicago's Comiskey Park has a gritty, Southside charm, Wrigley is well regarded for its vineland and daylight ball, and Yankee Stadium's outfield gap gives a view of the chugging people-mover that Billy Strayhorn immortalized in song: the A train. I've even borne witness to the wonders of a baseball field – encrusted in ice at the time, but no matter – in Ulaanbaatar, Mongolia, with an outfield so cavernous that nomads are able to live there year-round in their traditional felt domes – called *gers* – without fear of being awakened by tape-measure dingers (or roaring crowds. After all, it's not like baseball possesses the kinetic drama of archery, one of Mongolia's more wildly popular sports).

However, I defy anyone to find a ballpark as breathtaking as the home of the Palermo Athletics. The field was lorded over by three mountains that slouched to the base of the outfield. The scale of the rock engulfed the park, making it look like a patch of grass sprouting at the bottom of a primeval firepit. On the mountain beyond left field, a slab of stone had sheared away, revealing hard pink flesh the size of Long Island. The middle mountain was dotted with rows of houses with their doors and windows smashed, a Mafia housing project long since abandoned. The third mountain, by contrast, seemed to be in retreat, as if setting off to find more stone with which to build a bigger, more imposing wall.

At home plate, the batter must have felt like a club-waving caveman. To some of the weaker Peones batters, for whom the ball looked small at the best of times, it would have seemed no bigger than a Chiclet flying against the torrent of rock that filled the hitter's vision. As with Santa Margherita's duomo in Montefiascone, the setting imposed itself on the game, forcing the players to consider the power of the land as well as the players that it had produced.

The setting at Campo Palermo showed why the Athletics were so much bigger than the rest of the Italian clubs. It was obvious to me that the Wild Thing's gargantuan form was the product of his surroundings; he'd had no choice but to bulk up to match the fearsome rock, lest he become dwarfed by it. His broad shoulders and massive arms were a natural extension of the land, and as I watched him warm up before the game, I wondered whether, with the mountains at his back, his arm would be even more venerable than before, carrying with it the demands of the rising rock, on whose cliffs the gods were most assuredly perched.

To be fair, Pompo gave away nothing to the Wild Thing in terms of how his image played against the ballpark's grand stone theatre. While Novara stood upon the mound like a mastodon draped in coloured silk, Pompo rose from his dirt perch like a great tree. Having embraced his role as the team's ace, he took to the hill as if he demanded no less a setting. Their demeanour promised a battle of baseball giants, and that's exactly what the morning produced: two hours of breathtaking hardball.

Before the game started, I decided I'd sink into the event, observing the game as a fan who'd accidentally stumbled upon it. The season had been such an emotional ride that I wanted to step back for a change, to let the game unfold without my heartbeat racing at every pitch. But once things got under way, my voice came alive with the rest of the team: "*Attenzione! Franchayy!*" "*Grande, Pompo! Grande!*" "*Pensa casa!*" (Think home.) And when Maglio got ahold of a Pompo fastball, crushing it into right field to put Palermo ahead 2-0 in the first inning, I wailed long and hard before biting on my knuckle, seized by the glorious, horrible tension of the day.

In the second inning, the Peones answered the Athletics' lead, freeing my knuckle from its snare. They scored twice after a carousel of singles, stolen bases, and molti errori from Palermo, who, truth be told, seemed a little tight in the field. I'd assumed that the sheer power of the land would daunt the young Nettunese, but I hadn't considered the effect it might have on the home team, how the expectations of the Sicilian sporting gods might prove too demanding.

Pietro's strategy in games four and five, as it had been for the entire year, was to run, run, and run. The Peones' fourth inning was an exemplar of this style. It was also proof of how his management was both a plus and a minus when it came to the ways of winning baseball.

The Big Emilio started the inning by reaching on another error and was driven home by Chicca: 3-2, Peones. Next, Mario Mazza lined a ball to the shortstop, and as the infielder scrambled after the ball, Mazza kept running to second and Chicca ran past third, but, eventually, both were caught between stations as the shortstop returned the ball to the infield. By all rights, the infielder should have chased Chicca and prevented the run, but inexplicably he did not, choosing to nail Mario at second and allowing the Peones to vault into a two-run lead. The Peones' over-running had paid dividends for the blue and white, but in any other circumstance, with perhaps a more sure-handed shortstop, this kind of basepath abandon would have been fatal. I told Paolo, "Pietro's gotta resist his tendencies when it comes to sending guys. This is the semifinal, for cryin' out loud."

Paolo, ignoring the nervousness in my voice, said, "Yes, you are right. Now I must eat my salad and rice," and disappeared into the dugout's tunnel. He returned with his lunch and a piece of focaccia, which the fellows had imported from Nettuno in two oil-stained paper bags.

In the sixth inning, with the score 5-3 for Nettuno, Chicca laid down a bunt, but was thrown out after a flubbed hit-and-run by Mario Mazza, the second time they'd blown a fundamental play.

Chicca glowered at his teammate as he walked across the field into the dugout, returning to his place at the end of the bench. Mario eventually hit the ball hard, singling to centre, and was followed by the Red Tiger, who crushed a ball into the Sicilian skies. The ball climbed so high it was hard to know whether it would land in the glove of one of the outfielders or kiss the grass. Mario, sweep-stepping along the line to second, waited until the ball landed, then took off around the bases. He rounded third base as the right fielder – the Fly – gathered in the ball and lofted it to Carlos Novara, protecting home. Mazza, needing a clever slide to evade the tag, landed at home with all the grace of a man tripping over a sidewalk curb, tumbling into Novara's glove when he should have either swept around him or barrelled through the catcher.

As Mario got up from his fall, and made his way back to the dugout, Chicca sprang from his seat to assail the young second baseman: "*Porco Dio!* Tua scivola era *brutta!* Why can't you slide, man? What is your problem?"

"My leg! My leg is hurting me," said Mario, giving his teammate a series of quick-wristed duck beaks.

"*Fungooolo!* This is the playoffs! Do or die! Capito?" roared Chicca in a moment of leadership that left the rest of us bewildered. Mario argued a bit more – "If I hurt my leg, how can I play the rest of the game?" – then sat down and rubbed his sore gamba, aware that he'd failed to sacrifice his body for the team.

Mazza's non-slide loomed even larger as Palermo tied the game, 5-5. Guiseppe Leone doubled to Mario Simone, who collected the ball, threw it back to the infield, then turned and stared, hands on his hips, at the scoreboard in dead centre field just as a pack of pigeons burst from one of the black metal frames. With the score tied and the threat of a greater rally shading the scene, the Athletics suddenly found their voice, chanting "*Be-Pe, Be-Pe!*" as Guiseppe Acquaviva strode to the plate. This was followed by clapping and heavy foot stomping, at which point a teenager in the crowd found a sudden use for his hand drum, thumping a downbeat that echoed around the park.

The players shouted "*Be-Pe!*" on the one-two, leaving the three-four to rest. After recognizing the pattern of the chant – not that it possessed the technical complexity of "In the Court of the Crimson King" or anything – I decided that it was only right that I use my instincts as a musician to answer the home team's cheer. Though I held no particular animosity towards Beppe himself, I did my part as best I could, chiming in on the three-four with "sucks."

"*Be-Pe!*"

"*Sucks!*"

Realizing that the word *sucks* – while universal in sporting venues throughout North America – might not translate into Italian, I adapted my taunt:

"*Be-Pe!*"

"*Merda!*"

"*Be-Pe!*"

"*Merda!*"

This call and response persisted through the at-bat, and when Pompo threw a fastball down the middle of the plate, striking out Beppe Merda on five pitches, the Peones shouted as they ran off the field – "*Vai mogliamo mai!*" and "*Payyy-own-knees!*" – egged on, I liked to think, by your CanRock choral hoser.

The singing grew louder as the Peones caught fire. Solid Gold, who, as he had in game one, had looked terrible in his first few at-bats against the Wild Thing, rose up and lashed the ball into left field for a double. The Natural, batting second, did the same, driving home the go-ahead run. As the Wild Thing leaned in against the Big Emilio, the Emperor added to the repertoire with "Under Pressure" by Queen. The at-bat was the first of the day where the strength of each club was directly pitted against the other. Emilio raised his bat behind his head like a strong man about to strike a gong, while Giampiero, playing the required head game, shook off Carlos, nodded to his catcher, shook him off again, then threw. Every pitch in the at-bat was informed with this cat-and-mouse routine, as the boys sang:

"*Be-Pe merda!*"

"*Payyy-own-knees!*"

"*Unda presha!*"

To the sound of our voices howling across the field, the Big Emilio widened his eyes, drew back his bat, and swung with force. "*Stee-rike!*" Giampiero shook his fist. We sucked air and reeled on.

With their next turn at bat, Palermo promptly answered, tying the game at six. Maglio doinked a single, and was followed by the Wild Thing, who drove him in. With the go-ahead run on first, Pompo shook his head and pressed his eyes shut. Having ordered the universe of his thoughts, he stared at the Big Emilio and retired the next three batters in order, pitching with pinpoint location and a fastball that never lagged below the low 80s. After striking out the Lion to retire the side, the Peones' ace strode off the field as if thirty television cameras were trained on him. Head down, shoulders locked, staring at his footsteps, he looked like a superhero walking into a burning building. As he approached the lip of the dugout, he looked up to find fifteen palms raised, which he slapped, waiting until he was under the Peones' roof before sounding a raw, naked howl.

Just as Mario Mazza was about to step to the plate, it rained, causing a five-minute delay. I'd seen the weather swoop over the mountains, bolts of wet sunshine giving way to clouds and pelting rain. The players and I watched the great natural setting change with the day, pausing, if our nerves allowed, to savour the weather. The air grew cool with the rain, and as the clouds drew back and the sun broke through again, it brought with it renewed freshness and optimism. Which lasted all of a few seconds, until the terror returned to our spines and stomachs.

Mario Mazza made his way back to the dish, where he immediately poked the ball into right field, continuing his banner day at the plate. Mario Simone followed him. At first, he showed bunt, calmly holding the bat over the plate like a child fishing off a dock. But with Giampiero's delivery, he pulled back the wood and swung through the pitch, surprising everyone by singling to the gap. The bench exploded with excitement. Standing on first base, Mario clapped his hands and nodded to himself before steadying his batting helmet on his head and creeping towards second base, his great nose pointing like the barrel of a gun trained upon the Wild Thing's back.

As he fell behind 3-0 to the Red Tiger, you could see Giampiero – his hooded eyes trained impassively on home, his great arms resting at his side – try to summon the force of Mount Pellegrino as he paused between his third and fourth pitch, waiting a moment for the dark magic of the land to fill him. Then he screamed the ball at the plate, and the Red Tiger, trying for the element of surprise that had helped Simone reach first base, slap-bunted the ball weakly along the ground, forcing Mario Mazza at third.

Satisfied that the work of a greater force had conspired to help him weather the Red Tiger's at-bat, Giampiero looked over the Peones' ninth hitter – the light-hitting Emperor – and allowed himself to relax. He disobeyed what Pietro had told me was one of the cardinal rules of baseball: Quando un battitore è'debole, approfitta (When the hitter is weak, take advantage of him). Showing none of the concentration or determination that had guided the pitches thrown to the Red Tiger, Giampiero flicked the ball and hit the Emperor – il colpito – in the ribs. The enormous pitcher shook his head and swore at himself from the mound, understanding that, as Skunk Bravo stepped to the plate, the ripest of situations had turned into the most dire. The opportunity to erase the Peones had been squandered.

As he'd done all year, Skunk rose to the occasion, cracking a hit over the second baseman's head: 7-6, Peones. The Natural followed with a walk, Chicca reached on a wild pitch, and the Big Emilio also walked: 9-6, Peones. By now, Giampiero couldn't have found home plate with a road map and a compass. Balls sailed high, wide, and into the plate as his cursing – "Che cazzo!" – roared louder. Over four batters, he threw a total of two strikes. To save the inning from irreparable damage, Carlos, the Athletics' de facto manager, signalled for Umberto to change places with his brother, who flipped him the ball and stormed over to first base. The Wild Thing's meltdown reminded me of what the Serie A players from Messina had said: "If Novara can't find the zone, he's beatable, he's wild." But whether *wild* equalled *beatable* remained to be seen.

In the bottom half of the eighth, Palermo tried to bite back. Out of the gate, Maddonia tripled and was cashed in, narrowing the score to 9-7, Peones. This sent Giampiero Novara to the plate with the tying run at first. Because he was both the team's designated hitter and starting pitcher, he was allowed the chance for his bat to reclaim what his arm had frittered away. To a man, the players on both teams recalled what had happened the previous weekend, how Novara's three-run, extra-inning homer had turned a game that seemed as tight as a tenor's trill into a cakewalk, a Sicilian slaughter. Pompo knew it, Novara knew it, and Pietro, who'd bummed a smoke from the Natural and was dragging it down to its bitter end, knew it. The count ran to 3-2 before Pompo readied himself for the most important pitch of the Peones' season. Tense with concentration, Novara jerked the bat at his hip, waiting to explode at the ball. As it left Pompo's hand, the Wild Thing swung like Ulysses fighting the Cyclops, but he was about three years in front of the ball.

"Prendi posto somaro!"

"Take a seat, you donkey!"

The Peones leapt to their feet; the Athletics sank against their bench. Novara threw the bat across the field in disgust, knowing that Pompo had tricked him with a slow change.

"Dave, I am so nervous," said Mario Simone, chewing on a nail as he waited for his next at-bat. "Dave, mio cuore è non buono," said Emilio, tapping his hand to his heart. "And I'm sorry," he told me, apologizing for a season of shitfits, "I just get so excited." At one point, eight of the Peones were smoking, obscuring the dugout in a thick cloud. Mirko, who'd spent nine innings hollering at first base, sounded rougher than Tom Waits after a bender. Pietro, for his part, had the slumped, weary look of a sea captain after a wild storm, his face having aged with each at-bat.

Our collective anxiety was such that I wondered whether it might be just as well if the Athletics scored twenty-six unanswered runs to quell the sickening worry that had clenched our hearts. Maybe a bullet to the head would be best for everyone: a quick anodyne for all the suffering the game had brought on. However, just as soon as I began wishing for an immediate end to the day, the Peones – once again doing things as differently as possible from other teams – scored. Then they scored again. And again and again. Nine times, in total. Their first run was, in fact, so broad and fatal to the Athletics' chances that both sets of players on each side knew immediately which club would move confidently into the fifth game, and which would greet the event with the realization that one of their two chances to defeat the visitor had been wasted.

The run belonged to Chicca. After the previous weekend's triple-header, the third baseman had confessed to me over coffee at his bar: "Dave, I don't sleep all week. I put my head down, but it's impossible. I just think of the game, what had happened, everything that had happened. I close my eyes and I see the ball, the runners, the pitcher.

"Baseball," he said, "I love it. But it kills you."

On arriving home with the Peones' tenth run – scored on a squeeze play, this time with Chicca as the runner and the Big Emilio as the batsman – Chicca drove at the dirt with both feet. After the umpire's call – "*Salvooooh!*" – he bounded to his feet, his face twisted in triumph, his body smeared with basepath dirt, and howled a wordless "*Arggghwwaa!*" It was the look and sound of a man swept with passion; a look that scared me. Rooted to his spot in an apoplexy of joy, he pulled his blue batting helmet from his head and slammed it into the ground, where it skipped among the feet of the Peones rushing at him. Chicca greeted his teammates by high-fiving them as if he'd never thrown a high-five in his life; as if he'd seen them offered, but had turned away from such a stupid, vainglorious gesture. Having committed to the act, however, he slammed his palms at the others', all the while vibrating like a raw nerve. After descending into the dugout, it was impossible for him to sit still. Instead of slouching at the end of the bench, he paced the floor, punching his fist into his hand and shouting until, eight batters later, he walked out onto the field to hit again.

On the first pitch, he smashed a double.

The boys roared, "*Unda presha!*"

The Peones were alive.

30

BASEBALLISSIMO

Before the start of game five, Pietro told his players just two things: "Abbiamo vinto cazzo!" (We haven't won anything!) and "Don't eat too much focaccia!" You could see the fellows weigh these orders evenly before tearing into their bags of pizza, their voices and spirits high with victory. The joy of the day was reflected in the way Paolo, full-faced and happy, scraped the last of his lunch from his plastic tub, even though there was no chance he'd see action on perhaps the most important sporting day of the year; how Chencho tried to goad the scratch-throated Mirko into speaking by traipsing around the field with his gold towel draped over his forehead; in the way Fab Julie, game five's starter, flipped away his cap and ran on to the field to soft-toss with the Big Emilio; in the way the Emperor draped his arm around Fabio from Milan and pointed at the mountains, as if to suggest, Look where this team has brought us, look at what we've had to overcome to survive into the afternoon; and in the way the rest of the team devoured their enormous sandwiches, steeling their stomachs. They only had to look across the field to be reminded of what might have been: the Athletics sprawled in front of their dugout like the war dead, asking the sky why the great stone gods had smiled on the visitors, turning a blind eye to the hopes and dreams of their own.

I noticed that during the break between games, three rows of the grandstand had filled with two teams in full uniform – one from Messina, the other from Torino. I skulked over, observed the interlopers with a keen eye, made a few notes, then walked to the base of the screen, cupped my hands to my mouth, and shouted, "Anybody up there know how to speak English?"

The first person to raise his hand was Dante Carbini, a pitcher from Torino '48. My opening question to him was, "Hey, what's with the 48?" to which he replied, "1948 was the year of the very first team in Turin. We have a lot of respect for those players, so we thought we'd memorialize them on our jerseys."

"So there's a pretty deep tradition of baseball up north?"

"Oh yes," he said, sweeping the long hair off of his shoulders. "At least there was until three years ago, when it looked like the team would die. There were very few people coming to the park, very few sponsors, a typical story in Italian baseball. It was sad, but we fought to keep the club going, and we won."

"Congratulations," I said. "It must take a lot of work to keep a team going in a country that seems pretty indifferent to baseball."

"Well, it wasn't always that way. But even in Nettuno, things are different now."

"Yes, yes, I know."

"Nettuno in Serie A, for instance. Once upon a time, they used only players from Nettuno. They built up their teams with players who came from a hard corner of the city. Real ballplayers, you know? They had a chance to field a true local team, but no more. Now they're like all the rest. I think it affects baseball all throughout Italy to see this. There was a time when everybody respected Nettuno and everyone wanted to beat them. But not now. In order to have a strong national game, you need cities like Nettuno to be important. You need the real home of baseball to be above the rest."

"I think the Peones, in their own way, are trying to rediscover that," I said.

"They are all from Nettuno?" he said, gesturing to the blue and white, who'd started to warm up for the game throwing the ball in pairs.

"Ya, every one. And their coach is Pietro Monaco."

"Oh, I know Pietro Monaco," he said, smiling. "A great, great player. Where is he?" he asked.

"In the dugout. You want me to get him?"

"Yes, yes, please!" he said.

"What are you guys doing here anyway?" I asked. "Are you playing in another park?"

"You haven't heard?"

"Heard what?"

"Palermo scheduled us to play a game here at three-thirty."

"But that's when game five is beginning," I said.

"Yes, I know. They must have figured that the field would be available at that time."

I gave him a blank look.

"I guess they thought they'd been finished with you by then."

After a clutch victory, it's a trick even for the most wizened of teams to walk with their feet on the ground. To pull your head out of the skies after breathing the thin air of triumph takes a skill known to only the greatest, most emotionally balanced ballplayers. Winning do-or-die games in such a gutsy fashion has its drawbacks. As a coach or manager, the ideal is to have one's team reach its collective emotional and physical zenith on the last out of a championship game, not sooner, not later. As with the 1975 Red Sox and the 1987 Blue Jays, sometimes winning can come too early, in too great a dose. After finding the resolve and heart to press its foot across its opponent's throat, a team is often unable to crush the last breath out of the enemy, leaving the near-vanquished with just enough life to roll out from under the boot heel and strike back.

That said, without moments of triumph throughout a series, it's impossible to get to the point where the ultimate clutch victory is allowed to happen. By winning game four, the Peones had proven to themselves, and to the Athletics, that they could survive the threat of extinction. But since the Peones relied so desperately on their emotions to carry them – to the bottom, as well as the top – I couldn't help but wonder whether they'd climbed so high that they'd left no further room for their hearts to soar. It was also possible that they'd spent all they had to stave off elimination; whether, like Mirko's voice, they'd already played themselves hoarse. Could they put together back-to-back clutch victories, something they hadn't done all year? Did they have anything in reserve? Was the concept of reserve known in Italian sports?

The joy with which the Peones sprang onto the field to start game five showed the looseness that was both the team's charm and its Achilles heel. I figured that it was my job to sit at the other end of the scales, hanging a certain gravitas upon the affair, which more or less consisted of shouting "*Abbiamo vinto cazzo!*" as loudly and as often as possible. Had I been softened by a dozen or so gimlets, I might have even told the fellows the story of the old hockey coach Hector "Toe" Blake, Montreal's notorious taskmaster and perfectionist. During the 1986 Habs championship playoff run, he warned forward Brian Skrudland after they'd won the first round, "It's only round one!" After they defeated Hartford in round two, he said, "It's only round two!" He told them the same thing in the third round and, finally, after they defeated Calgary to win the Stanley Cup, he sat next to Skrudland in the dressing room, waved his hand, and scoffed, "Pffft. It's only one Cup!" Blake had won as many Stanley Cups as Pietro had won baseball titles. To both men, a victory meant little if it wasn't followed by another.

Fab Julie took to the hill to start the game. Considering the ravages of the team's pitching staff, it was probably more luck than masterstroke that Pietro had him going in the most crucial game of the year. Still, his presence managed to temper the game's action at a time when the hearts of the Peones were racing with visions of rolling in each other's arms across the dirt of the winning dugout. Fabio's face suggested a certain calm and civility. There was a friendly, light way about him, with hopeful eyes that flickered rather than smouldered. While Pompo or Fabio from Milan threw the ball with a tight, propulsive windup, Fabio whisked it through the air, tipping his body back before executing a modest leg kick that was more granny getting out of the back seat of the car than Bruce Lee trying to turn off a light switch with his foot. Fabio's manners were composed and measured, and his style of pitching allowed for a handful of hits, the odd home run, and very few strikeouts while giving up innumerable ground balls, delivered without surprise to his sure-handed infielders. If these qualities weren't enough to steady the scene, the Peones cheered him by name, a woman's name lending the diamond a certain tenderness and muting the testosterone that raged around the all-or-nothing event.

That said, Carlos Novara wrecked this elegant mood with a lead-off home run with a runner aboard. It felt like a bully tramping over a bed of tulips. Pietro reacted to the deadly hit by yelling to his pitcher at the top of his lungs, "*Troppo alto! Piu basso!*" (Too high! Get the ball down!). I thought his outbursts were a tad inappropriate considering the fragility of the game, but after the Peones failed to answer in the second inning, then were retired in order in the third, it was yours truly who began hollering "*It's now or never, Peones!*" and "*C'mon! Give me a good ending for my book!*" like an old woman shrieking after a purse snatching. Pietro walked over and said, "Dave, it's okay. Tranquillo, buono?" before holding out his hand, which I clasped like a climber pulling another across a treacherous rockface.

It was no surprise to see the Wild Thing back on the hill for Palermo. The Athletics were so desperate to win the game that they felt it necessary to burn their superstar to get past the Peones, even though, if they won, Giampiero would likely pitch twice in the championship game the following weekend. I thought this was a victory in itself for the young Nettunese, who'd grown accustomed to the big hurler, less daunted by his command of the ball.

Through the first three innings, Giampiero dominated, clearly unbowed by the events of that morning. But in the Peones' half of the fourth inning, something about him slipped. It wasn't anything you could put your finger on, but slowly, he became unglued. His head went first. He started arguing every ball that the umpire called against him, even pitches that sailed well outside of the strike zone. Sometimes, a minute would pass between deliveries so that the Wild Thing could cage his rancour long enough to throw the next pitch. Even though he was pitching a shutout, it was as if he'd suddenly been reminded of something terrible that had happened in his life, haunted by a ghost of baseball past. He was upset by every hit that got away from him, angry at himself, the umpire, his teammates, the game.

He lost his power and command. Carlos, the catcher, was forced to dive to his right and left to save the ball from going to the backstop. The umpire had to duck to avoid being hit, so did the batter. Finally, after walking the bases loaded, the Wild Thing pulled off his glove, walked off the mound into the home team's dugout, and disappeared through a small door.

There was silence throughout the field. The Fly crouched down in left and picked at the grass, while Maglio, in centre, took off his hat and glove and stood with his arms crossed, glowering at the empty mound. It was left to Carlos to pull off his catching gear, pile it to the right of home plate, and make his way to the mound, where he swept over Giampiero's cleat marks, then scraped the red earth with his own. After a time, the Wild Thing reappeared in the dugout soaked brow to chin, then returned to the field, where he stood for a few seconds over the catcher's armour, fuming. The entire Athletics infield crouched low to the diamond and watched as he slowly strapped on his brother's equipment, moved behind home plate, and motioned for Carlos to begin his warmup pitches, many of which sailed wide. After fetching the last of these six-foot strikes, Giampiero walked in front of the plate and fired the ball over his brother's head. He grunted, spat and swore.

Here stood a disgusted man.

There are moments of ignominy in every athlete's life, but there can be no more humbling experience than being forced to climb down from the diamond's royal hill to a position where you're close enough to read the underwear band of the opposing batter. It must have felt doubly humiliating for the Wild Thing, considering that, one minute he'd been grooving his cuciture past the hated Peones batters, the next he was crouching directly under them, as if in sub-servience. This is to say nothing of having to squat at the feet of the umpire, whom he'd baited all afternoon, or having to chase his brother's second-class slider, which Carlos threw with about as much accuracy as a blindfolded monkey.

I didn't want to leap to the conclusion about what this meant to the Athletics' fortunes on the day, but as Solid Gold stepped in to face Palermo's reverse battery, my heart jumped with the notion that the home team's demise – and the Peones' path to the final in Montefiascone – was imminent. Standing high on his toes in the batter's box, Solid Gold cracked the ball into centre field, tying the game at 3. The next batter, Chicca, immediately tore into Carlos's delivery and pushed the Peones into the lead. Mario Simone singled, the Red Tiger followed with a hit, and as the inning ended, the Peones were ahead, 6-3, and Carlos and Giampiero were screaming at each other as they strode off the field.

The Peones dugout roared with life. They sang and shouted and cheered: "*Amo Fabutimmo!*" At first, they'd watched the Wild Thing's meltdown in disbelief, but after understanding that it was real – the Palermo ace, their best player, had removed himself from the game! – they hit the roof. With each Peones run, the players left their feet, spinning and frugging and swatting the air in sport-ing ecstasy. Every high-five burned the palm, every "Forza! Cazzo Peones!" tore across the tongue, every smile was tearfully happy, every fist gripped as if beating down an old door swaying from the force of their blow.

Casting away my better judgment, I roared in chorus with my teammates, thrilled at sharing something so dear and deep and special with them. There was hugging, laughing, singing. Mario Simone grabbed a phantom microphone, planted his feet, and belted, *"Simplee da best!"* The Emperor paraded around an enormous crostata – for all intents and purposes, a chocolate cake – passing it down the dugout as if at a party. Mario Mazza was not rubbing his leg. Chicca was laughing and smoking. Even Solid Gold, after his RBI, had climbed into the dugout and winked sideways at me. Only Skunk Bravo held his form, peering out at the field the way a stormwatcher might look for a gathering of clouds. I spared a second to look myself, but saw nothing and launched into song: *"Be-Pe, mer-da!"*

The dugout laughed. But I wondered what I'd done.

It wasn't until the sixth inning – neither the Peones nor the Athletics had scored in the aftermath of Nettuno's rally – that I saw that the Peones' cascade of runs had been an isolated incident. Carlos had managed to stem the tide by finding a weapon that neutralized the visitors: a sidearm – and occasional three-quarter – delivery, which he used to throw his slider. The Peones' lack of hitting came from two places: not knowing how to pick up the ball as it shot at them from below the belt, and not digging-in as they had that morning. Their at-bats were cushioned by the lazy awareness that the lead was theirs, and that by showing the Wild Thing what-for, they'd paved the way to certain victory.

In the seventh inning, Palermo got to Fab Julie, putting two runners on base before the veteran managed to wriggle off the hook, forcing Acquaviva to hit into a tailor-made double-play ball. While game three had been a great accomplishment for the placid right-hander, this moment in game five was, I think, Fab Julie's finest hour. He coaxed the Palermo batter into reaching for a slow curve – a slurve, they used to call it in the bigs – and he spun atop the mound, eyes widened, to see the ball shoot across the field to Kid Mazza, who whirled and threw the ball to Skunk at second, who, in turn, swept the bag with his foot before throwing to the Emperor, who stretched to get the runner.

In the eighth inning, Fabio was again hit hard, allowing baserunners at first and third. In the dugout, Pietro asked Pompozzi, "Come stai?" (How do you feel?) Wanting the ball, Pompo told him that he felt fine but, later, Pietro said that he hadn't been convinced. Still, he told Pompo to put on his uniform. Pietro kept Fabio in the game to face Maddonia, who promptly dribbled a ball to Skunk Bravo: one out, runners holding. But with the heavy-hitting Leone coming to the plate, Pietro knew he had to make a move. You could see his eyes fall on Fabio from Milan, who was still too broken down to use. Pitò was an option too, but his stuff was only slightly better than Fabio's, even if it had greater velocity, a quality that would only play into the Athletics' free-swinging hands. This left him with two choices: his tired-armed ace or il pazzo mancino. Walking to the mound to take the ball from Fab Julie, he decided, without much inner debate, upon whose shoulders the fate of the Peones' season would fall. Fabio came off the hill and tipped his cap to the fans, including the players from Messina and Torino, who stood and applauded his fine work. A breeze fluttered his sleeve as the reliever dashed past him towards the mound.

Chencho.

In a sense, it was perfect that the season came down to Chencho, the player who most embodied the Peones' extremes of emotion. Chencho was as coiled as he was loose. One minute, his gyrating face would have the team in stitches, the next he'd be calling the umpire's mother a sailor's whore. Chencho was the truest Peone, its hiccuping id. While he was passionately devoted to winning, he also used the sanctity of the playing field like a bawdy playhouse. He was the worst crotch-hiking Lothario, but had been married the longest of any of the players. He embodied the Peones' style, their season, their playoffs. And now, he had the ball.

By choosing Chencho, Pietro had decided to go out with the kind of flair and style I'd hoped from him all year. He saved the grandest, most flamboyant gesture to the end, for every pitch that Chencho threw was full of peril and adventure. Each at-bat was grand theatre, the characters having assembled together in one final closing scene. Chencho's character had manifested into a kind of joker devil, his gestures and booming voice expressing his fear. Every cry to the umpire or slap of the glove rattled with nervousness and tension. Snakes grew out of his eyes, and he popped a tail. He was a wild, quivering beast as he slung the ball at the plate with the whole of his screaming heart, jumping towards the plate as if trying to shake himself from his crawling skin.

First, Leone hit a sacrifice fly to the Red Tiger: 6-4, Nettuno. Then, Giampiero dragged his club to the plate. As in game one, the Wild Thing stood there knowing that he could atone for his meltdown with a single swing of the bat. Chencho looked in to his catcher, nodded, and threw. The Wild Thing tripled, slamming the ball to the farthest reach of the park and clearing the bases to tie the score at six.

Chencho fell into a crouch and pounded the dirt with his fist, then looked up in time to see Maglio step to the plate. There were certainly more daunting hitters in Italian baseball than the heart of the Palermo order – it was, after all, Serie B – but, at this moment, they possessed the stature of Murderer's Row. The same green-and-gold colours that had made Canseco, McGuire, et al, appear so thick-chested and trunk-legged against the civil blue of the Jays also magnified the Palermo hitters. Maglio placed his batting helmet on his head, dug his feet into the dirt like a bull scraping his hooves, and cast his big, dark, dreadful eyes on Chencho.

There are many instances in pro sport where an athlete's failings and weaknesses are laid naked, but there are few positions other than baseball's short relief where these truths are displayed in such harsh light. The soccer player who puts the ball over the goal in a shootout is in a similar spot, but the fact that the game has been sent into penalties implies a certain achievement in itself. Field-goal kickers suffer the same raw exposure, but at least their faces are obscured by helmets, and basketball's stricken free-throw shooter has likely scored a bucketful of points before being called to the floor.

But the short relief has to stand willingly in front of a firing squad. At times, every baseball fan wonders whether closers exist solely to blow leads. After failing to cement victory for his team, a closer's performance is unequivocally about failure, nothing more. No smitten reliever ever says, "Hey, at least I threw two strikes past him!" Worse, this failure is displayed on the mound for all of the crowd to see, so that the fans may point at him as if at a heretic, shouting him from the field.

Chencho was spared this terrible fate for the time being, though it didn't look that way at first. Once the ball left Maglio's bat, it seemed certain that the Wild Thing would score and Palermo would take the lead into the ninth inning. The ball flared into the opposite field – Chencho had tried to jam him, but the slugger had fought back, extending his thick wrists over the plate – the Red Tiger in pursuit. A mad orange streak running across the field, he flew, almost sideways, at the ball, which landed with a thud into his mitt. He left a long muddy trail where he'd slid. Rising slowly from the earth, the Tiger stood and screamed at Chencho, *"Porco!"*, furious that the mad reliever hadn't put the game away. On the mound, Chencho looked like he was going to vomit. He made his way down the hill, threw his glove into the dugout, and attacked the back wall with his fists.

Chencho stopped before he could do any real damage to his hands, and as he passed me, I whispered through my clenched throat: "Positivo, Chench. Positivo." He threw his head into his hands and moaned.

In the Peones' ninth, Mario Simone, whose tight, pursed face was the opposite of Chencho's, singled to start the inning. He immediately stole second, pushing open a gate that had seemed locked. To a man, we rose against the dugout step, and watched, achingly, as one batter went down after another, the Emperor striking out to end the inning. Pietro tried desperately to urge on his hitters, but was loath to pinch-hit Paolo or any of the other Aces for those of his starting nine. Mario Simone had come tantalizingly close to scoring, but he couldn't be pushed home. The last thing I remember in the inning was Skunk Bravo holding a bat over his shoulder in the on-deck circle. In my heart, I knew that if he could get to the plate, he would cash in the go-ahead run, and the Peones would win. But as the little shortstop stood there, stranded behind the Emperor, my heart of hearts told me, Take a good look, stronzo. A good, long look.

In the bottom of the inning, Umberto Novara slashed Chencho's curveball to the right of the mound. He crushed it with such authority that it seemed certain to find the outfield grass. As it left the bat, Chencho dived after the ball only to have it skitter past him. Chicca sped into the hole from l'angolo caldo, collected the ball, and hurled it to the Emperor. With the umpire's call – "*Out!*" – there were cries from the deepest parts of the outfield, to say nothing of the dugout, where Pietro shouted, "*Bravo Chicca!*", his hands cupped to his mouth, the veins in his neck as taut as piano wire.

The good times lasted for the Peones as long as it took Manny Manno, the Athletics' weakest hitter, to walk to the plate, where he was promptly hit in the back by Chencho's loose slider. Putting the lead-off runner on is never the best idea, let alone in the fifth game of a deciding series. Pitching from the stretch, Chencho collected himself long enough to strikeout Acquaviva, who seemed overanxious trying to bring home his teammate, but lost Carlos to a single, putting runners at first and second with one out.

The next batter was Giampiero Novara, whom Pietro decided to walk. The move was unconventional. In walking the Wild Thing with runners on first and second and one out, Pietro was putting the potential series-winning run at third base. With Manny Manno just ninety feet away, it allowed for the game to end on a wild pitch, an infield error, an overthrow to first, a hit batsman, a passed ball. Suddenly, it narrowed the Peones' margin of error to nothing, forcing Chencho and his fielders to play perfect baseball to survive the bottom of the tenth.

It's easy to weigh an event after pulling it around for a while, yet every time I think about what happened in that final inning, I wonder about Pietro's call. But, in sports, you never know, even when you think you know. Giampiero's performance had been so complicated that he could have just as easily thrown his bat into the stands and returned to the dugout as slam the ball into the mountain face, winning the game right then and there. For Pietro to allow that to happen, he would have to believe that Chencho could somehow draw on his passion and determination and hatred of the opposition to overcome the heart of the Palermo team. While it's true that coaches are relied on for cold, even-minded decision-making in frenetic moments, it's also part of the job description to land the occasional dream on the head of a tack. As Pietro stepped from the dugout and passed his hand through the air, Chencho pressed his hands together and begged: "Noooo! Perche? Noooooo!" For an instant, Pietro looked into Chencho's eyes, searching for a sign that the words of il matto sinistro were more than just pleas of desperate pride.

"Chencho, walk him," he ordered.

The pitcher turned his back and swore, spinning about the field in search of support, but finding only faces gripped with tension. The Big Emilio stood behind home plate, barked at the mound, and held out his arm in a semaphore. After four wasted deliveries, the Wild Thing stood at first, Carlos at second, and Manny Manno at third, with nowhere to go but home.

Before Maglio approached the plate, I watched him in the on-deck circle. His eyes were rolled back in his head, his chest heaving as he breathed. I was encouraged to know that the Athletics – well, at least Maglio – also felt overwhelmed by the tension of the situation, that this heart-wrenching affair affected him as much as it affected the visitors. Watching both the pitcher and the batter was like seeing two people forced into a barrel and flung over Niagara Falls. From the bench, the Black Aces and I bit our fingers, our voices tightening with each ticking second. Only Paolo had the courage to speak:

"Let's go, *Chencho!* You can do it! *Pensa casa!* Relax, he's yours. You own this *cazzo* batter!"

I desperately wanted to join my friend, but could not. The thing I wanted to do most was to scream at Chencho: "Get this goddamned hitter out and we'll drink a big friggin' bottle of cacchione!"

It had to be said. It would have loosened up the boys and freed the scene. But I could not speak. Instead, I slunk behind an old filing cabinet in the corner of the dugout and peered through my hand. My heart shouted, Chencho is sexy! Chencho is beautiful!

"Novara contro Navacci!"

Ball one.

Ball two.

Ball three.

"*Steeeerike!*"

Ball four.

Maglio never lifted the bat off his shoulder. Chencho had tried to groove four unhittable pitches off the corners of the plate, each sailing either high or wide and low. After being required to waste four pitches in order to walk Giampiero, Chencho now found that the strike zone eluded him. With the umpire's final word of the day, Chencho ran home and pleaded with il arbitro to reverse the call. The Big Emilio also roared at him too, demanding that the pitch be called a strike. Pietro, who'd inexplicably refused to visit Chencho to suggest a pitch sequence or calm him down or tell him just to throw the ball down the plate and let the gods do their thing, charged from the dugout and pushed his face into the umpire's, insisting that he reverse his call. It was something he hadn't done all year, and a revealing sign that the game had got to him too.

The Old Bugger was one of us, after all.

It had to happen. It simply wasn't possible that a team that had flown so high would be allowed to float victoriously out of the ballpark. The baseball gods wouldn't let that happen. The Athletics knew better than to mail in their performance without rising to meet their opponents at the crest of the action. After all, the Novaras, for all of their dramatics, were seasoned ballplayers. When it was all over, Umberto, the youngest sibling, told me that if Palermo had lost the semifinal, they'd be forced to cease operations as a team. Since travel costs had become prohibitive for them (while Sardinia was subsidized by FIBS, Palermo was not), the only way they could survive would be to move up to Serie A2, where there was more money and the trips were less rigorous. If baseball in Palermo were to survive, they'd have to defeat Nettuno, and then beat Montefiascone (which they did, in three games, to win the league and a reprieve from organizational death). Another thing he told me was that the team had caught up to Fabio's pitching. Seeing him twice in two weeks, he told me, was plenty of time to adjust. All they had had to do was keep his brother in the game, he said, and the rest took care of itself.

The Emperor cried. Tears slid through his hands, which he held to his face to hide his grief. The rest of the boys screamed a torrent of profanity until exhausted. Then they either lay down on the dugout bench or escaped into a tunnel underneath the stands to sob in private. Chencho sat alone on the dugout step, staring at the Athletics running a victory lap, clapping their hands and swinging their fists over their heads. Mirko made his way up the right-field line, pushed his face into his Peones cap, slumped to the ground, and he filled his hat with a long, low moaning. The only person I thought I might talk to was Paolo, but when I approached him, he held up his head. "Dave," he said. "I am too angry."

Pietro walked the infield alone, his arms crossed, eyes stabbing the ground. It was hard to know what the old veteran was thinking, whether he was replaying every move over in his head or lamenting the state of his devastated pitching staff or bitterly asking how he'd let the bird fly from his grip, an escape that nobody on the Peones had really noticed until it was a fading dot in the watery sky. As always, Pietro struck a sartorial figure, his pose suggesting that even though the game had ended, the Peones had lost, and their season – my season – was over, baseball in Nettuno would echo as long as Pietro stamped the grass. The game, the teams, the players would exist beyond the wins and losses as long as Pietro held form. The

Peones and their coach had wanted to keep true Italian baseball alive, and even though their season was done, from the way Pietro tipped back his head and searched the sky before making his way back to his team, I knew that they had.

Once Palermo had completed their victory lap, Umberto Novara crossed the diamond holding a great stainless-steel tray, making his way to the Peones' dugout. Every player looked at him except the Emperor, who lay across the bench, his face covered by his hands.

"Ragazzi, here, for you," said Umberto, lowering the tray to belt height.

I shouted, probably too excitedly, considering the fresh hurt of losing, "Bravo! Pizza!"

"No, no," corrected Umberto. "This is not pizza. This is sfincione. This is like pizza, but not pizza. It is a Sicilian specialty."

The crust was layered in a kind of bechamel paste, with tomatoes and olives scattered about.

"Please, fellows," said Umberto. "Enjoy. It's the tradition of our team to offer sfincione to our friends, such great players from the home of Italian baseball."

Fab Julie, Mario Simone, and Mirko reached in first, then the rest followed. Soon, the entire team was clustered around the tray, easing their sadness and unrequited baseball dreams with a tomato and bread anodyne. Even the Emperor roused himself from his deep sorrow to try the exotic flatbread.

He took two pieces.

EPILOGUE: A PLAY AT THE PLATE

The losing hurt, but it would pass. Chencho was the only player who disappeared from view – I didn't see him again before leaving Italy – while the rest of i giocatori were back promenading around the Borgo, calling out to me and grabbing me by the neck with both hands whenever we met across the cobblestone. For my part, I refused to remove my Peones hat from my head (in fact, I refused to take it off until I finished this book), its spiderweb of white sweat stains and blue-brown hue calling attention to itself among the impeccably groomed Nettunese. I was asked a few times each day what had happened in Palermo. I told people the same, long Bertoluccian epic about how the boys had missed the finals by a whisker, and how their play surely promised a new era of winning baseball, leaving out the details of Chencho's demise and the fact that, with their crushing loss in Sicily, one-quarter of the Peones would probably either retire or move laterally through the wilderness of Italian minor league ball.

When I talked about game five with the Peones, the first word that passed their lips was "Chencho." Paolo suggested to me,

"Really, Chencho should have just thrown strikes. He should have let Maglio hit the ball, instead of throwing it this way, that way," he said, moving his hand like a sidewinder. "Chencho is stubborn. With the bases loaded and the count 3-1, he should have just pointed the ball at the middle. He should have thrown it. But, upffft. Chencho. He doesn't learn." Unlike Paolo, Fabio From Milan was less critical of Chencho's fatal pitching sequence. "Chencho is crazy," said Fabio. "He doesn't think like you or me. He did what he did because he was Chencho. No other thing could have happened," he said, shrugging and turning over his hands.

The Emperor organized a team dinner on the eve of our departure at Peyote's, the Italo-Mexican trattoria on the edge of town. Only Chencho – and Paolo, who was nursing a cold – was missing from the table. I felt bad that il matto sinistro had balked at the invitation, because I wanted to single him out as one of the Peones who'd made me feel comfortable during my stay. Nonetheless, I climbed on a chair at the head of the table and spoke Italian for twenty minutes, something I couldn't have imagined doing at the beginning of my trip. I roasted every player with jokes written on a scribbled sheet of foolscap, which Janet had helped me prepare. The guys took their licks to great bursts of laughter and applause, but when I got to Pietro – "I'll always remember Signor Monaco playing for hours on the diamond in the heat of the sun, taking one hundred ground balls, fielding even a few of them cleanly!" – it was almost as if they were too wary to laugh. In the middle of my bit, Pietro turned and asked Janet, "What does he mean by this? Why is he saying these things?" But later on he told me, "Dave, you did very good up there. Very good. Very nice discorso," he said, nodding his head appreciatively.

Over the course of the evening, we feasted on seven courses, more: antipasto, pizza, three kinds of pasta, seafood, risotto, bruschetta, bistecca, suppli, and verdura, to say nothing of an inexplicable panoply of Mexican dishes: tortillas and nachos buried under melted Parmesan cheese. There were great caraffes of cacchione, bottles of grappa and beer, bowls of olives and trays of proscuitto, salami, and a myriad of cheeses. With the exception of my discorso, our table had been a constant rattling of life, the players shouting, jibing, and calling out to each other, passing Lorenzo from lap to lap, filling Cecilia with gelato and dolci. Near the end of the night, I was sitting across from Pietro, who had opened the door through which I'd passed into the Italian minor leagues. With the season at my back, and six notebooks filled with scribblings (to say nothing of bus tickets, café receipts, wildflowers, gum wrappers, and clippings from *Il Granchio* stuffed between the pages), I didn't know what to say, or how to thank him. Finally, I said, "Thank you for sharing your life and your team with me. Soon, the story of the Peones will be on the shelves of every bookstore in North America," overstating the prospects for a work that, in fact, had yet to be written. Pietro turned his ear and gestured for me to repeat myself. Humouring him, I translated what I'd said into broken Italian, but it was impossible to know whether I made any sense. My voice was swallowed by the din, lost in the culinary music of my team.

ACKNOWLEDGMENTS

I'm usually quite fastidious when it comes to compiling a list of who to thank (or not to thank) for their assistance in the creation of a book. You can imagine, then, what kind of forehead-ripping consternation came over me when I realized that, for *Baseballissimo*, no such list existed. Of course, there were the usual suspects – Fred and Jo (my parents), Mel and Norma (the in-laws, who helped me with my Italian), Cathy (my sister), and Phil and Luca (and now, Amelia), Melanie Morassutti (and, in a way, Dwayne), Julia Hambleton, Laura Lunetta (and family), and the Rheostatics, evermore. There's also my kind and sagacious editor, Dinah Forbes, and my agent, David Johnston, who suggested that I write about baseball in Italy rather than wrestling in Newfoundland (Heritage Canada can take up whatever concerns they may have with him). But apart from these names, it seems that I've forgotten, en masse, every other person who helped to arrange my travel or find my bearings abroad. I hate saying, with a dismissive giggle, "To those people who did everything: you know who you are!"

But, well, you do.

Of course, a few names dangle – Chris Ralph, who arrived in Nettuno from San Francisco with two friends (John and Geoff) to make a film about the very subject that I was covering, but who nonetheless shepherded our family around the Boot with a merry smile; Geddy Lee, who sent me a great, heavy book about Italian wine, if one egregiously lacking in a chapter on cacchione; Mike Downie and Nick dePencier, who waited on my return before going to Mongolia; and Peter Alegi, Jeff Z. Klein, Chris Young, and Dave

Merritt (and Melanie Morassutti), each of whom read bits and pieces of this book. Still, as I sit here awash in the emotional relief – and crushing fatigue – of having built this prose castle over the last two and a half years, I'm perfectly aware that I've already forgotten to mention Riccardo Schiroli, Cathy Bidini (again, for her lovely photos), Howie Starkman, Mark Leno, *TORO* magazine, Gord Cumming (Baseball Jesus), the Rebels (and the Morningstars), Gary Bedingfield, Roger Kahn, Dock Ellis, George Plimpton (who passed away while I was in the late stages of this book), Warren Zevon (whose demise preceded the paper lion's), Laura Ferri, Nicoletta Barbarito, Paolo Chirumbolo, Fred Thornhill, Maria Antonietta Marcucci, Sante de Franceschi, Heather Sangster, Kong Njo, Mark Weinstein, SABR, Cafe Faema, Peter Haidasz, and the *Toronto Star*, who ran a story about our first trip to Nettuno. This is to say nothing of Guided by Voices, Super Furry Animals, and Gilberto Gil (among others), whose glorious sounds painted the air whenever the alternative was the humming silence of a writer not writing. And, before ending this book, I must thank the 2002 Nettuno Peones and their coach, Pietro Monaco, for their help and support, not forgetting the assistance of Silvano Casaldi and the great Giulio Glorioso. Andy Pafko once said, "I would rather play baseball than eat." But the Peones proved that you can do both things, and do them well.

Oh, hold on.

Right.

Thanks, above all, to my charming and beautiful wife, Janet, and our delicious children, Cecilia Abel and Lorenzo August, without whom none of this would have been possible.

Please write:
P.O. Box 616
Station C
Toronto, Ontario, Canada
M6J 3R9